Cotton Bales, Keelboats, and Sternwheelers

A History of the Sabine River and Trinity River Cotton Trades, 1837-1900

Second Edition
ISBN: 9798843076122

Copyright © 1995
By W. T. Block
Published by WTBLOCK.ORG

Forward

A book that utilizes primary sources to trace the steamboat cotton trades of the Sabine and Trinity rivers has been long overdue, and *Cotton Bales, Keelboats, and Sternwheelers* does just that. Beginning in October, 1837, when the 3rd U. S. Infantry blew up and cleared the Sabine River of logjams and obstructions, the first sternwheeler, the 133-foot *Velocipede*, steamed all the way to Pendleton, Sabine County, and back without suffering any mishap. During the 63 years between 1837 and 1900, *Cotton Bales* traces the voyages of 84 steamers, many of which eventually sank in Sabine's murky depths.

The most famous of them, Uncle *Ben*, was also a cottonclad Confederate gunboat at the Battle of Sabine Pass, and *Cotton Bales* explains all activities of the Sabine's Confederate fleet. In 1857, Uncle *Ben* traveled the 800 river miles to Belzora, near Tyler, Texas, and brought down 3 loads of 1,000 bales of cotton on each voyage. The Confederates scuttled the gunboat Josiah Bell south of Orange, but its powerful engine powered equipment in Lutcher and Moore's Upper Sawmill for 50 years thereafter.

Perhaps of especial interest to the descendants living in the Orange vicinity today were the steamboats *Dura*, Capt. Tom J. Davis; *R. E. Lee*, Capt. J. J. Jordan; *Una*, Capt. Wiley Phillips; *Charles Lee*, Capt. Charles Davis; *L. Q. C. Lamar*, Capt. H. T. Davis; and the *Emily P.*, Capt. W. D. Bettis. The book also includes many steamers used only in the logging industry. The boats sailed interchangeably in both the Neches and Sabine Rivers.

Steam boating on the Trinity spanned a much shorter time period than that on the Sabine, but the cotton bale volume was greater. As many as fifteen steamers at one time scoured the Trinity River landings for cotton in 1871-72, but the trade ended abruptly in 1874 due to rail competition. *Cotton Bales* covers the voyages of 104 sternwheelers on the Trinity from 1838 to 1894, including two voyages of the *H. A. Harvey* and *Job Boat No. 1*, each of which went all the way to Dallas. The *L. Q. C. Lamar*, mentioned earlier, was the last large sternwheeler to sink in Trinity in 1892, nine miles south of Liberty.

Cotton Bales truly recovers a memorable time span in East Texas history, when rural settlers, upon hearing the boat's whistle around the bend, knew that mail, passengers, and new merchandise were arriving in town and honeymooners would soon be sailing for Galveston.

Table of Contents

Table of Figures

To the Reader

Many years ago, I recognized the need for a well-researched story about the steamboat cotton trade of the Trinity and Sabine Rivers for the years 1837 until 1900. While researching my masters thesis around 1970, I read of the steamboat Uncle Ben carrying out on three trips, 1,000-bales loads of cotton in 1857 from Belzora, east of Tyler in Smith County, down the Sabine River to Sabine Pass. About the same time, I learned that two stem wheel steamboats, the Job Boat #1 in 1868 and HA. Harvey in 1893, sailed up the Trinity River from Anahuac all the way to Dallas. These stories were all published at the time the events occurred. Later, upon crossing the Trinity River near Dallas or the Sabine near Longview, I began to realize that any mature jackrabbit, however gaunt, could cross either river in one giant leap, so how was it possible for 100-foot boats to reach there?

Later, I learned too that the old-time rivermen claimed that some flat-bottomed stem wheelers "could navigate in heavy dew." And I soon realized from old newspaper microfilm that the Trinity and Sabine Rivers remained at flood stage, sometimes a mile wide, during the shipping seasons for each of several years during the 1850's. In fact, there is indisputable proof that in 1849, an iron-hulled, square rigged steamer ran all the way to Fredonia in Panola County, near Longview, and carried out a load of cotton without encountering low water at any time.

It is my sincere hope that this volume will answer many of the Texas river buffs questions about early commerce on either river. And long lists of river boats and sailors are included for genealogical research as well.

I am deeply indebted to the Charles W. Fisher Collection at Sam Houston Regional Library at Liberty, Texas for photographs of some Trinity River steamers, and to Dr. Howard Williams and the Orange County Historical Society for many steamboat pictures and old Sabine River scenes.

–W. T. Block

Part 1—Sabine River Trade

Chapter 1—The Sabine River's Physical and Economic Background

At the southeastern extremity of Texas, there are three bodies of water which together share a common name, Sabine Lake, Sabine River, and the Sabine Pass, the latter being a tidal inlet which connects the lake and river to the Gulf of Mexico. As far north as the thirty-second degree of north latitude, near Joaquin, Texas, they collectively represent the common boundary between the states of Texas and Louisiana. The Sabine Pass is a five-mile-long inlet or estuary, which connects Sabine Lake, a seven by fourteen mile tidal lagoon, with the sea. Together they form the confluence of a total of three rivers, the Angelina, the Neches, and the Sabine, which with their countless tributaries, drain about 40,000 square miles of Eastern Texas and Western Louisiana. This combination of a river, a tidal lagoon, and a tidal inlet or estuary is quite common to the geography of the Gulf Coast Prairie of both Texas and Louisiana, and is also shared by two neighboring streams, the Calcasieu, and Mermentau Rivers of Louisiana.

If the Sabine, known by the Spanish as the Rio de los Flores or as the Rio San Francisco de las Sabinas (cypresses), had a voice, there is no stream of Texas that could equal the romance or stories it would have to tell—of the Hasinai Caddo or Attakapas warriors and dugouts upon its surface, or of Lafitte piracy, African slave-smuggling, French fur-trading, cotton freighting, customhouse border conflict, frontier violence, and even Civil War battles that occurred within its shadows.

A century ago, it sliced through some of the most beautiful and extensive pine, cypress, and hardwood forests in North America. But the virgin forests, amounting to some thirty-five billion board feet of lumber, have long since been cut away and replaced today only by second-growth (both smaller and subsequent) timber. Flowing almost 1,000 river miles from its source north of Greenville, Texas (near the South Sulphur fork of the Red River) in Hunt

County, the Sabine River is particularly noted for its serpentine meanders in the hilly uplands, which make the river distances approximately double the airline distances between points.

Probably unique in the history of the American rivers is the fact that the Sabine was once an international boundary which had to be negotiated by treaty with three foreign countries, namely, Spain, Mexico, and the Republic of Texas. Under Spain and Mexico, its west bank as far as the Trinity River was designated as a 20-league border reserve in which Anglo-American settlement was forbidden. Between 1803 and 1829, both Spain and Mexico feared American encroachment into Texas and reserved the border strip for the settlement of Indian tribes, such as the Creek and Seminole nations, who were considered to be hostile to the United States.[1]

Since long treatises have been written on the eastern boundary of Texas, suffice it to say that these represent some of the most interesting reading in American history, but they are not particularly pertinent to a study of the early commerce and navigators of the Sabine River.[2] The one exception is the steamboat voyage of the "Albert Gallatin" in May 1840, when the steamboat carried the Texas-United States Boundary Commission surveyors and two granite markers north to the 32nd parallel. Since this is perhaps the best account of an early-day steamer voyage on a Texas river, the commission's daily journal will be quoted at length in Chapter 3. The "Albert Gallatin" was the fifth steamer to ascend the river after 1837.

There were many early descriptions of the Sabine, most of which praised the beauty of the adjacent forests but minimized the worth of the adjoining farmlands. One source noted that, although the Sabine River drains only a few thousand square miles, the volume of its water discharge into the Gulf of Mexico ranks third among the Texas rivers, primarily because of the humidity and rainfall common to East Texas.[3] Writing in 1840, George Bonnell observed that:[4]

*...The land upon this river for the first 200 miles from
the mouth is generally of an inferior quality except
the bottom lands along the river and its tributaries.
These are sometimes extensive and rich. The upland
is generally covered with a lofty growth of pine
interspersed occasionally with prairie. This pine is of
fine quality and a rich trade in lumber, tar, pitch, and
turpentine may be carried on from that river. The
bottoms are well-adapted to the cultivation of corn,
cotton, and sugar ...*

Writing in 1848, Victor Bracht, an early German immigrant and writer, noted that "magnificent forests are found along its banks... It is, however, subject to tidal overflow."[5] In 1856, Jacob DeCordova listed 61 tributaries of the Sabine River, which makes them much too numerous to recite in detail.[6] In 1840, William Kennedy, the British consul at Galveston, wrote extensive volumes about Texas and listed the major tributaries on the Texas side of the stream, giving in addition an excellent description of the river's early navigability, as follows:[7]

*...The land which around the bay {Sabine Lake} is low
and destitute of timber, is of inferior quality for
agriculture and well-adapted to grazing. The
steamboats have ascended the Sabine to a
considerable distance from its mouth. A raft {logjam}
deemed by some as an insuperable obstacle to its
navigation, was removed {blown up} in four weeks by
order of the War Department of the United States.
The first attempt to navigate the river by steam was
made in 1837, by Captains Wright and Delmore of
the Velocipede, which ascended as high as Gaines'
Ferry. The Velocipede was in length 125 feet, in
breadth 32 feet, and drew 6 feet of water {these
figures are in error as will be revealed later}. In May
1839, a steamboat plied regularly between the
settlements on the river. The Sabine periodically*

overflows its banks. The tributaries from the west are
Bevil Creek {Cow Bayou}, Adams, Cypress, Big and
Little Cow {creeks}, Palo Gaucho, Patron, Teneha,
and Cherokee creeks

During the eighteenth century and decades before any Anglo-American settlement in Texas began, two trade routes, both of which crossed the Sabine River, developed between Texas, Louisiana, and Mexico. The most important of these evolved after 1713 along a route between Natchitoches, La., Nacogdoches and San Antonio, Texas, eventually ending at Nuevo Laredo, Mexico. This became known as the King's Highway, crossing the river at a point later to be known as Gaines' Ferry. Much less important was a southerly route which is still known as the Old Spanish Trail, which evolved after 1770 and crossed the Sabine at Ballew's Ferry, 10 miles north of Orange, Texas. This trade route, also known as the Atascosita or Opelousas Trail, developed primarily for the movement of Texas cattle to the New Orleans market, reaching its zenith during the 1850's when more than 40,000 steers annually made the long trek to the Crescent City. The effects of the cattle movements were reflected at the Sabine and Neches River ferries, where the respective county governments set the crossing fees per head for swimming cattle and horses and stipulated how many ferry "hands" must be employed for purposes of crossing cattle. The Old Spanish Trail, however, was never important as a trading route for manufactured wares. Under the Texas Republic, Gaines' and Ballew's ferries were the points on the international boundary where postal routes crossed from Texas (or Mexico prior to 1836) into the United States.

Under international treaties, the waters of the Sabine River, Sabine Lake, and Sabine Pass, to the west bank or Texas shore, were ceded to and left under the jurisdiction of the United States. That circumstance, coupled with the high tariff rates of the Texas Republic, resulted in rampant smuggling across the Sabine River and festering border conflict on Sabine Lake and the Sabine Pass, which was resolved only after Texas received statehood. Since Texas customhouses were maintained at both Sabine Pass and

Galveston, manufactured goods entering the young republic by water could not evade the Texas duties, leaving East Texas wholly dependent on the New Orleans market via an overland route to Grand Ecore, Shreveport, or Natchitoches, La., and thence south along the Red and Mississippi watercourses. One small town on the Bolivar Peninsula, Rollover, owes its name to the early smugglers for it was once known as "the rolling-over place." Smugglers would unload their barrels of merchandise, roll them some 1,200 yards across the peninsula, and then sail around to East Galveston Bay and retrieve the barrels on the north shore of the peninsula.

As a result, the trans-Sabine River smuggling of manufactured wares flourished. As late as 1843, many East Texas planters:[8]

> *...even as far west as Crockett on the Trinity River,*
> *have been furnished with goods from the Shreveport*
> *market at a cheaper rate than they could purchase*
> *them at Galveston or Houston ...*

To the detriment of the Texas merchants, steamboats and schooners anchored in Sabine Lake, River, or the Sabine Pass (which were then territorial waters of the United States), defied the Texas revenue officers, often with the support of an American cutter patrolling in the Lake, and sold merchant wares indiscriminately to Texans and Louisianans alike.[9] In July, 1840, Stephen H. Everett, a Texas Senator as well as a Sabine Pass cotton factor, complained that from Barney Low's ferry, then in Jasper County, to the mouth of the Sabine, there was no store on the Texas side of the river, all of the merchants having relocated on the Louisiana shore.[10] As late as 1845, Austin and Clapp, prominent merchants of Sabinetown, moved their store across the river to Camp Sabine, a U. S. army outpost, where they sold their goods for 20% less. The move proved so lucrative to the merchants that they operated a free ferry for the use of their customers.[11] Under the Texas republic, Sabinetown (now extinct but then in Sabine County) was the largest river port on the Sabine and the commercial hub of East Texas, second only to Nacogdoches.

Because of pressure from the East Texas planters and merchants, the Sabine customs officers became reluctant to enforce the tariff laws and manipulated them to suit their own purposes. When in 1840 the collector seized goods belonging to Thomas H. Brennan, a prominent Beaumonter, the owner sued the revenue officer, won judgment, and the collector resigned.[12] Deputy collectors along the river were openly defied and threatened with guns. On one occasion, wagon smugglers at one Sabine River ferry severely assaulted a customs collector before proceeding westward into Texas with their wagon and smuggled wares.[13]

The border conflict over Texas tariffs reached its zenith during 1844-1845. Up until that time, the masters of the New Orleans cotton schooners "William Bryan," "Lone Star," "Louisiana," "Cabot," and "Robert Center" (each a U. S. flag vessel), while loading cotton from Texas keelboats or flatboats in Sabine Lake, consistently ignored the Sabine Pass customs collector's demands to pay Texas tonnage fees. They argued that they were within the territorial waters of the United States; and since that was the case, they were not subject to Texas laws, and realized that the collector had no means to enforce his demands. The cotton schooners were often protected by the New Orleans revenue cutter "Woodbury," which often patrolled in the lake (and whose master was the United States collector at the Garrison Ridge on the Louisiana shore). But the latter two circumstances were greatly altered in 1844 when the Texas cutter "Santa Ana" also began patrolling in Sabine Lake and delivered two cannons to the Texas collector at Sabine Pass which were mounted at the customhouse. On April 17, 1844, Texas Collector W. C. V. Dashiell attempted to sink two of the schooners when they refused to stop, forcing them to call at the customhouse and execute over their protests bonds for Texas tonnage fees. Thereafter, an undeclared customs war continued in Sabine Lake, with considerable diplomatic wrangling between the Secretaries of State of both countries, until Texas' entry into the Union in February 1846, negated the cause for the hostilities.[14]

Apart from French fur traders, the first commercial navigator and keelboatman of cotton on the Sabine River is believed to have been Rezin Green, who gave his name both to Green's Bluff, the original name for Orange, Texas, and perhaps also to Green's Bayou, adjacent to Garrison Ridge on the Louisiana side of Sabine Lake, where the United States customhouse was built in 1839. However, the master of the U. S. cutter "Woodbury" and the first U. S. collector at Garrison Ridge was also a Captain Green, from whom the bayou's name may have been derived. Whether Rezin Green and Captain Green were one and the same is unknown at this writing. Green is sometimes credited as being the first settler at Orange. In 1836 Rezin Green served a 90-day enlistment in Capt. Franklin Hardin's company in the Texas Army, and in the following year, he was also the first associate justice for Jefferson County, Texas.

In May 1839, when Captain Green was appointed as the first United States collector for the port of Sabine Lake, his appointment had nothing to do with the customs conflict with the Texas collector, which still had not developed as of that year. Since as of 1839, there were a number of schooners under construction at New Orleans which authorities believed were intended for a resurgence of the African slave trade between West Africa, Cuba, and the Sabine River, Capt. Green was ordered to use his cutter "Woodbury" to prevent any renewal of the illicit commerce, which under both Texas and American law was chargeable as piracy.[15]

The flat boating or keel boating of cotton is believed to have begun on the Sabine River about or during the year 1830 and was certainly in use on the nearby Neches River during that year. In 1830 Thomas F. McKinney began the keel boating of cotton there, beginning on the Angelina waterway, between Nacogdoches and Sabine Lake. The earliest flatboats were little more than a raft of logs, or a box built of rough sawn lumber which had to be "poled" and/or floated with the river currents during the winter river freshets, and they lacked conventional steering equipment. Hence, they could not proceed into the lake or beyond the mouths of the rivers. Later, all such craft were built of rough sawn lumber, having much the appearance of box-like barges, and at the journey's end, many of them were dismantled and sold for house and bridge timbers at Sabine Pass. (There was always a great demand for lumber at treeless Sabine Pass before the first sawmill was built there in

1846.). Keelboats were much more elaborate models, often with a pilot house and crew's quarters aboard, but they were still dependent on current movements or sails for propulsion. Hence, a keelboat was rarely dismantled, and they usually were "poled," towed, or sailed back upstream to the point of origin. Such a craft was the keelboat "T. J. Rusk," which carried cotton from Nacogdoches County to Sabine Lake, beginning in 1844.[16] As opposed to the Sabine River, where steam navigation began in 1837, steam boating on the Angelina/Neches waterway did not begin until 1846, when Robert Patton (who also owned the "T. J. Rusk") built the steam packet "Angelina" at Pattonia, Nacogdoches County, and left on his first voyage to Sabine Pass.

In 1840, a San Augustine editor reported that S. Steadham and Van Dusen owned five keelboats at East Hamilton on the Sabine River, near Sabinetown, which would carry cotton to the mouth of the river at 50 cents per hundred-weight.[17] In 1843 the Houston "Telegraph and Texas Register" observed that:[18]

> ...Capt. J. Wright is now building a large and substantial keelboat which will be completed in a few days. This boat ...will ply regularly between Hamilton and Sabinetown. Arrangements have already made by Messrs. C. H. Alexander and Co {then of Sabinetown, later of Sabine Pass} to procure a new and substantial steamboat to ply between Sabine Pass and the upper landings on the river ... The cost of transportation of cotton from the upper landings of the Sabine to New Orleans by this route will be $3.25 a bale. The cost of transportation of cotton from San Augustine to New Orleans for land carriage ...is now $7.50 a bale ...There was cotton in town {San Augustine} the other day which had been brought in wagons for 130 miles.

In 1841, the cost of shipping cotton overland from Sabinetown, via Natchitoches and the Red River, to New Orleans varied from $6.50 to $7.50 a bale as opposed to $3.50 a bale to ship via keelboat or steamboat from Sabinetown to Galveston.[19] The high shipping costs notwithstanding, the majority of East Texas cotton continued to move overland to market throughout the 1840's, partly because of the inadequacy of steamboat facilities, and during the six months prior to April 1, 1842, 3,850 bales of East Texas cotton were freighted by wagon to Natchitoches, La., for transshipment to New Orleans via the Red River.[20] The keel boating of cotton on the Sabine, however, remained a popular mode of movement for the fluffy commodity until the late 1870's, and as late as 1879, a keelboat belonging to Captain Moffat of Town Bluff, Tyler County, wrecked at Yellow Bluff on the Neches River, disgorging 260 bales of cotton into the water.[21]

From a number of early maps and published sources, the following river mileages on the Sabine, beginning at Sabine Pass, appear to be as nearly correct as the writer can determine. Most of the mileages were reprinted weekly in several area papers over a long period of years:[22]

Sabine Pass	0	Low's Landing	350
Pavell's Landing	24	Fullerton's Landing	355
Orange	40	Sabinetown	361
Ballew's Ferry	54	Crow's Ferry	369
Niblett's Bluff	58	Pendleton	374
Princeton	—	Patterson's Ferry	380
Sudduth's Bluff	110	Hamilton	414
Salem	110	Haley's Ferry	445
Donohoe's Ferry	161	Brown's Bluff	452
Belgrade	171	Myrick's Bluff	459
Stark's Landing	191	Logansport	514
Bayou Lanacoco	220	Rose's Bluff	544
Hickman's Ferry	252	Pulaski	580
Burnham's Landing	261	Fredonia	609
Burr's Ferry	281	Grand Bluff	664
Bevil's Ferry	300	Camden	744
Toledo	306	Bacon's Bluff	774
Snell's Landing	308	Water's Ferry	849
Belzora	879		

It is of particular interest that of the many river ports that at one time or another lined the Sabine River, only Orange, Texas, and Logansport, La., remain today as towns of considerable worth. Another exception is Sabine Pass, Texas, which actually must be considered a seaport adjacent to the gulf rather than a river port. The cause lies principally with the development of rail facilities along the Sabine, for as the river trade subsided, the river ports were abandoned as new towns were developed along the railroads. And Orange and Logansport were the only old river ports which likewise became railheads during the nineteenth century. In 1861 the Texas and New Orleans Railroad completed trackage to Orange, which was operational only for a few months and abandoned. The line was completely rebuilt and reopened in 1876. In 1881 the line linked up with the Louisiana and Western Railroad to form the present Southern Pacific route. Logansport became a railhead after the Civil War when the Houston East and West Texas Railroad was completed between Houston and Shreveport.

The largest of the Sabine River ports, which in time regressed to ghost towns or returned to forest, was Sabinetown. By 1840 it was already a shipping center of considerable note. By 1850 it had grown to some 800 houses and business firms and for a time, it actually rivalled Nacogdoches as the commercial center of East Texas. After the Civil War, it retrogressed rapidly, however, and only a possible historical marker might reveal its former location in the forest today.

Other river ports that for a time enjoyed prosperity but eventually disappeared included Salem, Belgrade, Pendleton, East Hamilton, Toledo, Fredonia, Camden, Pulaski, and Belzora. Belgrade, for instance, which showed great prospects at its beginning in 1836, was soon a victim of the tariff laws of the Texas Republic. In 1845, the editor of Houston "Morning Star" observed that:[23]

> *... this once flourishing town that made such a*
> *respectable appearance on the maps of Texas five*
> *years since has dwindled away to the smallest of*
> *small hamlets. It is now but four houses and one*

small store. Being situated close to the Sabine where
the facilities for smuggling are very great, no large
mercantile house can be maintained in it ...

No list of the principal merchants and cotton factors along the Sabine River is known to exist. The following, gleaned from a number of old newspapers, must suffice, however, and is believed to contain at least half of the most prominent cotton merchants along the river between 1840 and 1880. Beginning at Sabine Pass and moving inland, they are as follows: Stephen H. Everett, Sabine Pass; Niles F. Smith, Sabine Pass; C. H. Alexander and Co. (after 1855), Sabine Pass; Hutchings and Sealy (before 1854), Sabine Pass; Otis McGaffey, Sabine Pass; Mathew H. Nicholson, Sabine Pass and San Augustine, Bondies, Roehte and Co., Sabine Pass, Pattonia (on the Angelina River), Nacogdoches, and Fredonia; John Clements, Sabine Pass and Bevilport; Keith and Vaughan, Sabine Pass; Eddy and Adams, Sabine Pass; Craig and Keith, Sabine Pass; John McRae, Sabine Pass; A. Pavell and Co. (until 1865), Shellbank; F. Pavell and Co. (after 1866), Shellbank; A. G. Swain, Shellbank; Hugh Ochiltree, Orange; Dennis Call and Son, Orange; Alexander Gilmer, Orange; C. Warner, Orange; Wingate and Burr, Orange; S. Fairchild, Orange; T. S. McFarland, Belgrade; W. A. Ferguson, Jasper; Hines and Ford, Burkeville; G. B. Burr, Burr's Ferry and Orange; J. J. Snell and Co., Toledo; Morris and Beckum, Toledo; Augustus Hotchkiss, Sabinetown and Sabine Pass; C. W. Hotchkiss and Co., Sabinetown; Austin and Clapp, Sabinetown; C. H. Alexander and Co. (before 1855), Sabinetown; James F. Thorne and Co., Fredonia; and Robert S. Patton and Co., Pattonia and Belzora.

Unlike the Trinity River, where the cotton trade ended rather abruptly by 1874, the Sabine River was to enjoy a lucrative trade until long after the railroads arrived. For one thing, no railroad paralleled the Sabine until 1895, when the Gulf, Beaumont and Kirbyville line was built. And although the East Texas Railroad from Beaumont to Rockland was built in 1881, any cotton carried on it would otherwise have gone to market on the Neches River. Also, unlike Trinity, where the plantations owned the steamboats, the trade of the Sabine remained principally in the hands of the merchants, many of whom doubled as steamer and schooner captains, or the independent steamboat owners. However, the volume of cotton trade on the river at no time equaled that of the Trinity in its heyday around 1873, or for that matter, perhaps the Brazos River as well. To some degree, this was attributable to the competition of the wagon freighters to points on the Red River, who prior to 1846 had no difficulty returning with merchandise that had evaded the Texas tariffs. Also, the lands along the Trinity and Brazos had won much acclaim and in fact, probably were more adapted to cotton-growing. Since only two railroads intersected the Sabine River prior to 1900, the sternwheelers of the Sabine River were still much in demand as cotton carriers. Those steamboats operating on the lower river carried cotton back to Orange, and those on the upper river carried their cargoes to Logansport, La. And when the cotton trade finally waned about 1900, the packets were still needed to help build the railroads; to supply the logging tram roads at such points as Salem, Laurel, Belgrade, Deweyville, Elizabeth, and Sudduth's Bluff; to tow the log rafts along the river and barges of rough and finished lumber to the export docks at Sabine Pass. After 1876, steamboats often could move no faster that one or two miles an hour due to floating logs which surrounded them. In the early days, a few steamers were built along the stream, but many more were destined to find a watery grave within Sabine's depths. An account of the Sabine River's cotton trade, as well as the steamers' contributions to the logging and timber trade and early day passenger service, are sagas that the writer deems most worthy of historical preservation.

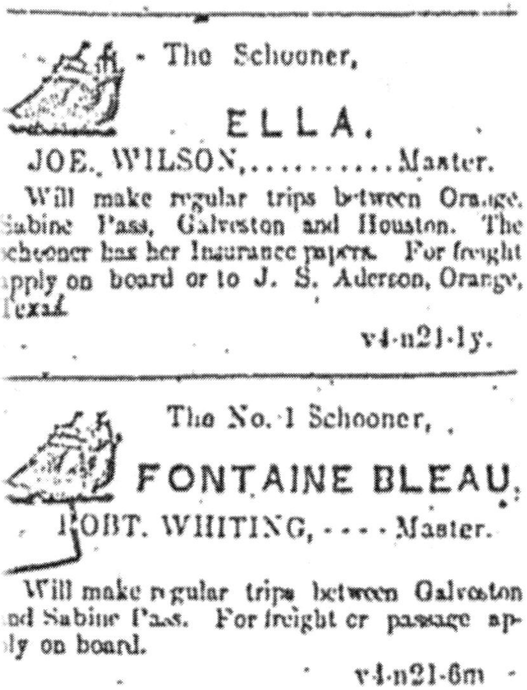

The Schooner,

ELLA.

JOE. WILSON,..........Master.

Will make regular trips between Orange,
Sabine Pass, Galveston and Houston. The
schooner has her Insurance papers. For freight
apply on board or to J. S. Aderson, Orange,
Texas.

v4-n21-1y.

The No. 1 Schooner,

FONTAINE BLEAU,

ROBT. WHITING, ····Master.

Will make regular trips between Galveston
and Sabine Pass. For freight or passage apply on board.

v4-n21-6m

Figure 1 - Ads for Schooners

Endnotes—Chapter 1

[1]Odie B. Faulk, THE LAST YEARS OF SPANISH TEXAS (The Hague: Mouton and Co., 1964, 69-70.

[2]For the boundary history, see Robert and Pauline Jones, "Texas' Eastern Boundary," TEXANA, III (Summer, 1965), 124-153.

[3]J. L. Clark, TEXAS GULF COAST: ITS HISTORY AND DEVELOPMENT, I (New York: Lewis Publishing Co., 1955), 83.

[4]G. W. Bonnell, TOPOGRAPHICAL DESCRIPTION OF TEXAS, Austin, 1840 (reprint: Waco, 1964), 9.

[5]V. Bracht, TEXAS IN 1848 (San Antonio: Naylor Company, 1941), 7.

[6]Jacob Decordova, TEXAS: HER RESOURCES AND HER PUBLIC MEN (Waco: Texian Press, 1969), 82.

[7]William Kennedy, THE RISE, PROGRESS AND PROSPECTS OF THE TEXAS REPUBLIC (Reprint: Fort Worth: Molyneaux Craftsmen, 1944), 24.

[8](Houston) *Telegraph and Texas Register*, August 2, 1843.

[9]R. E. L. Crane, "The History of the Revenue Service and Commerce of the Republic of Texas," Ph. D. dissertation, Austin, The University of Texas at Austin, 1950, pp. 280, 285.

[10]*Ibid.*, p. 280.

[11](Houston) *Morning Star*, March 8, 1845.

[12]Crane, "History of the Revenue Service," p. 277.

[13] *Morning Star*, August 4, 1843.

[14]G. P. Garrison, DIPLOMATIC CORRESPONDENCE OF THE REPUBLIC OF TEXAS, II (Wash. D. C.: 1908-1911), 320-322; E. C. Barker and A. W. Williams, THE WRITINGS OF SAM HOUSTON, IV (Austin: Pemberton Press, 1970), 270-271; *Morning Star*, March 11, 1845; *Telegraph,* March 12, 1845.

[15]*Morning Star,* May 1, 1839; Kennedy, *op. cit.*, 761.

[16](San Augustine) *Redlander*, January 20, 1844.

[17](San Augustine) *Journal and Advertiser,* December 17, 1840.

[18](Houston) *Telegraph and Texas Register*, October 4, 1843.

[19]*Telegraph,* August 18, 1841. In 1852 it cost $8.75 a bale to ship from Nacogdoches, Texas, to Natchitoches, La.

[20](Houston) *Morning Star*, May 10, 1842.

[21](Galveston) *Weekly News*, May 12, 1879, quoting Beaumont *Lumberman*.

[22](Galveston) *Tri-Weekly News*, December 22, 1869; (Beaumont) *News-Beacon*, February 22, and August 19, 1873; J. H. Eaton, "Sketch of the Sabine River from Camp Sabine to the Gulf," *House Document 365,* 1838; J. D. Graham and T. J. Lee, "Map of Sabine River, Lake, and Pass," Texas-United States Boundary Commission, 1840.

[23](Houston) *Morning Star*, January 23, 1845. See also F. C. Chabot (ed.), A JOURNAL...THOMAS S. MCFARLAND (San Antonio: 1942), 22ff.

Chapter 2—The Matchless Sabine River

Its Ships, Sailors, Snags, and Sandbars

Almost from the beginning, it becomes virtually impossible to separate the trade of the Sabine River from that of the Neches, its watery neighbor to the west, with whom it shares its outflow into Sabine Lake. Many sternwheelers had a long record of service in both rivers, while others were associated principally with a single river. Oftentimes, this was determined by the place of residence of the captain and/or owner, especially if he operated a store or plantation along the river, as with G. B. Burr of Burr's Ferry, J. J. Snell of Toledo, both of the Sabine, or Andrew Smyth and William Neyland of Bevilport, on the Angelina/Neches. With the mouths of the Sabine and Neches Rivers emptying into Sabine Lake only five miles apart, the trade of the two rivers tends to fuse before reaching Sabine Pass. And it most certainly fused when commodity shipments became mere statistics at the Sabine Pass customhouse. Hence, it is nigh impossible to state with any degree of accuracy how many bales of cotton, etc., were shipped from either river. Among timber products, such items as barrel staves and fence pickets came only from Orange on the Sabine, as least until 1880. Suffice it to say that at all times a probable two-thirds or more of all export items listed at the customhouse before 1880 originated at points along the Sabine River. For one thing, Sabine steamers went inland a total of 800 river miles, to Belzora, near Longview, Texas, whereas shipping on the Neches usually went only to Rockland on the Neches and Pattonia on the Angelina. As early as 1861, shippers at Beaumont had the option of shipping to Galveston or Houston by rail as well as by sea (although the rail line from Beaumont was out of service between 1867 and 1875), a circumstance generally denied to the Orange and Sabine River shippers until 1876.

If steamboats moved from the Neches River to the Sabine, or vice versa, at will, the same can almost be said for some of the Trinity River packets. Such steamers as the *Early Bird* moved to the Sabine River only after all cotton had been moved from the Trinity landings. The *Early Bird* and many other Trinity packets belonged to the plantation owners along the river. In 1872, thirteen steamers attempted to divide the Trinity trade between them when seven would have sufficed. In 1874 seventeen steamboats returned to the river at a time when much cotton was being diverted for trans-shipment on the newly-constructed railroads running parallel to the river. The cotton shipping season there lasted only about one month, after which many packets, such as the *Tobe Hurt, Wren,* and *Ida Reese*, were sold to Sabine River owners. During the 1872-1873 carrying season, the Trinity River trade ended in February, whereas there were still several thousand bales awaiting at the Sabine landings for transportation. Although some packets were transferred permanently and others only temporarily removed to the Sabine, the three mentioned were soon to meet ignoble ends in a short span between 1873 and 1875. The *Tobe Hurt* burned while tied up at Orange, whereas both the Wren and the *Ida Reese* were to find permanent graves in Sabine's murky depths.

Unlike the Trinity steamer and cotton trade, which was well-recorded by numerous old river men in the Galveston "News" of 1893, no lengthy lists of Sabine River packets or of its steamboatmen are known to exist. The longest list, one prepared by Captain William Wiess of Beaumont in 1910, records some 36 boats that he recalled over his lifetime, the earliest being around 1855, but he made no attempt to connect them with either the Neches or the Sabine. No one knew better than Capt. Wiess that any packet that had ever sailed in the Neches had probably sailed in the Sabine River as well. Hence the writer has had to depend upon old newspaper accounts and steamer ads, as well as other scraps and bits of information available over a span of sixty years, as well as customhouse records, in order to compile his list. The following 80-plus steamboats are all known to have plied the Sabine on at least one voyage, and a few remained in the Sabine River trade over a long span of years. Many others remained over a long span of years because they sank there, never to be raised. But most of them also sail in the Neches or in other rivers as well.

The following list of 81 names is as follows:

Ace	Fleta	Orleans
Ada	Flora	Patrick Henry
Adrianne	Florilda	Pearl Plant
Alamo	General Bryan	Pearl Rivers
Albert Gallatin (1), 1840	General Rusk	Pelican State
Albert Gallatin (2), 1870	Grand Bay	Philadelphia
Angelina	Henrietta	Pioneer
Belle Sulphur	Ida Reese	Powhattan
Bertha	J. J. Warren	Robert E. Lee
Bertha Roebuck	J. L. Webb	Rough and Ready
Big Ben	James L. Graham	Rufus Putnam
Bonnie	Jeff Davis	Sabine (1), 1844
Buffalo	John H. Bills	Sabine (2), 1860
Ceres	John Jenkins	Scioto Bell
Charles Lee	Josiah H. Bell	Stonewall
Colonel Woods	Juanita	Sunflower
Comargo	Kate (1), 1850	T. J. Smith
Cora	Kate (2), 1870	T. J. Emory
Dennis Call	Lark	Tobe Hurt
Dime	Laura	Tom Parker
Doctor Massie	Liberty	Tom Davis
Dura	Lizzie	Una
Early Bird	L. Q. C. Lamar	Uncle Ben
Effort	Maude Howell	Velocipede
Emily P.	Mary Falvey	Vicksburg
Era No. 8	Mustang	Washington
Extra	Neches Bell	Wisconsin
Fannie	Ogden	Wren

Since no list of Sabine River steamboatmen has ever been found, the writer has also been forced to compile a list from steamboat ads, crew lists in census records and Civil War records, other newspaper accounts, courthouse records, and whatever other sources were available to him. However, it is intended to apply equally to the Neches River, and many names will also appear on the list of old Trinity River sailors. In fact, some names are much better known for their tenure of service on the Trinity, Brazos River, or Galveston Bay Trade. As an example, Capt. James Havilland brought the steamers Philadelphia and Ogden to the Sabine River and the packet Lafitte to Sabine Lake (where he bought a load of cotton), but he is much better known as a Brazos navigator or in the Brazos-Galveston Bay trade while carrying cargoes for McKinney-Williams and Co., cotton merchants of Galveston Island. Although altogether, several hundred men probably plied the Sabine as captain, clerks (supercargoes), mates, engineers, cooks, crewmen, even as musicians, no more than about 140 names, as follows, can be compiled at this late date:

S. G. Allardyce	A. F. Gripon	John Orr
J. M. Allardyce	Cato Gripon	Augustus Overhue
Joseph Ables	Green Hall	T. A. Packard
William Amiss	George W. Hawley	Robert L. Patton
C. L. Anderson	Charles Hausinger	Moses L. Patton
John Barnhart	James A. Havilland	William Peake
Jacob Berg	John A. Heard	S. N. Peters
John G. Berry	E. P. Hemmingway	John Payne
W. D. Bettis	F. P. Hemmingway	Wiley Phillips
L. L. Bettis	R. D. Hines	George Pomeroy
George Bondies	J. Hord	S. Pomeroy
D. A. Brandenberg	J. W. Ingram	Jules Poitevent
John Brown	A. Johnson	Julius Pratt
Pearl Bunn	Cave Johnson	John J. Price
Charles Burch	J. P. Johnson	W. P. Rabb
Neal Burch	George Jolly	M. Reid
Sherman K. Burch	Warren Jones	David Rigsby
Increase R. Burch	E. Jones	James Robertson
Martin Carey	J. J. Jordan	W. E. Rogers
Fielding Carey	Wilson Junker	Theodore Roehte
Jack Caswell	E. I. Kellie	C. F. Runck
Stephen Chenault	Abel Ketchum	H. Clay Smith
John Clements	— Lancaster	Elias T. Smith
Abel Coffin, Jr.	William Lapham	Niles H. Smith
B. Cooper	W. O. Loving	Andrew Smyth
John Crossman	J. M. Liles	Aaron Sheffers

Joseph Cummings	S. Mansfield	J. J. Snell
J. O. Dannell	J. H. Maratta	John Stewart
C. Davis	Frank Maratta	William Stewart
E. Davis	Charles Martin	Hiram Stewart
H. T. Davis	H. F. S. Martin	John H. Sterrett
J. M. Davis	Arthur Magill	Peter D. Stockholm
Capt. Delmore	James McCall	Jerome Swinford
John Dorman	John McCall	Eberle Swinford
Mike Dyer	M. McCarty	A. T. Skinner
Luke Falvel	W. H. McKnight	Doc Truitt
J. C. Tichenor	Capt.–Miles	William Wiess
A. Fox	H. Mellier	Napoleon Wiess
Robert Frazier	— Medford	T. C. Whittle
James Fullerton	Green Moore	L. E. Wilson
Robert Gibson	A. J. Moore	J. D. Wildey
John Gibney	L. Nicholson	John Woods
G. Godwin	Andrew Nicholson	Capt.–Wolf
Bud Goskill	William Neyland	Isaac Wright
Ben Granger	Capt.–Norris	George Wolford
Sanford Gregory	Henry Orr	W. W. Wolford
	P. A. Work	

No figures are available which apply solely to the cotton commerce of the Sabine River. Export figures at the Sabine custom house applied equally to the Neches River. But at no time before or after the Civil War does the writer believe that the Sabine River trade ever exceeded 15,000 bales in any given year. Until 1846, eighty percent of the cotton trade went directly to New Orleans on American schooners which bypassed the customhouse, and any Texas tariff or tonnage fees were evaded. Unlike Trinity, the Sabine River trade experienced much competition from cotton freighted overland to Natchitoches or Grand Ecore, Louisiana, or else was shipped to New Orleans via Jefferson, Texas, Caddo Lake, and the Red River. Until 1856, the river rarely attracted more than two steamboats in any given year, and these usually did not reach the landings beyond Logansport. During the years around, before, or after 1850, the river was often at flood stage due to monsoon rains in Northeast Texas, and in 1857, the "Uncle Ben" made at least three trips inland all the way to Belzora, Smith County, carrying out 1,000 bale loads on each voyage. Often, there would have been long waiting periods at the landings to get cotton to market, and an even longer wait to realize a cash return in gold. Although insurance was available on cotton shipments as far back as 1845, perhaps farther, the rates aboard steamboats were high, and still higher for keelboats. And frequently cotton shipments were lost in the river after a steamboat sank, all of which left the planter confused regarding the preferable cotton route to market.

For whatever value to this treatise they may contain, exports at Sabine Pass for the year ending July l1, 1858, consisted of: 15,176 bales of cotton; 6,120,000 shingles; 210,000 oak barrel staves; 1,063,000 feet of lumber; 1,543 cattle hides; 2 casks of horns; 30 barrels of potatoes; 7 barrels of beans; 325 barrels of lime; NOTE 115,000 pounds of tobacco; 125 loose deer hides; 9 bear hides; 25 bundles of deer hides; 45 sacks of rice; and 135 barrels of Sour Lake mineral water. A. M. Truitt of Burkville, who in 1857 was engaged in Sabine River channel clearance (raft and snag removal), thought that between 60,000 and 70,000 bales of cotton would reach Sabine Pass during 1859, but such gross exaggerations, miscalculations, or exorbitant guesses were quite common in the old records and newspaper accounts.[24]

In 1859, Sabine Pass exported 18,393 bales of cotton; 6,096 cattle hides; 1,099,000 feet of lumber; 5,669 heads of beef cattle to New Orleans; 7,000 hoop poles; 11,919,000 shingles; 97,000 barrel staves; 28,700 pounds of tobacco; 55 barrels of molasses; and 18 bales of deer skins.[25] When one realizes that cotton shipments there decreased to only 6,500 bales in 1866, he or she can readily visualize the unfortunate plight the East Texas cotton planters which resulted from the Civil War and the effects of defeat, all of which reduced the Sabine carrying trade to only a small fraction of its antebellum size in 1860.[26]

In 1881, the Sabine and East Texas Railroad was completed to Rockland on the Neches and in subsequent years all the way to Dallas. Later the Gulf, Beaumont, and Kansas City Railroad was constructed to Kirbyville, Texas, and eventually completed to Longview, Texas. The many sawmill and logging tram roads which reached the Neches and Sabine Rivers were soon tied into these main lines. By 1895 it appears that the movement of cotton on the Sabine had effectively ceased, except perhaps for a few occasional bales. A few steamers remained at Orange until after 1900, but their role had degenerated to excursion service, mail, or freight service to isolated Johnson's Bayou, Louisiana, or towboat service for log rafts, and lumber barges moving along the river or to Sabine Pass, or freight service to supply the tram logging roads, carrying principally corn for the mule teams and oxen. As a result, the tiny remnant of sternwheelers soon gave way to the conventional and more efficient screw-propeller tugboat with an internal combustion engine, which is still the mainstay of the Sabine River trade. But for purposes of this monograph, the writer defines the river packet as a steam-driven, sidewheel or sternwheel boat employed primarily in the cotton-carrying trade.

In truth, the river steamers lingered on the Sabine River far longer than on any comparable Texas river, principally because of the logging, tram road, and railroad construction activities which existed between 1875 and 1910. Its heyday long since removed, the steamboat had bowed once more to the rails it had helped to construct. But with its passing, there lingered for decades to come a certain nostalgia and fond memories of yesteryear for the many old settlers along the Sabine and the old steamboatmen of Orange, who missed the sternwheeler's shrill whistle below the bend and regretted its demise.

Endnotes—Chapter 2

[24]TEXAS ALMANAC, 1859, pp. 150-151.

[25]*Ibid.*, 1861, p. 237.

[26]*Ibid.*, 1867, pp. 124-125.

Chapter 3—The Sabine River's Antebellum Sternwheelers

The first steamboat movement on the Sabine River and the first channel clearance in that stream did not occur as a consequence of legislation or other action on the part of the Republic of Texas or the needs of its citizens. It came about because the United States army needed to reduce exorbitant wagon-freighting costs to its troops stationed in Western Louisiana, namely at Fort Jessup near Many and at Camp Sabine, on the eastern banks of the river opposite Sabinetown. The wagon freighters were primarily East Texans and cotton carriers who had to make the long trek to Natchitoches, La., in order to haul the commodities of East Texas to the Red River for trans-shipment to New Orleans. They also had to freight manufactured wares, etc., on the return trips, but because of the bulk of the cotton bales, the return loads usually utilized only a fraction of their wagon trains' carrying capacities. Obviously, the traffic in military goods was a boon to the freighters, but they nonetheless took full advantage of the U. S. Army to overcharge at prices up to $6.00 per hundred-weight, or roughly twice the rate charged the East Texas planters to transport a 400-pound bale of cotton.

The events of 1836 in East Texas were also to have an adverse effect. To begin with the Texas Revolution caused U. S. President Andrew Jackson to send an army of 4,000 men to occupy Fort Jessup and Camp Sabine, necessitating the need to pay exorbitant wagon freight rates to supply them. Some historians believe that had Mexican General Antonio de Santa Ana been successful in driving the Texans across the river and Mexicans had crossed the Sabine in pursuit, Jackson had full intent to order the invasion of Texas by American troops. In 1836, thousands of Texans neglected the planting of cotton during that spring and fled eastward to escape the Mexican army, or else enlisted in the Texas army. In fact, the years 1836-1837 saw comparatively little cotton planted anywhere in Texas since corn was in greater demand to replenish the food supply and replace the dwindling supply of livestock. Hence, with little cotton available to haul and their livelihoods threatened, wagon freighters of necessity turned to military transporting full time in some instances and increased their freight rates charged the army whenever cotton was unavailable. Thus, the military authorities' decision to clean out the river and ship freight via steamboats, even though no steamboat up to 1837 had ever ascended the river, was a logical result.

Early in 1837 the American Congress authorized expenditures to include the mapping of the Sabine Lake and River, the removal of snags and overhanging trees, and the blowing up of a number of "rafts," or permanent logjams, so that the fallen trees could float out to sea and "open the navigation of the Sabine River" to steamboats. During the summer of 1837, the army sent Major W. G. Belknap and a detachment of the 3rd U. S. Infantry Regiment to Sabine Lake, where they set up a temporary camp on a marsh "chenier" or ridge on the Louisiana shore of Sabine Lake, after which the engineers began mapping the region. To the present day, that oak-studded "chenier" in the marsh is known as Garrison Ridge from the army garrison that occupied it. The project of blowing up some twenty obstructions to shipping was accomplished by Lieutenant J. H. Eaton and his men in a span of four weeks. Upon completion of their assignment in December 1837, Major Belknap contracted the services of Captain Isaac Wright and his Vermillion River (Louisiana) steamer, the "Velocipede," who tested, as the following letters in House correspondence of the 25th U. S. Congress reveal, the navigation of the Sabine all the way to Gaines' Ferry:

Camp on Sabine Lake (La.). March 23, 1838,

Maj. Gen. A. Macomb

Washington City

I have the honor to enclose, herewith, a sketch of the Sabine River, from Camp Sabine to the sea, together with a statement of the acting assistant quartermaster showing the expense incurred in rendering it navigable for steamboats, and the copy of a letter from the master of the steamboat "Velocipede," on making his first trip. The chart...was made by Lieutenant J. H. Eaton, of the 3rd Infantry, after a most careful and minute examination...

W. G. Belknap

Major, U. S. Army

Sabine Pass, Texas, March 23, 1838

Major Belknap

From your report of the navigation of the Sabine River, I have been induced to make the trial, with the steamboat "Velocipede," of 143 tons burden, 133 3/4 feet in length, 30 foot beam, with guards of 14 feet, drawing five feet of water; and I am pleased to inform you that I have succeeded in ascending and descending to and from the town of Sabine {Sabinetown}, a distance of about 300 miles without the least injury to my boat.

Your success has been beyond the expectations of the oldest inhabitants on the river; and your labor has enhanced the value of all lands adjacent to the river at least 200 percent...

The price of freight, from Natchitoches to Camp Sabine, has heretofore cost about five or six cents per pound; and by the Sabine River, from New Orleans to Camp Sabine, the freight will cost two cents per pound.

Isaac Wright

Captain, Steamer "Velocipede"[27]

For all the effort and expense that the United States Army put into that first Sabine River channel-clearing project, it seems to have derived very little benefit therefrom, and it probably returned to its old method of wagon-freighting in order to supply its forces in Western Louisiana. Too, with East Texas in friendly hands again, the large number United States troops stationed in Louisiana was probably reduced quickly. (Around 1830, the strength of the U. S.

Army is known to have dropped to as low as 6,000 **men** at times, and for 4,000 to be stationed in Louisiana at a time when the Louisiana Purchase was opening to western settlement and the plains Indians were increasingly hostile made no sense.) On Captain Wright's second voyage in the river, Thomas S. McFarland, the developer of the townsite of Belgrade and an early Texas Senator, recorded in his journal on April 15, 1838, that:[28]

> ...The steamboat "Velocipede" arrived here this morning at sunrise. She discharged a considerable quantity of provisions which was much wanting, not only here, but all over the country. This is her second trip to...the upper landings...as high as Pendleton.

Two weeks later McFarland reported that the packet had returned to Belgrade after experiencing "much difficulty" on the route and got up as high as the Town of Hamilton. On her way down she was snagged and received injury otherwise."[29] It is of interest that neither record of Captain Wright's voyages mentioned any cotton cargo aboard, but as late as March, the cotton along the river probably had already gone to market via wagon freight and the Red River. Wright evidently found little prospect for establishing a profitable commerce along the river and took the steamer back to Vermillion Bay, Louisiana.

Further proof that the army made little, if any, further utilization of the Sabine for hauling freight stems from the fact that only one other vessel arrived in the river in 1838 as well as only one packet in 1839. In 1838 the steamer Ceres came to the Sabine, McFarland noted, ascending as high as Salem, where it also sank.[30] Capt. Peter D. Stockholm, a veteran Sabine River pilot then residing in Beaumont, confirmed McFarland's statement, adding that "Captain Reid brought the Ceres around from Shreveport," reaching almost to Belgrade where the packet ran up on a sunken log and foundered.[31]

On February 15, 1839, Captain Miles brought the 125-ton Texas steamer Wisconsin, with "general sundries" and eight passengers aboard, from Vermillion Bay, La., and ascended the river as far as Sabinetown. On a second voyage begun on March 31, the Wisconsin ascended to Sabinetown with passengers and general cargo.[32] On still a third voyage, the vessel returned to Sabinetown, but was subsequently snagged and sunk while descending the river.[33] No record has been found concerning the volume of cotton carried on the Wisconsin, but it becomes apparent that, in view of three voyages, a profitable commerce was already available on the river. Otherwise, it would be highly illogical to assume that Capt. Miles would have returned to the Sabine for a third voyage unless he had been obtaining profitable cargoes and, for lack of space, had left quantities of cotton at the landings on his second voyage.

In 1839, the packet Rufus Putnam entered the Galveston Bay trade, and one of its advertisements noted that it was "provided in case of fire with chain wheel ropes."[34] Over a span of thirty years, its master and owner, Captain John H. Sterrett, brought no less than ten steamboats to Texas, a number of which sank in the Texas rivers. Late in 1839, one source revealed that Sterrett had contracted with the Sabinetown merchants "to bring down about 4,000 bales of cotton" to the coast.[35] On January 6, 1840, the Rufus Putnam cleared the customhouse in route to Sabinetown, but shortly after entering the river, the ill-fated packet struck an underwater snag or obstruction opposite Eaves Plantation near Salem and sank. The Texas-United States Boundary Commission map of 1840 marks the site of the Putnam's sunken hulk plainly.[36]

There is no doubt that 4,000 or 5,000 bales of cotton reached the coast during the 1839-1840 shipping season, but the bulk of it must have arrived at the mouth of the river on keelboats such as Steadham and Van Dusen's fleet at Hamilton. On September 1, 1839, August Hotchkiss of Sabine Pass advertised for "10 or 15 vessels of lawful tonnage" to carry cotton from Sabine Pass to New Orleans during the coming winter.[37] Hotchkiss was at the time the first cotton merchant at Sabine Pass of which there is any record, but he returned to Sabinetown in 1842 and reopened his store there.

Hence after only two years of steam navigation on the Sabine River, already the river had chalked up quite a list of victims from among the first four packets to sail there. Three of them were already submerged as rotting hulks beneath its murky surface, and the fourth, the Velocipede, had sustained serious, but not fatal, damage on its second voyage. Unfortunately, a high rate of snag victims was to tarnish the river's history for many decades to follow.

According to Capt. Stockholm, another vessel of the year 1840 was the packet Washington. A veteran of the Red River trade, the sternwheeler belonged to a Shreveport master, Capt. J. S. Brown, who brought the vessel around to Sabine Pass. Capt. Reid then took over as master and, with Pilot Stockholm at the wheel, steered Washington to Fullerton's Landing below Sabinetown. For some unexplained reason, the steamboat remained moored at the landing throughout the summer of 1841, and it is probable that engine trouble or low water was the cause. During an especially low water period, when the entire hull was out of the water on a sandbar, the vessel's ribs cracked and the ship timbers dried out, opening seams or leaks which quickly filled with water when the first river freshet arrived. There was no record of any effort to refloat Washington, nor is it listed among customhouse arrivals and departures for that year.[38]

On March 20, 1840, Captain H. Mellier brought the steamer Albert Gallatin from New Orleans and cleared Sabine customs, bound for Sabinetown with general cargo. According to the Thomas McFarland journal, the packet passed Belgrade on March 27, eventually ascending the river as far as Pendleton. On April 12, the river boat "was heavily laden with cotton" upon reaching Belgrade on the return voyage.[39] At the time of her first voyage in the Sabine, the sternwheeler carried an advance party of surveyors of the Texas-United States Boundary Commission (then in session at Orange and Sabine Pass) as far north as Gaines' Ferry, one of whom, civilian engineer George Gordon Meade, some 23 years later was to subject Gen. Robert E. Lee to his worst defeat at the Battle of Gettysburg and turn the tide of civil war in favor of the North.[40]

Apparently, the captain of the Gallatin sold his first Sabine River cargo to some New Orleans-bound cotton schooner anchored in Sabine Lake for, according to customs records, the steamboat cleared for Sabinetown again on April 15 and for a third time on May 8. On May 19, 1840, the packet sailed for Galveston with 119 bales of cotton, hides, and sundry produce.[41] While descending from her fourth voyage late in June, 1840, the Gallatin ran on a log and grounded on a mud flat in the Sabine, where the boat remained stranded for several days.[42] On December 23, 1841, while engaged in the Galveston Bay trade with Houston, the Albert Gallatin exploded and sank in the bay with a loss of fifteen persons killed and scalded by high pressure steam.[43] At the time, the packet was racing another steamer.

Probably the best account of an early-day steamer voyage on a Texas steamer, and certainly the best for the Sabine River, resulted from Gallatin's fourth voyage upriver. On May 22, 1840, the packet left Orange with the remainder of the boundary commission members as well as the two granite boundary markers which were subsequently erected at the 32nd parallel (near Joaquin, Texas, one on each side of the river. During the 1960's, one of the markers was re-located in the swamps near the Sabine, but the other has not been found.).43 The lengthy quote, which follows, is from the daily journal of the boundary commission:[44]

> May 1840–On the evening of the 22nd, the commissioners, surveyors, clerks, etc., on the part of the United States and Texas, together, with Major Graham and Mr. Daniel Wilbur and Andrew B. Gray, the last two engineers on the part of Texas (army), embarked near Huntley {Orange} on board the steamboat Albert Gallatin, for the purpose of surveying the river and marking the boundary as far as the 32nd degree of latitude. The same evening the party proceeded upriver about 16 miles, as far as Ballew's Ferry, passing the mouth of Cypress Creek and Old River on the Texas side.

> May 23–At about 11:00 o'clock A. M., left Ballew's Ferry where the boat had lain all night, and continued the work of tracing

the boundary upriver. We proceeded this day about – miles. For 30 miles after leaving Ballew's Ferry, the river winds in a continuous succession of abrupt sinuosities {serpentine curves}. The bank contains here and there patches of pine, though much of the timber is of those kinds that usually flourish in lowlands.

May 24th–Started at sunrise and proceeded this day – miles. This portion of the river is by no means so crooked as that which we traveled yesterday. We passed by the town of Salem, situated on one of the mouths of Big Cow Creek. About sundown, reached the town of Belgrade, where the boat lay for the night. Belgrade is said to have once been the seat of the Biloxi Indians.

May 25th–Started at 5:30 A. M. We this day found the navigation of the river for several miles above Belgrade somewhat difficult, it being obstructed not only by the extreme crookedness of the river, but also by a raft {logjam} of about 3 miles in length, commencing about 2 miles above Belgrade. We proceeded that day as far as Hickman's {Landing}, situated on a high bluff on the Louisiana side of the river and about half-mile by land south of Thompson's Ferry. The boat lay for the night at Hickman's, being – miles, more or less, by the course of the river from Belgrade. Mr. Wilbur and Maj. Graham were engaged on shore until three hours after midnight in making astronomical observations for the latitude and longitude of this point. The sky was very clear and favorable for their observations.

May 26–At sunrise, left Hickman's and proceeded this day within 14 miles of Sabinetown. The boat lay during the night opposite White's, situated on a bluff on the east bank, or Louisiana side, of the river, the atmosphere remaining remarkably clear and favorable for their observations. The banks of this portion of the river are in general more elevated than any we have yet passed, some of the bluffs as high as 14 feet above the present level of the river, which is just now unusually high. Today we passed the path of a recent tornado, which has prostrated the trees and cane on the banks of the river. Its course was observed to be 72 degrees west to north 72 degrees east, and the track to be from 300 to 400 yards wide. It is thought to be the same tornado which occasioned such dreadful destruction of human life and property at Natchez on May 7th.

May 27th–At sunrise, the boat started and about 8 A. M. reached Sabinetown, a flourishing village situated on the Texas side of the river. The boat lay there discharging freight until 4 o'clock P. M., when we started for Gaines' Ferry, where we arrived the same evening. Here we joined Captain Pillans and Lieutenant Lee, who had availed themselves of the first trip of the Albert Gallatin to ascend as high as this point. After the temporary adjournment of the joint Commission at Sabine Pass, Mr. George G. Meade {later to be the Union commander at Gettysburg}, who had been appointed an assistant in the astronomical department of the United States, joined the Commission at this place on the first of April.

May 28th–Not having arranged the means of transportation higher up the river, we obliged to lay at Gaines' Ferry during the day. An agreement was, however, finally made with the captain of the Albert Gallatin to convey the party as high up the river as the 32nd degree.

May 29th–We accordingly left Gaines' Ferry this morning at noon, having taken on board the instruments and camp equipage previously sent to this place. We proceeded this day about 35 miles, our boat lying during the night at a high bluff five miles from the village of Hamilton. The night was clear, but the density of the forest on either side was such as to prevent the engineers from observing.

May 30–Started at 6:00 A. M. and about 9 o'clock reached Hamilton, on the west side of the river, where we took on wood. The river up to this point from Gaines' Ferry is very crooked and the navigation a good deal interrupted by the overhanging trees. We proceeded this day – miles to a point ascertained by observation to be in latitude 37 degrees, 48 minutes, 30 seconds. Here Maj. Graham, Mr. Wilbur, Lieutenant Lee, and Mr. {George Gordon} Meade were occupied until one hour after midnight making astronomical observations. Above Hamilton, a portion of the river for several miles is wide and quite straight, but during the latter part of the day, our progress was again obstructed by trees and the crookedness of the stream.

May 31–Started at 6:00 A. M. We had not gone more than three miles before we were stopped by a raft in the river, which detained us nearly seven hours. At 1:30 P. M., the raft being removed, we started and ran for the rest of the day, meeting, however, with occasional obstructions... The night was clear, and the engineers were engaged on shore until past midnight in observing for latitude and longitude.

June 1st–Started at 6:00 A. M. From this point the character of the land and timber began to change, the former being higher on both sides of the river than heretofore, and the latter consisting chiefly of white and red oak, hickory, white maple, pine, and cypress...

After Albert Gallatin left the Sabine River for Galveston Bay, it appears that the trade of the river may have declined somewhat for the next two years, if judged solely on the basis of steamboat arrivals. The unknown variable, however, is the volume of cotton that arrived on the coast via keelboat or flatboat, and Sabine customhouse records do not reflect an accurate figure prior to 1847. During the years 1841-1842, there are indications that the cotton trade was unprofitable for those steamers that were moving on the stream, or until 1843, the year when the packet Sabine entered the Sabine River trade, where it remained until the exigencies of the Mexican War forced its removal to the Rio Grande River.

According to customhouse records, only two river steamers navigated the Sabine River during the year 1841. On February 8, Captain J. Hord brought the American packet Patrick Henry from Berwick Bay, La., and entered the river. Whether or not the packet came in search of cotton is uncertain, but on March 1, the captain cleared for Galveston with a load of lumber loaded at Huntley (or Green's Bluff, now Orange).

On January 21, 1841, Captain James Havilland brought the American steamboat Philadelphia from New Orleans and cleared customs with four passengers and mixed cargo for Sabinetown. Was the U. S. Army still moving cargo to Camp Sabine? Such was not clarified, and by the time of its second voyage in the river, Capt. Havilland, by then of 'Sabinetown,' had changed the vessel's registry from American to Texas. On March 11, Havilland arrived at the customhouse and cleared the same date for Sabinetown to load cotton.[45] Following his second voyage, the captain moved his packet to the Brazos River, where on April 13, 1842, the Philadelphia was driven aground at the mouth of the Brazos during a storm and became a total wreck. The steamer had 450 bales of cotton aboard.[46] The following November, Capt. Havilland, as master of the new, 138-ton McKinney-Williams and Co. steamboat Lafitte, was back in Sabine Lake, where he loaded a cargo of cotton bound for the Island City.[47]

Two sternwheelers are also recorded as navigating the Sabine River during the year 1842. In February 1842, the packet General Bryan arrived at Sabinetown, where it immediately loaded a cargo of cotton belonging to C. W. Hotchkiss and Co. While descending the river, General Bryan:[48]

...ran aground of a sunken log, tore off a portion of her bottom, and immediately sank. General Bryan had on board about 400 bales of cotton and a lot of

groceries for some of the landings below ...The boat,
it is believed, will be a total loss...

The following November, the packet Mustang advertised that it would sail from Galveston on the 28th on a "trading excursion" in the Sabine River. Captain John Singer quoted passage aboard at $50 a person to Sabine Pass or $100 to Sabinetown.[49] Evidently the steamboat made only one Sabine River voyage for, two months later, the Mustang was navigating the Brazos River, where it sank a year later with a large cargo of cotton aboard.[50]

In the year 1843, it appears that there was a significant increase in Sabine River cotton trade as well as in transportation on the river. On September 30 of that year, the Houston "Morning Star" printed a lengthy article on Sabine navigation, the editor crediting such merchants as C. H. Alexander of Sabinetown, who come to realize that in order to keep steamboats permanently in the river, it would be necessary to transfer ownership from the independent steamer captains, who moved from river to river at the slightest whim or promise of increased profits.[51] Although no more than 15% of the cotton exports received Texas customhouse clearance, the increased activity was likewise visible at Sabine Pass, where 2,039 bales were registered with the collector in 1844 as opposed to only 805 bales in 1841.[52]

On January 27, 1843, another ill-fated packet, the 139-ton Pioneer under Captain A. Fox of New Orleans, cleared customs, bound for Sabinetown. After a month in the river, it sailed for Galveston with a load of cotton. On its second voyage in April, the Pioneer's crew mutinied while in the river, and were subsequently jailed in Galveston to await trial in admiralty court. The vessel was later auctioned by order of that court, and when the new owners attempted to sail the steamer to Matagorda Bay, the Pioneer ran aground, a total wreck, near Pass Cavallo.[53]

As perhaps the Sabine River's first merchant-steamer captain, John G. Berry of San Augustine bought the packet Big Ben, which traded up and down the river, delivering freight and merchandise and loading aboard cotton and other commodities.

Years later, he was also to own and command another boat of similar name, the Uncle Ben, perhaps the most famous steamer ever to ply the stream, for it often made the 800-mile voyage to Belzora, near Longview, in Smith County.[54] In 1843, C. H. Alexander and Co. of Sabinetown purchased the "substantial light draught steamer John H. Bills," with Captain Frisby as its master. In December 1843, the new packet Sabine, "built this summer at Louisville, Kentucky, expressly for the Sabine River trade," arrived on the river, captained by Charles H. Donne.[55] Earlier, another order had been placed at Louisville for the steamboat Colonel Woods, which arrived in 1844.[56]

In 1888, Captain Peter Stockholm recounted that he had piloted the packet Scioto Belle up the Sabine to Hamilton in 1842. It is probable, however, that the esteemed and veteran river pilot's memory erred somewhat regarding the exact year since 45 years had elapsed at the time of his writing. And a number of primary sources place the Scioto Belle in the Sabine River trade only during the year 1844.[57]

The 95-ton Scioto Belle, under Captain Isaac Wright (and formerly of the Velocipede), arrived from New Orleans on February 11 and cleared customs for Sabinetown with general cargo and passengers. A month later, the packet sailed for Galveston, heavily-laden with cotton. After a second voyage to Sabinetown in April, at which time the steamboat was under a new skipper, Captain E. Jones, the Scioto Belle sailed for Galveston in ballast on May 4, 1844, having apparently disposed of its cargo to the New Orleans schooners at anchor in the lake. Perhaps, too, the steamer failed to find any more cotton along the river for May of 1844 would be woefully late in the shipping season for any 1843 cotton still to be awaiting shipment.[58] The Weekly News reported that the sternwheeler was "new, substantial, and of light draft," and planned to enter the Trinity River cotton trade immediately.[59]

In March 1844, the 134-ton Colonel Woods, the other steamer "built expressly for the Sabine trade," cleared customs for Sabinetown. At the end of its first voyage Captain John Woods lightered 502 bales aboard the New Orleans schooners Robert

Center and Cabot, then at anchor in Sabine Lake. At the end of its second voyage on May 4, the steamboat cleared for Galveston in ballast, having apparently lightered its second cargo aboard the lake schooners as well or else, had failed to locate any bales left at the river landings. This packet, however, did not return to the river after its second voyage, and other sources reveal that it soon engaged in the lucrative Galveston Bay trade. Due to a number of steamboat mishaps in Texas in 1844, Colonel Woods for a short time was the only vessel left in Texas' inland cotton-carrying trade.[60]

No other steamer of the 1840's was to enjoy as lengthy or lucrative career in the river as did the 106-ton Sabine. The packet was soon owned jointly by its new master, D. A. Brandenberg, and Capt. John Sterrett of Houston. Its pilot, Capt. John Clements, had begun his Sabine River career as a keelboater of cotton during the late 1830's, and with the possible exception of Peter Stockholm, knew the Sabine River's shoals, currents, snags, and channels better than any other pilot of that era.

Over a span of four shipping seasons, 1843 to 1846, it is uncertain exactly how many voyages the steamboat completed in the river, but it probably averaged about four each year. On one occasion in May 1845, Brandenberg lightered 300 bales aboard the New Orleans schooner William Bryan and immediately returned to Sabinetown.[61]

In March 1845, a Houston newspaper editor reported that the Sabine was then:[62]

...plying between the Sabine Pass and landings as high as Hamilton. The boat has made two trips in the river this season and Capt. B.(randenberg) experienced so little difficulty in the passage that he expressed his determination to continue in the Sabine River trade...

In 1846, Brandenberg advertised that the Saint Louis Perpetual Insurance Company would insure cotton shipped on his packet at cheaper rates than cotton shipped on the river by either barge or keelboat.[63] By November 1846, the Sabine had been transferred to the Galveston Bay trade, and again in 1847 to South Texas during the Mexican War, where the packet was snagged and sunk shortly after entering the Rio Grande River.[64]

As might be expected for a river with such extensive forests along its banks, the timber products industry, comprised principally of hand-made lumber, shingles, and barrel staves, began its development along the lower Sabine shortly after the Texas Revolution. As late as 1875, forty years after the first Sabine River, water-powered sawmill had been built, an estimated thirty billion board feet of long leaf pine and five billion feet of cypress still stood on both banks of the river. And with the passing of time, the movement of logs and lumber along the lower stream would replace the transportation of cotton and breathe new life into the steamboat trade until long after its heyday had vanished elsewhere. As early as 1837, Robert E. Boothe built one of the pioneer sawmills of Texas, run by waterpower, at a point on the Sabine, north of Orange, and could cut 1,500 feet of lumber daily. About 1843, Robert Jackson constructed a steam-driven sash sawmill at the "Narrows" of the Sabine, on the Louisiana side of the river near Deweyville, and utilized an engine and boilers recovered from a steamboat wreck, probably the Rufus Putnam.[65] In February, 1844, Captain Christian Warner, an early Orange merchant, sailed the sloop William Wallace, loaded with 56,000 shingles and 4,000 barrel staves, from Green's Bluff {Orange} to the Island City, proving that timber products were already an important commercial product of the river, and many more lumber cargoes are recorded among early customhouse records of the Republic of Texas. By 1853, at least five steam sawmills were in operation at many points along the lower river (including the mills of John Merriman, R. A. Neyland, R. H. Jackson; Brosser, Wood and Co.; and the Empire Mills), principally in the vicinity of Orange, turning out vast quantities of lumber, shingles, fence pickets, barrel staves, wood lathes, and wagon spokes.[66]

With timber resources so conveniently available, it was inevitable that an early shipbuilding industry should also develop. Although there is no record of a steamboat being built on the banks of the Sabine during the 1840's, adequate facilities for such construction were available at Green's Bluff {Orange} by 1845, for in January 1846, Charles Baxter's yard completed construction there on the new schooner Creole for Captain John Pederson.[67] In 1849, Captain Peter Stockholm, the pilot, bought a half-interest in Baxter's shipyard. (Stockholm had been apprenticed to a ship carpenter in Brooklyn as early as 1830, and he utilized his off-season months in repairing and building ships.) In June 1849, the partners signed a contract with Moses L. Patton, master of the first Neches River steamboat, the Angelina, to rebuild completely that vessel's superstructure, to include "new wheelhouses, new plumber blocks, new upper guards, new lower guards, facings and moldings from stem to stern, and slight repairs to the cabin, main deck, and ceiling..."[68]

Between 1846 and 1850, the Angelina, owned by two brothers, Robert S., and Moses L. Patton of Pattonia, Nacogdoches County, was the first steam carrier on the Angelina-Neches waterway.[69] and the foregoing document is the only known record which places that steamboat in the Sabine River. The brothers had keelboated Nacogdoches County cotton on the Neches River as early as 1836, and they built one early-day keelboat, the T. J. Rusk, which was complete with wheelhouse and rudder. However, R. S. Patton was a major Sabine River steamboatman as well, shipping from his plantations at Belzora in Smith County. Since there is no account, however, of a sternwheeler plying the Sabine River during the years 1847-1848 (all of them had gone south to the Mexican War), it seems only logical that the Angelina would not have passed up the opportunity to carry cotton on the Sabine after the Angelina-Neches River trade was finished. In April 1849, a Galveston editor recorded that:[70]

> *...the steamer Angelina had been making regular trips. She arrived at the Pass on the 18th with full freight. By the same accounts, a number of flatboats on the Sabine and Neches were on their way down, bringing in altogether about 3,000 bales ...It is*

*computed that at least 6,000 or 7,000 bales of cotton
will be shipped from the Sabine this year...*

Hence, in lieu of inadequate steam transportation, it appears that most of the cotton along the Sabine River was once again moving via keelboat or flatboat. In February 1850, the Angelina was snagged and sunk in the Neches, eight miles above Grant's (Wiess) Bluff (south of Evadale). At the time, the vessel was ascending the river with a load of rough lumber which Patton probably had purchased at Orange.[71]

It becomes quite obvious that a lack of cotton could not have been the principal cause for the decline of the Sabine River steamboat trade during the years 1847-1848. The shortage of transport facilities was sorely felt by the merchants along the river, who had no other recourse except wagon-freighting for obtaining merchandise or keelboats and wagons for shipping cotton. And the convening in 1849 of three Sabine River navigation Conventions clarifies one cause for the lack of steamers (the writer believes that exigencies of the Mexican War was the other cause). With no clearing of the Sabine River channel impediments throughout the 1840's, the many obstructions (such as log rafts, overhanging trees, and underwater snags) in the stream had discouraged the steamboat owners to the point of abandoning the Sabine River for the more lucrative Trinity, Brazos, Galveston Bay, or transporting Mexican War soldiers and supplies.

In May of 1849, a number of San Augustine and Sabine County merchants and planters, led by Gen. John G. Berry, met at Shelbyville to initiate plans for clearing the river of navigation hazards; to determine the approximate costs and extent of the work needed; and to solve how to fund the project. Solicitation for private subscriptions went out to all the neighboring counties that depended on the river trade and to the adjacent Louisiana parishes of Desoto, Sabine, and Vernon. Upon adjournment, a second Sabine River Navigation Convention was scheduled to convene at Henderson, Texas on July 4, 1849, with invitations extended for delegations from Cherokee, Smith, Rusk, Panola, Shelby, Newton, and Jasper Counties as well.[72] Between conferences, a committee was appointed to determine the extent and costs for minimal channel clearance that would render the river passable and safe for steamers.

For reasons not stated, the second convention assembled at Sabinetown on July 16, with John G. Berry as permanent chairman and J. S. Noble as secretary. A number of resolutions were adopted, and delegations in each county and parish were authorized to solicit and collect funds for the project. A third river conference was then rescheduled to meet on August 3, 1849, at Milam, Texas.[73]

Some clue to the river clearance work that apparently resulted from the conventions is visible in the following facts. Prior to 1849, no packet had ever attempted to ascend the Sabine beyond Logansport, La., which is 514 river miles from the Gulf of Mexico. In 1850, only a year after the conferences, a steamboat travelled all the way to Belzora in Smith County, 18 miles northeast of Tyler, Texas, and 879 river miles from Sabine Pass, opening up a new market for the many upper Sabine River counties. Two of the next two vessels to sail to the upper reaches of the river were not sternwheelers at all, but were V-bottom, deep sea steamers. One, the Liberty, was a 200-foot, square-rigged, IRON steamship that sailed all the way inland on a river freshet to Fredonia, Rusk County, and carried out a load of cotton.

During the 1850's, the State of Texas began expending public funds for maintaining the Sabine River channel, and in 1852, the state legislature approved a $33,000 appropriation for that purpose.[74] In 1856, the Texas Legislature appropriated $300,000 for the improvement of the Texas rivers and harbors, voting to expend on the Sabine an amount equal to that authorized by the State of Louisiana.[75] In the summer of 1857, Captain Robert S. Patton, the pioneer navigator and merchant of Belzora and Pattonia, arrived at Orange with his steamer Uncle Ben, prepared to execute his contract with the State of Texas for channel clearance. Patton, however, died at Orange shortly after his arrival there, and his contract was reassigned to John G. Berry of San Augustine, who also bought the Uncle Ben from Patton's estate.[76]

Two other contracts were assigned for Sabine River clearance in the year 1857, 'section No. 1' of the river going to A. M. Truitt and Co. of Burkeville, who weas to:[77]

...improve the navigation of the same from Turner's Ferry to Logansport, distance over 400 miles. Section No. 2, on the same river, has been awarded to T. M. Likens and Co. as the best bidders, to improve said river from Logansport to Bacon's Bluff, distance 200 miles or over...The first section was awarded at a little over $31,000, and Section 2 at $20,000... These contractors will proceed at once to the work and will lose no time till contracts are completed.

In November 1858, J. H. Parsons, an assistant engineer for the State of Texas, returned to Orange after touring the Sabine, where he inspected the work performed by Truitt, Likens, and Berry, and he certified their contracts for payment.[78] In 1859, the State appropriated another $15,000 and signed a contract with Captain David Bradbury of Galveston to build a dredge boat at Sabine Pass for cutting a channel through the Sabine River bar.[79]

To view the Sabine River today in the vicinity of Longview, Texas, and to realize that steamboats as large as the 135-foot Uncle Ben once navigated the tiny stream as far inland as Smith County defies belief. But old-time East Texans always insisted that the shallow-draft "river steamboats could navigate in heavy dew." Actually, the boats never attempted to go far inland except on the river freshets, and between 1849-1851, torrential winter rains kept the upper Sabine River at flood stage for months on end. The second and third vessels, respectively, the General Rusk and the Liberty, to reach the upper river after the channel clearance of 1850 were not river boats at all, being considerably larger than the Uncle Ben, and instead were ocean-going steamships with V-bottom, deep sea hulls! The masts of the 2,500 bale Liberty, a square-rigged ship 200 feet long with a solid iron hull (one of the first iron vessels ever built), "tore down all the trees bending over {the Sabine}." Incidentally, the writer expects readers to be skeptical about this occurrence, so he invites them to consult the articles in the "Texas Republican" which verify it. In 1851, a Sabine River booster, living at Pulaski, Texas, wrote to a Marshall, Texas, editor as follows:[80]

> *...Some two years ago, a few enterprising men met in the form of a convention to devise ways and means to have our river navigated, and many of our citizens laughed in our faces, and told us that the Sabine was little more than a spring branch, and that they would never live long enough to see a steamboat run up it. Now let skeptics laugh at those who put their shoulders to the wheel ...There is no one now that will pretend to doubt that the Sabine is a better navigable stream than the Red River ...*

After the Sabine River conventions of 1849, there survives a record of only two packets entering the river during the remainder of that year. In September, the steamboat Ogden, under Capt. James Havilland, left Houston to go to the Sabine River "to take on board a large number of beeves for the New Orleans market."[81] This appears to have been the initial voyage of a new trade that would eventually carry thousands of East Texas cattle by sea to the Crescent City. By 1858, 5,000 heads of cattle were being exported annually from Sabine Pass to the New Orleans market, nearly all of them transported on the steamer Jasper, which carried 80 beeves on each of its weekly voyages except during the cotton-shipping season. The Jasper belonged to an association of New Orleans butchers, and each winter it carried 5,000 bales of cotton to market.[82]

In December 1849, the steamer Buffalo, under Capt. J. P. Border, entered the Sabine River trade and later became the first packet ever to travel the entire 879 river miles to Belzora.[83] The following march, a Galveston editor observed that:[84]

> *...the steamer Maria Burt is now at Sabine Pass discharging a full freight of merchandise for*

*shipment on the Sabine River, some of it to be sent
as far as 800 miles up the river ...The steamer Buffalo
is still running on the Sabine and the business of the
country is steadily improving. The Sabine and Neches
and all their tributaries are booming with water, and
the whole country is said to be flooded ...*

This and numerous other accounts reveal that the shipping season between 1849 and 1851 lasted very long because of the unusually heavy and continuous rainfall throughout Northeast Texas which kept the upper Sabine River so long at flood stage. That factor gave the early steamboat skippers sufficient cause to challenge the stream farther inland and eventually to extend the river commerce as far north as Smith County around Longview and Gladewater.

The Buffalo made three voyages in the Sabine River, but on a return voyage late in March 1850, it was snagged and sunk. Two months later, Dr. Niles F. Smith of Sabine Pass reported while on a visit to Houston that the owners already had the Buffalo "partially raised" and expected to have the packet back in service within few weeks.[85] In 1851, the Buffalo entered the Trinity River trade, but it transferred again to the Brazos in 1852.[86]

During the late 1830's, the Patton brothers, Moses, and Robert, settled at Pattonia on the upper Angelina River, 12 miles south of Nacogdoches, where they were number among the pioneer keelboaters of cotton and later became the first steamboaters on the Neches-Angelina watercourse. In 1846 Robert Patton built the packet Angelina, which his brother Moses was to captain for the next four years. About 1849, however, Robert Patton foresaw the cotton-carrying potential of the upper Sabine, and he decided to become one of the pioneer navigators of that stream as well. He already owned extensive acreage suitable for cotton in Smith County. He sold out to his brother Moses at Pattonia, leaving the latter in control of the Angelina-Neches. R. S. Patton then moved to Smith County, where he was soon in the shipping and cotton factoring business again at a new place that he built called

Belzora, 18 miles northeast of Tyler, as well as at Florence, or Patton's Ferry, located about two miles downstream.[87]

It appears that Patton's first Sabine River venture may have been disastrous. In a history of Smith County published in 1948, the author reported that the first proponents of upper Sabine navigation built a packet named the Ben Henry, loaded it with cotton, and sent it forth from Belzora "on its maiden journey toward the Gulf." Since Ben Henry was never heard from again, it appears likely that somewhere it became just another steamer casualty buried within Sabine's murky depths.[88]

Other upper Sabine River ports included Camden, Grand Bluff, Walling's Ferry, and Fredonia, all of them located in Rusk County, and Pulaski in Panola County.[89] At Belzora, Patton entered the shipping business with his son-in-law, John Cleveland Rusk, and Patton was to name his next Sabine River packet after an old friend, Gen. Thomas J. Rusk, who was his son-in-law's father.[90]

Where R. S. Patton acquired the General Rusk is unknown, but the steamer appears to have enjoyed two or three shipping seasons in the Sabine. Patton is also known to have keelboated cotton at intervals between Belzora and Fredonia, so it appears that due to low water the Rusk was not always able to ascend the river to its home port of Belzora. As stated earlier, the new packet was actually a V-bottom, deep sea steamer with a much deeper draft than a flat-bottom sternwheeler. Until 1851, the last year that the Sabine remained at flood stage, it didn't matter, and the deep sea steamship could reach the upper river with no problem. In March 1851, a Pulaski, Texas, correspondent noted that:[91]

> ...On the 2nd instant, the steamer Gen. Rusk left this place on her downward trip heavily-loaded with cotton. This is the second trip she has made as high up as Smith County. The steamship Liberty left this place {Pulaski} for Grand Bluff and Fredonia, heavily-laden with freight for other points upriver. She is a fine looking vessel with an iron hull...

As far as the writer can determine, the sidewheeler Liberty, which was also square-rigged with cross spars and square sails, did not return to the Sabine River after its initial voyage to Fredonia,[92] but the General Rusk remained in the river for at least two, and perhaps three, shipping seasons. Other accounts noted that the steamship ran only in the daytime, tying up at night, to avoid snagging or wrecking.[93] In 1852 a Galveston editor observed that "the steamer General Rusk has all the business she can do in the Sabine."[94] By 1853, it appears that Patton had decided to shed the deep sea steamer for a more shallow draft vessel, and the General Rusk soon went into coastwise service between New Orleans and the Texas ports. In 1859 she was the largest of more than 300 vessels which cleared the Sabine Pass customhouse during that year.[95] And in 1861, whenever Lt. Richard W. Dowling, the hero of the Battle of Sabine Pass, and his men of Co. F, 1st Texas Heavy Artillery were transferred from Galveston to Fort Brown on the Rio Grande, the soon-to-be-immortal Davis Guards were transported aboard the "former Sabine River steamer" General Rusk.[96]

Very possibly, Patton may have ordered a new packet for the Sabine River trade, but if so, the ill-fated vessel never arrived. In May 1852, the Nacogdoches "Chronicle" reported that the "steamboat Francis Jones {was} lost in route from New Orleans to Sabine Pass. She was intended for the Sabine River trade."[97] During the 1853-1854 shipping season, the steamboat John Jenkins made a number of voyages on the river, but the only record of these that the writer has located appeared after the packet had transferred to the Trinity. In September 1854, a San Augustine editor recounted that:[98]

> ...the steamboat John Jenkins, formerly running the Sabine, is well-known to the citizens of this country. While being hauled out on the ways to undergo repairs at San Jacinto, she sank at the stern...The John Jenkins, under Capt. B. Allen, moved to the Trinity after its last Sabine River voyage in March, 1854.[99]

In 1911, the Jenkins was one of seventeen recalled by Robert E. Russell as travelling the Sabine River during the early years of his residence at Orange, as follows: the Pearl Plant, J. Jenkins, Kate, Cora, Bertha Roebuck, Sunflower, Belle Sulphur, Florilda, Pearl Rivers, Doctor Massie, J. J. Warren, Rough and Ready, Sabine, Ida Reese, Era, Grand Bay, and the L. Q. C. Lamar (Writer's Note: Specifically, Era No. 8. There were 13 Era-class steamers, Nos. 1-13, all built at Shreveport and some of which ran in the Trinity River.)[100]

There were two steamboats named Kate on Sabine-Neches waters in Russell's lifetime, and it is not entirely clear whether he referred to one or both vessels. Russell, who born at San Augustine in 1847, was only six years old when the Kate No. 1 moved permanently to the Trinity in 1853, so his reference was probably to the second steamer of that name. However, he resided first at Sabine Pass in 1850 and later moved to Orange.

Both vessels named Kate were primarily associated with the Neches River, and both eventually sank in the Trinity River. The first steamboat, a 1,000-bale sternwheeler, was on the Neches River between 1849 and 1853, sailing regularly between Pattonia and Sabine Pass. The packet belonged to its captain and clerk, respectively, Capt. George Bondies and Theodore Roehte, who owned stores at Pattonia, Nacogdoches and Sabine Pass. Since Bondies-Roehte and Co. also owned a half-interest in James F. Thorne and Co. of Fredonia, Rusk County, on the Sabine River, the Kate probably had ample cause to travel in the Sabine River as well whenever the Angelina-Neches River cotton crop had been hauled to market, but no known record confirms its presence on the Sabine. After the Patton brothers, Bondies and Roehte were the second firm to tap into the Nacogdoches County cotton crop which, by 1845, amounted to about 12,000 bales annually. In 1853, Bondies-Roehte and Co. closed their stores and moved the Kate to Magnolia, Anderson County, on the Trinity, from whence they brought down many 1,000 bale loads of cotton to Galveston during the next three years.[101] In 1856, the Kate sank, "a total wreck," at Wheeler's Landing on the Trinity with a full cargo of cotton aboard.[102]

The second Kate, a much smaller steamer with a screw propeller, came to the Neches River in 1869 and usually towed a 400-bale barge on its regular voyages between Bevilport on the Angelina and Sabine Pass. Sometimes the packet travelled as far inland as Pattonia as well. The Kate was the first screw propeller steamer on Sabine-Neches waters. The small packet belonged to her captain, Charles Hausinger, and she was based at Smith's Bluff, near Port Neches, where Hausinger resided. According to advertisement in the Beaumont and Sabine Pass newspapers, the Kate made regular stops at Beaumont, Concord on Pine Island Bayou, Bunn's Bluff, Wiess Bluff, Bevilport, and Pattonia.[103] The Kate was small enough that it could navigate any of the large bayous along Sabine Lake or its tributaries. Following its transfer to the Trinity River, the Kate collided with some sunken logs at Moore's Bluff, south of Liberty, and sank in December 1873. Although raised and repaired on that occasion, it sank again the following year and was considered a total wreck.[104]

Other than Robert Patton, Captain John Clements probably contributed more to the Sabine River's early history and commerce of the 1850's than any other individual. His service on the river began as early as 1840, when he began "poling" the keelboats during the turbulent river freshets, and was to continue until 1860, when he bought the resort hotel at Sour Lake and retired from maritime pursuits. Altogether he brought five steamers to the Neches-Sabine waterways, the first of which was the Pearl Plant, and later Doctor Massie, Mary Falvey, Juanita, and Sunflower as well.

Clements first arrived at Bevilport on the Angelina in September 1852, where he acquired a cotton warehouse for his commission business, and he also occupied the "large and commodious warehouse" at Sabine Pass formerly occupied by John G. Berry and Hugh Ochiltree of San Augustine. In 1853, Clements took over much of the cotton trade abandoned by Bondies-Roehte and Co. in 1853, and later, by John Hutchings and John Sealy, when this illustrious pair of entrepreneurs moved from Sabine Pass to Galveston in 1854. Soon afterward, the Pearl Plant began making three round trips monthly between Bevilport and

Sabine Pass.[105] By 1856, the steamboat had transferred to the Sabine River, where it remained for five years until the Civil War began.[106]

In March 1858, the packet was lightering cotton over the Sabine River bar at a time when 10,000 bales had already been freighted down the river, 9,000 of which had already been carried to New Orleans aboard the cattle-carrying steamer Jasper.[107] In 1862, D. R. Wingate of Sabine Pass bought the Pearl Plant and attempted to run the blockade with about 500 Bales of cotton. When faced with impending capture by the Union blockaders offshore, Wingate chose instead to run the packet aground at Texas Point, set the vessel ablaze, and he and his crew then waded ashore.[108]

In 1856 Clements brought the steamers Mary Falvey, under Capt. Luke Falvel, and Doctor Massie to the Neches River trade, where both packets often travelled as far inland as Nacogdoches County. In February 1856, Doctor Massie sank at Town Bluff, blocking the Neches for a few weeks, but the hull was soon raised, repaired, and placed back in service.[109] By May 1856, both the Falvey and the Massie were freighting cotton in the Sabine River. During that month, Dr. Abel Coffin of Sabine Pass reported that 10,000 bales of Sabine River cotton had already reached the coast, and another 5,000 bales were awaiting transportation at all the river landings between Orange and Belzora.[110] In 1857 and 1858, the Falvey and Massie were again active in both the Neches and Sabine River cotton trades.[111] On October 18, 1856, Captain Clements sold his interest in the 102-ton Doctor Massie (by then captained by John Dorman of Sabine Pass) to Charles H. Alexander (who had just moved his cotton commission business from Sabinetown to Sabine Pass) for $1,800. Alexander was another merchant who moved to the coast, expecting to fall heir to some of the cotton factoring trade abandoned by Bondies, Roehte and Co. in 1853, and later in 1854 by John Hutchings and John Sealy when the entrepreneurs moved to Galveston. The Doctor Massie, a new packet built at Spear's Mill on Buffalo Bayou in 1854, was 93 feet long, 20 feet wide and drew five feet of water, a draft which leads the writer to believe the vessel may have had a V-bottom, deep sea hull.[112] The steamer's fate after 1861 is unknown.

Alexander, however, was heavily engaged in blockade-running activities during the early years of the Civil War, and he possibly sent the vessel to sea with a load of cotton.

Between 1856 and 1860, Henry R. Green was a Galveston newspaper correspondent and schoolteacher at Beaumont, and he reported on a number of steamboat trips aboard the Sabine River packets. In November 1859, he rode the Mary Falvey on a voyage to Concord on Pine Island Bayou and to Bunn's Bluff and Wiess Bluff on the Neches. At that time, the Falvey had just been purchased by Charles H. Ruff, a Beaumont merchant and saloon owner. Green was favorably impressed with the steamer, referring to Captain Charles Burch as a "popular commander, sociable, generous and clever..." He was equally complimentary of Ruff and of Doc Truitt, the mate. Green added that the packet was "fitted up in fine style...having good accommodations, excellent fare, and kind and gentlemanly officers."[113] The Falvey too was removed from service in April 1861, tied up at Sabine Pass, and its fate thereafter is not recorded in the Galveston or Houston newspapers, the 158 volumes of The War Of The Rebellion, or the Jefferson County Archives. Ruff, however, was a partner of C. H. Alexander in ownership of the steamer Uncle Ben and the blockade-running schooner Tampico, and most likely the owners sent the Falvey abroad with a load of cotton, from which voyage she never returned.

In December 1857, Green reported that Henry Clay Smith and Henry B. Force, both of Orange, were building their new packet, the T. J. Smith, at Town Bluff, Tyler County on the Neches River. Perhaps the fastest steamboat of its day on Sabine-Neches waters, the sternwheeler was built expressly "to ply between Beaumont, Sabine Pass, and Orange as a mail boat.[114] In September 1858, Green rode the Smith to Sabine Pass from Beaumont and wrote that:

> *...this craft is just one hundred feet long, wide in proportion, four feet in the hold, runs like lightning with a thunderbolt after it, neatly finished, comfortably arranged, and well worthy of the patronage of shippers and the travelling public...*

Green complimented C. L. Anderson, the captain as "courteous and accommodating" as well as Arthur Magill, the chief engineer (who with his wife, soon-to-be Confederate heroine Kate Dorman, owned the famed Catfish Hotel on the waterfront at Sabine Pass), of whom he said was "scientific in his line, very careful, and experienced."[115]

By 1859, Clay Smith was the captain and sole owner of the T. J. Smith. And perhaps Magill was not so "careful" as Green had intimated, for on November 1, 1859, the Smith's boilers blew up, killing Magill instantly.[116] After Clay Smith defected to the Union Navy in 1862, the Confederate government confiscated the steamer. The last record of the packet indicated that the T. J. Smith was tied up in 1863 in an inoperative condition at Lake Charles, La., and as the Calcasieu River was not blockaded until a year later, the Smith too probably went to sea with a load of cotton.[117] On September 8, 1863, Clay Smith piloted the Union gunboat Sachem at the Battle of Sabine Pass and was the only member of the crew to escape death or capture, luckily perhaps because of the Confederate price tag on his head.

At the beginning of the 1855-1856 shipping season, Robert Patton's last river boat, Uncle Ben, appeared on the Sabine and was to enjoy a number of profitable seasons until the Civil War began. One account referred to the packet as a "fine new steamer," although another source indicated that the vessel was built in 1853. Apparently, the upper Sabine was again at flood stage as it had been a few years earlier because, by March 1856, Ball, Hutchings, Sealy, and Co. of Galveston were receiving large cotton shipments via the Sabine River from Smith and Rusk Counties. In April 1856, the Weekly News recorded that the steamboats were again ascending "the Sabine to a point opposite Tyler in Smith County."[118]

Following Robert Patton's death in the fall of 1857, John G. Berry of San Augustine bought and captained the Uncle Ben between 1858 and 1860. During the winter months of 1858, the packet accounted for one-third of the cotton exported at Sabine Pass, as is recorded in A. M. Truitt's letter from Burkeville, Texas, dated July 1, 1858, as follows:[119]

*...the steamer Uncle Ben made five successful trips,
two which were as high up as Belzora in Smith
County, a distance of nearly eight hundred miles,
carrying out nearly one thousand bales each trip, this
season. Also, the Pearl Plant and other boats have
done considerable in the Sabine trade, and without
the least difficulty save for leaning timber. The
steamer Uncle Ben is now laid up at Hamilton, in
good condition, and ready for the fall and winter
trade. Her owners design never taking her out of the
Sabine trade...*

In 1860 Berry sold Uncle Ben to Charles H. and Otto Ruff, well-known merchants of Beaumont, and Charles H. Alexander, who had grown to become the largest commission merchant at Sabine Pass, for $8,000. After the war began, the owners soon leased the steamer to the Confederate States government (details of which will appear in the next chapter), and in a year's time the steamboat earned more than $17,000 in charter fees for Ruff brothers and Alexander.[120]

And Truitt's prediction was to become a fact. Except for the Civil War, when the Sabine cotton trade was largely non-existent (most cotton along the river belonging to the Confederate States government), the Uncle Ben remained on the river until 1867, when the vessel was snagged, a total wreck, and found a permanent watery berth beneath the Sabine's murky surface. Only the steamer's bell survives today, mounted "at the high school at Center, Texas."[121] But before consigning the vessel to its watery grave, the Uncle Ben was to play a significant role as a cotton-clad gunboat in two battles of the Civil War, which will appear in Chapter 4, "The Sabine's Confederate Steamers."

In 1859 a second steamer named Sabine appeared on the river. The packet belonged to the Burch brothers of Sabine Pass, and Capt. Charlie Burch soon left his command as master of the Mary Falvey to become the pilot on the Sabine. Its 15-member crew list enumerated in the 1860 census would indicate that the steamboat was well-equipped to accommodate both freight and passengers. The crew included Increase R. Burch, master; Sherwood Burch, clerk, or supercargo; L. Nicholson, chief engineer; Andrew Nicholson, second engineer; Bud Goskill, steward; John Barnhart, cook; Leon Wilson, saloon keeper; T. C. Whittle, musician; John Brown, seaman; James Robertson, seaman; J. W. Ingram, laborer; R. Frazier, carpenter; J. Cummins, carpenter; and David, Rigsby, cabin boy.[122]

The Sabine was tied up at Sabine Pass in April 1861, and its fate thereafter is not recorded in the Civil War records. Increase R. Burch soon became captain of a Confederate artillery company, and Charles Burch served as a pilot or captain on a number of Confederate gunboats and transports. Like other vessels of that era, it seems most likely, too, that the Sabine was either sold or sent abroad as a blockade-runner.

Another of the antebellum Sabine River steamers listed **by R. E.** Russell was the Sunflower. Captain Clements purchased the vessel sometime during the mid-1850's and for a period of time, served as its captain.[123] On May 15, 1860, Clements sold his interest in the Sunflower to Captain William Neyland, a wealthy cotton merchant and large-scale planter and slaveholder of Bevilport, Jasper County, for $1,500.[124] Abel Coffin, Jr., a steamboatman and hardware merchant of Sabine Pass, recorded in 1863 that he had sailed for years as engineer on the cotton steamer, and later, on the same vessel when it was a Confederate tender. While employed on the packet in 1857, he met and married his wife, Pauline, daughter of Simon Wiess, the pioneer cotton merchant of Wiess Bluff (and middleman of Neches River commerce because Wiess Bluff was as far up the Neches as sternwheelers could travel during summer or low water season). While a participating Confederate in the offshore battle against the Sabine blockade flotilla on January 21, 1863, Coffin wrote a history of the battle on the flyleaf of a copy of Macaulay's Essays, the book being the only souvenir he was able to obtain from the library of the captured blockader Morning Light. Until his recent death, the book was still owned by his grandson, A. W. Coffin, of Wiess Bluff, Jasper County. The Sunflower's role as a Confederate tender will appear in a later chapter. In January 1867, after the 1,000-bale packet entered the Trinity River cotton trade under Captain D. E. Connor, the Sunflower was snagged and sunk at Patrick's Landing, north of Swarthout, with 553 bales of cotton aboard.[125]

Other antebellum Sabine River steamers mentioned by Russell are less well-known. Nor can it be stated with exact accuracy what years that some of them plied the river. Captain Peter Stockholm commanded the Bertha Roebuck for a few years before and during the Civil War,[126,] but the only factual information available came later when the packet served as a Confederate transport and tender. The Belle Sulphur, mentioned by Russell, may have sailed on the Sabine River before or after the Civil War, but in any case, it could not have been on the Sabine for more than a short season, or after all the cotton had been picked up along the Trinity. The Belle Sulphur is best known as a Galveston Bay or Trinity River packet. An 800-bale sternwheeler, the Sulphur was a new boat when it arrived at Houston in 1859, and it immediately entered the Trinity cotton trade.[127]

The Grand Bay appeared on the Sabine River for the first time in 1860 and remained there throughout the Civil War as a transport and tender. In April 1861, the steamboat was ferrying crossties from Wiess Bluff to Sabine Pass for the Eastern Texas Railroad. The packet probably belonged to John Stamps, a wealthy Sabine Pass resident who was the chief stockholder and prime contractor for building the railroad. However, the packet's ownership by the railroad is uncertain, and the writer has also seen indications that it may have belonged to Craig and Keith, a prominent cotton commission firm at Sabine Pass before the Civil War. At any rate, Craig and Keith assumed responsibility for the steamer's debts during an estate settlement in 1865.[128]

The steamboats Ace and Dime were small steamers that were on the Sabine River between 1860 and 1861, and during the next four years, both of them were to render valuable service to the Confederate Army's "navy," the Texas Marine Department, principally because the sternwheelers could navigate the larger bayous along the river and Sabine Lake with ease. The Dime was built in Orange in 1860 by Captain Tom Davis when he was awarded the mail contract between Orange and Sabine Pass.[129] The Dime and its barge carried fresh water to Sabine Pass and also travelled up Johnson's Bayou in Louisiana to carry mail, supplies, and commodities. The Confederate careers of both steamers will be documented later. Still another packet, the Jeff Davis, arrived on the river early in 1861, hauling railroad materials, and was to become another of the Confederate tenders on Sabine waters.

Two of the largest and best known steamers ever to ply the Sabine River arrived in 1859, and each was eventually to find its final berth (one a storm victim; the other, a suicide) beneath the river's surface. The Josiah H. Bell was an 1,800-bale boat of white oak construction with a V-bottom, deep sea hull, and the 220-foot Florilda, the largest sternwheeler ever to ply Texas' inland waters, could accommodate 2,500 bales. However, neither packet was engaged in the Sabine cotton trade. In the spring of 1859, when rails of the Texas and New Orleans Railroad were rapidly approaching Beaumont from Houston, both steamboats were purchased by the T. and N. O. Railroad to freight rails, crossties, and bridge timbers to points along the Neches and Sabine Rivers and their tributaries.

Between 1854 and May 1859, the Bell had enjoyed a long and lucrative trade in the Trinity River and was certainly to leave its mark on that stream. With its sturdy construction of 6-inch oak timbers and deep sea hull, the Josiah Bell also had a sharp prow which could navigate the rivers with no fear of snagging, and according to one writer, other steamboats depended on the Bell to break up log rafts and plow through other obstructions in the Trinity. On one occasion, the Bell dug a new channel through the mudflats of the Trinity delta near Anahuac by gouging its sharp prow into the bank repeatedly, and once it cut through a long horseshoe bend of the river, north of Liberty, which saved miles of travel.

At the end of the Civil War, the Bell was in an Orange shipyard, being converted to a blockade runner. On May 25, 1865, only a day after the Confederate flags were lowered from Forts Griffin and Manhassett at Sabine Pass, the shipyard employees, determined that the steamboat does not fall into the hands of Union troops, removed the Bell's 400-horsepower marine engine. They then towed the hull four miles downstream to an unused channel of the Sabine River and scuttled it. In 1905, a history of the Lutcher-Moore Lumber Company at Orange stated that the engine had been in continuous use for fifty years, forty of them in the Orange sawmill industry, without "suffering so much as a sheared pin."[130]

According to the census records, officials of the Texas and New Orleans Railroad may have used the steamer Florilda as floating office space as well as a freight carrier. The crew members, enumerated at Beaumont in 1860, were as follows: T. A. Packard, captain; John J. Price, clerk; Frederick Donn, mate; James Fullerton, chief engineer; Joseph Ables, second engineer; Augustus Overhue, pilot; John Hahn, laborer; Henry Schram, laborer; William Amiss, laborer; Jerry Harrington, watchman; Mike Dyer, cook; Mike McCarty, laborer; J. E. Hutton, railroad civil engineer; W. Herbert, civil engineer; David Scott, physician; and Bridget Gallagher, cook.[131] This is the only occasion that the writer ever noted a female among the crew of a Texas inland steamboat. After the Civil War began, Price, the clerk, replaced Packard as the Florilda's master.

In August 1859, while Florilda was freighting rails between Sabine Pass and Beaumont, Henry R. Green booked passage on the "capacious vessel" to Sabine. Green found the seaport filled with "steamships, steamboats, and schooners," a result of the flourishing cotton exports and rail imports because of the two railroad construction projects then in progress in Southeast Texas. That night, Green attended a ball aboard the vessel, hosted by Florilda's:[132]

> ... gentlemanly commander, and where there was a
> great deal of beauty, funny dancing, dreadful music,
> a few ugly men, much pleasure, exchanges of
> friendly feelings, and the most stupendously
> accursed wine that was ever administered to saint or
> sinner...

The sad demise of these two fine steamers at the bottom of the Sabine River following the Civil War came about as a result of fate or act of Providence rather than by river mishaps such as snagging. According to R. E. Russell of Orange, the sidewheeler Florilda was out of service and tied up at Hugh Ochiltree's wharf when a devastating hurricane destroyed Orange on September 13, 1865. The packet "went down that night and still rests on the bottom of the Sabine. She struck the bank in front of the Ochiltree house...and her upper parts were blown off and ended up in the Cove..."[133] Of some twenty boats tied up or anchored in the harbor at Orange that night, only an aged, ex-slave ship, the schooner Waterwitch, avoided capsizing or being blown ashore. Nevertheless, the Waterwitch also went down during a hurricane at sea a few weeks later.

In 1893, W. A. Bowen, an old Trinity River steamboatman, authored a long article about the former gunboat Josiah Bell. He wrote of the decision of the workmen to remove the engine and sink the hull, rather than let the proud ship be claimed as spoils of war by the Union forces. Bowen added that: [134.]

...the Bell had a deep-water hull...paid little attention to snags and willows, but rushed right on, breaking through them like they were weeds and shoving snags and sawyers out of the way ...The Bell was being fitted (out as a blockade-runner) for sea at Orange when Lee surrendered, and our people sank her there ...

Because Federal troops were expected to arrive at Orange at any moment for occupation duty, the old Sabine River workhorse was sunk in an unused horseshoe bend of the river that the Bell had used her sharp prow to plow through and turn the course of the river. In recent years, there has been some talk of attempting to raise the hulk, but no action has ever resulted from it.

A study of the antebellum Sabine River cotton trade would be incomplete without some knowledge of what the cotton bale potential of that stream might have been. The agricultural census of

July 1, 1860 is the best available source for the eleven Texas counties which lie adjacent to, or in proximity of, the river. This is not to intimate that all of the cotton bale figures, which follow, could be construed to have been available for shipment on that waterway. Harrison County, for instance, had its own river port and route to the cotton market – via steamboat from Jefferson and thence via Caddo Lake and the Red River to New Orleans. The Sabine River, however, is the south boundary of that county, and the writer believes that perhaps as much as 7,000 bales probably went to market via that stream. Also, some counties, such as Jasper and San Augustine, found that the Neches River may have been a preferable route for shipping cotton. The upper five Sabine River counties, in 1859, produced almost four times, 57,659 bales, than the six lower Sabine River counties. And if all of that cotton had gone to market via the Sabine, the river would have required ten more steamboats than are known to have been plying that stream during that year. In addition, the figures reflect how greatly entrenched slavery had become in the upland counties as opposed to the lower Sabine River counties, and how adaptable the upland county soil was to cotton-growing as opposed to the pine timber regions to the south.

The cotton production of the eleven Sabine River counties in 1859, as revealed in the 1860 Agricultural Schedules, is as follows: Smith County, 9,148 bales; Rusk County, 12,737 bales; Panola, 8,218; Upshur, 7,550; Harrison, 20,006; Shelby, 3,389; Newton, 2,091; San Augustine, 3,901; Jasper, 3,792; Sabine, 2,127 bales; and Orange County, 262 bales; total, 73,221 bales. No cotton figures for the West Louisiana parishes were researched, but an additional potential of 10,000 bales was probably available in that region. Calcasieu Parish produced around 4,000 bales, most of it in the north part of the parish and in proximity of the Calcasieu River. Some of the cotton grown in Vernon, Sabine, and Desoto parishes may have gone to market via the Red River, but generally most planters found it cheaper and more convenient to ship via river boat instead of wagon freight.[135]

Equally impressive and worthy of mention were some of the largest Sabine River planters of that year, as follows: William

Garrett, San Augustine County, 350 bales; J. M. Burroughs, Sabine County, 250 bales; B. F. Hammond, Rusk County, 300 bales; B. R. Harris, Panola County, 216 bales; D. R. Wingate, Newton County, 350 bales; L. J. Davis, Upshur County, 291 bales; J. C. Traylor, Jasper County, 232 bales; William Neyland (captain and owner of the sternwheeler Sunflower), Jasper County, 225 bales; A. F. Crawford, Jasper County, 200 bales; and W. S. N. Biscoe, Smith County, 180 bales. Harrison County's eight largest cotton growers produced an average of 244 bales each, but the writer chose not to include their names. Generally, it would appear that there were more small cotton planters along the Sabine River as opposed to the Trinity regions, particularly Walker County, where the seven largest planters averaged 368 bales each.[136]

Much like the Trinity River trade, the few years preceding the Civil War were exceeding prosperous for the Sabine River planters and would witness an average of four or five steamers on the river during each shipping season and a volume of 20,000 bales annually reaching Sabine Pass by 1861. The late 1850's would also witness considerable efforts to clear the river of obstructions and deepen Sabine's bar. Likewise, there were no known mishaps or steamer wrecks in the river during the late antebellum years. After an interlude of rebellion, sorrow, and military defeat, the Sabine River cotton trade would rise again to its earlier level, but only after many steamboats and steamboatmen had gone off to war. And many of them never returned, of course, but a nucleus of planters and river men remained to rebuild and revive the trade, for the East Texas farmers knew only one way of life – COTTON – and a route to market was indispensable for that frontier pattern of living. Despite the suppression of human slavery, the planters devised an alternative method, share-cropping, which would keep the American Negro tied to the soil in the South for generations to come. But before that post-bellum period's cotton commerce on the river can be resurrected for the reader, the role of Sabine's steamers and steamboatmen during the War of the Rebellion warrants immediate attention.

Endnotes—Chapter 3

[27] *House Document No. 365,* 25th Congress, 1838, Library of Congress.

[28]F. C. Chabot (ed.), A JOURNAL OF THE COINCIDENCES AND ACTS OF THOMAS S. McFARLAND (San Antonio: Yanaguana Society, 1942), 32.

[29]*Ibid.*

[30]*Ibid.*, p. 61.

[31](Galveston) *Weekly News*, April 19, 1888.

[32]"Arrivals and Departures," R. C. Doom, collector, March 31, 1839, Sabine Bay Customs Records, File 4-21/10, Texas State Archives, to be hereinafter abbreviated only as 'File 4-21/10.'

[33]Chabot, *op. cit.*, p. 61; *Telegraph and Texas Register*, July 24, 1839.

[34](Houston) *National Intelligencer*, June 30, 1839.

[35](Richmond, Tx.) *Telescope*, April 4, 1840.

[36]"Entrances and Clearances," J. D. Swain, collector, March 31, 1840, File 4-21/10; J. Graham, "Map of Sabine River, Lake, and Pass," Texas-U. S. Boundary Commission, 1840, Texas General Land Office.

[37](Galveston) *Civilian and Galveston Gazette,* November 4, 1840.

[38](Galveston) *Weekly News*, April 19, 1888.

[39]"Entrances and Clearances," J. D. Swain, collector, March 31, 1840, File 4-21/10; Chabot, *op. cit.*, p. 61.

[40]W. T. Block, "The Romance of Sabine Lake, 1777-1846," *Texas Gulf Historical and Biographical Record,* IX (November 1973), 33-35.

[41]"Amount of Fees Collected," and "Entrances and Clearances," J. D. Swain, Collector, June 30, 1840, File 4-21/10.

[42](Houston) *Morning Star*, July 11, 1840.

[43]See also Texas Historical Commission, "Post Marks Historic Border," *The Medallion*, May-June 1977, p. 1; *Telegraph and Texas Register*, December 29, 1841.

[44]Reprinted from (Beaumont) *Journal,* December 24, 1905. The boundary journal was then a part of the G. W. Smyth Papers at Beaumont, now compiled in Austin.

[45]"Entrances and Clearances," J. P. Pulsifer, collector, March 30, 1840, File 4-21/10.

[46]*Telegraph and Texas Register*, April 20, 1842; (Galveston) *Civilian and Galveston Gazette*, April 16, 1842.

[47]"Abstract of Imposts," Niles F. Smith, collector, January 31, 1843, File 4-21/10.

[48]*Telegraph and Texas Register*, March 9, 1842; (Houston) *Morning Star,* March 3, 1842.

[49] (Galveston) *Texas Times,* November 6, 1842.

[50](Washington-on-the-Brazos) *Texian and Brazos Farmer*, January 28, 1843; *Telegraph and Texas Register*, November 29, 1843; February 8, 1849.

[51]*Morning Star*, September 30, 1843.

[52]Crane, "History of the Revenue Service," Ph. D. Dissertation, p. 309.

[53]"Abstract of Imposts" and "Quarterly Return," Niles F. Smith, collector, January 31 and April 30, 1843, File 4-21/10; *Telegraph and Texas Register*, April 12, and June 21, 1843.

[54]G. L. Crocket, TWO CENTURIES IN EAST TEXAS: A HISTORY OF SAN AUGUSTINE COUNTY (Dallas: 1962), 222; C. F. Burns, "Transportation in Early Texas," Unpublished M. A. Thesis, St. Mary's University, p. 75.

[55](San Augustine) *Redlander*, December 9, 1843.

[56]*Ibid.*, January 13, 1844.

[57](Galveston) *Weekly News*, April 19, 1888; W. T. Block, EMERALD OF THE NECHES: THE CHRONICLES OF BEAUMONT, TEXAS, FROM RECONSTRUCTION TO SPINDLETOP (Nederland, Tx.: 1980), 380.

[58]"Arrivals and Departures," also "Quarterly Return," and "Tonnage Fees Collected," W. C. V. Dashiell, collector, April 30 and July 31, 1844, File 4-21/10.

[59](Galveston) *Weekly News,* May 11, 1844.

[60]"Arrivals and Departures" and "Tonnage Fees Collected," W. C. V. Dashiell, collector, April 30, July 31, 1844, File 4-21/10.

[61]*Weekly News*, April 19, 1888; "Quarterly Return" and "Arrivals and Departures," W. C. V. Dashiell, collector, January 31, April 30, and July 31, 1845, File 4-21/10.

[62]*Telegraph and Texas Register*, March 26, 1845.

[63] (San Augustine) *Redlander*, March 12, 1846.

[64]*Telegraph and Texas Register*, November 9, and December 28, 1846; May 31 and June 14, 1847.

[65]*Weekly News*, August 6, 1891.

[66](Nacogdoches) *Chronicle*, August 16, 1853; *Weekly News*, February 22, 1844, and May 10, 1859.

[67]Galveston Admiralty Court lawsuit, Baxter Versus Pederson, quoted in *Weekly News*, February 11, 1850; Vol. F, p. 61, Deed Records, Jefferson County, Texas.

[68]Vol. A, p. 69, Personal Property Records, Jefferson County, Texas.

[69]Lois F. Blount, "Story of Old Pattonia," *East Texas Historical Journal,* V (March 1967), 12-22.

[70]*Weekly News*, April 20, 1849.

[71]*Ibid*., March 11, 1850.

[72](Nacogdoches) *Times*, April 28, 1849; (Marshall) *Texas Republican,* June 15, 1849; *Telegraph and Texas Register*, May 17, 1849.

[73](Marshall) *Texas Republican*, August 16, 1849; (Nacogdoches) *Times*, June 16, 1849.

[74](Clarksville, Tx.) *Standard*, February 22, 1852.

[75] H. P. N. Gammel, THE LAWS OF TEXAS, IV (Austin: Gammel Book Co., 1898), 427-431.

[76]*Weekly News*, December 8, 1857; Estate of R. S. Patton, Probate Records, Smith County, Texas.

[77](Galveston) *Weekly News*, October 13, 1857.

[78]*Ibid*., November 16, 1858.

[79]*Weekly News*, April 5, 1859.

[80](Marshall) *Texas Republican*, April 12, 1851.

[81]*Telegraph and Texas Register*, September 16, 1849.

[82]TEXAS ALMANAC, 1859, p. 237; (Galveston) *Weekly News*, August 4, 1857, March 9, and June 8, 1858.

[83]*Texas Republican*, April 12, 1851.

[84]*Weekly News*, March 11, 1850.

[85]*Telegraph and Texas Register*, May 2, 1850.

[86]*Weekly News,* May 27, 1851; (Galveston) *Semi-Weekly Journal*, May 10, and March 22, 1852

[87]Blount, "Story of Old Pattonia," p. 18.

[88]Albert Woldert, A HISTORY OF TYLER AND SMITH COUNTY, TEXAS (San Antonio: Naylor Co., 1948), 31, 130.

[89]D. H. Winfrey, A HISTORY OF RUSK COUNTY, TEXAS (Waco: Texian Press, 1961), 83.

[90]Blount, "Story of Old Pattonia," p. 18.

[91]Letter, A. R. to editor, Pulaski, Tx., April 5, 1851, as reprinted in (Marshall) *Texas* Republican, April 12, 1851.

[92]See also *Telegraph and Texas Register*, May 16, 1851.

[93]*Ibid.*, January 31 and May 16, 1851.

[94](Galveston) *Semi-Weekly Journal*, March 22, 1852.

[95]TEXAS ALMANAC, 1861, p. 2l37.

[96]F. X. Tolbert, DICK DOWLING AT SABINE PASS (New York: McGraw, Hill: 1962), 30.

[97](Galveston) *Semi-Weekly Journal*, May 10, 1852, quoting the (Nacogdoches) *Chronicle*.

[98](San Augustine) *Redlander*, September 9, 1854.

[99](Nacogdoches) *Chronicle*, April 4, 1854.

[100]MSS, Robert E. Russell, "A History of Orange, Texas," January 25, 1911; and published in (Beaumont) *Enterprise*, April 23, 1922.

[101](Nacogdoches) *Times*, March 24, 1849; (Nacogdoches) *Chronicle*, August 7, 1852, and November 8, 1853; *Weekly News*, April 11, 1854; Blount, "The Story of Old Pattonia," pp. 19-20.

[102](Galveston) *Weekly News*, April 1856, and March 28, 1867.

[103](Sabine Pass) *Beacon*, June 10, 1871; (Beaumont) *Neches Valley News*, April 27, and July 27, 1872; Blount, "Story of Old Pattonia," p. 23; W. T. Block, SAPPHIRE CITY OF THE NECHES: THE HISTORY OF PORT NECHES, TEXAS, FROM WILDERNESS TO INDUSTRIALIZATION (Austin: Nortex Press, 1987), 66.

[104](Galveston) *Tri-Weekly News*, December 19, 24, 1873.

[105](Nacogdoches) *Chronicle*, October 30, 1852; December 13, 1853.

[106]Burns, "Transportation in Early Texas," Unpublished M. A. Thesis, St. Mary's University, p. 75; (Galveston) *Weekly News*, May 27, 1856; March 7, 21, 1857.

[107]*Weekly News*, March 9, 1858.

[108](Galveston) *Daily News*, February 18, 1899; Thomas A. Wilson, SOME EARLY SOUTHEAST TEXAS FAMILIES (Houston: Lone Star Press, 1965), 13.

[109]*Weekly News*, May 27, 1856, and March 9, 1858.

[110]*Ibid.,* May 27, 1856. As early as January 1856, Doctor *Massie* was carrying cotton on the Sabine River. See *Weekly News*, January 10, 1856.

[111]*Ibid.*, March 7, 21, 1857; March 9, 1858.

[112]Vol. B, pp. 145-147, Personal Property Records, Jefferson County, Texas, Archives.

[113]*Weekly News*, November 9, 1859; (Nacogdoches) *Chronicle*, March 2, 1858.

[114]*Weekly News,* December 12, 1857; September 21, 1858.

[115]W. T. Block (editor and compiler), "Beaumont in the 1850s: Extracts From The Writings of Henry R. Green," *Texas Gulf Historical and Biographical Record,* XI (November 1975), 67.

[116]File 170, Estate of Arthur Magill, 1860, Probate Records, Jefferson County, Texas, Archives.

[117]WAR OF THE REBELLION–OFFICIAL RECORDS OF THE UNION AND CONFEDERATE ARMIES. (Washington: 1880-1911, Series I, Vol. XXVI, Part 2, p. 337.

[118]*Weekly News*, March 11, and April 1, 1856; March 21, 1857.

[119]Letter of A. M. Truitt, July 1, 1858, in TEXAS ALMANAC, 1859, p. 150.

[120]Vol. C, pp. 105-109, Personal Property Records; and File 195, Estate of Otto Ruff, 1863, Probate Records, Jefferson County, Texas, Archives.

[121] (Port Arthur, Tx.) *News*, September 5, 1971; (Beaumont, Tx.) *Enterprise*, October 24, 1974.

[122]Manuscript Census Returns of 1860, Schedule I, Population, Jefferson County Texas, residences 327, 328, 372.

[123](Beaumont) *Enterprise,* September 21, 1910.

[124]Vol. B, pp. 297-299, Personal Property Records, Jefferson County, Texas, Archives.

[125]*Weekly News*, January 11, 1867.

[126](Beaumont) *Enterprise,* September 21, 1910.

[127]*Weekly News*, September 6, 1859.

[128]File 205, Estate of Thomas Snow, Probate Records, Jefferson County, Texas, Archives.

[129](Galveston) *Tri-Weekly News*, April 4, 1861.

[130](Galveston) Daily News, June 11, 1893; MSS, "History of the Lutcher-Moore Lumber Co., Orange, Texas," published in (Beaumont, Tx.) *Enterprise,* October 15, 1905.

[131]Manuscript Census Returns of 1860, Schedule I, Population, Jefferson County, Texas residence 288.

[132]W. T. Block, compiler, "Beaumont In The 1850s: Extracts From The Writings of Henry R. Green," *Texas Gulf Historical and Biographical Record*, XI (November 1975), 74-76.

[133]MSS, R. E. Russell, "History of Orange, Texas," January 25, 1911, p. 7; reprinted in (Beaumont) *Enterprise*, April 23, 1922.

[134](Galveston) *Daily News*, June 11, 1893.

[135]Manuscript Census Returns of 1860, Schedule IV, Products of Agriculture, in Smith, Rusk, Panola, Upshur, Harrison, Shelby, Newton, San Augustine, Jasper, Sabine, and Orange Counties, Texas.

[136]*Ibid.*

Chapter 4—The Sabine River's Confederate Steamers

When the attack at Fort Sumter, South Carolina, signaled the beginning of hostilities between the northern and southern states, the normal channels of trade and commerce in East Texas ground to an abrupt halt as thousands of young men enlisted in military companies bound for Virginia. Within days, three companies of men from Orange County, one from Tyler Company, and one from Newton County were arriving at Sabine Pass, seeking transportation to New Orleans or Morgan City, La. Steamers, often lacking crews or cargoes, quickly tied up as well. As of April, 1861, there were at least thirteen, and possibly fourteen steamboats, permanently domiciled on Sabine-Neches waterways, as follows: the Uncle Ben, Pearl Plant, Sabine, Mary Falvey, Doctor Massie, Ace, Dime, Grand Bay, Sunflower, T. J. Smith, Bertha Roebuck, Josiah H. Bell, Florilda, and Jeff Davis. As of 1861, Falvey, Massie and Sabine disappeared from the local scene almost immediately, which is why the writer suspects that they were either sold or sent abroad with cotton and never returned. Perhaps the Pearl Plant might have disappeared also if it had not run aground at Texas Point with a load of cotton and had to be burned to prevent its capture. Being a fast packet, the T. J. Smith was perhaps the vessel most adaptable for blockade-running, but being a scow or flat-bottom boat, she would have had to ply a course between Sabine Pass and Mexico in order to remain near the coast and avoid heavy seas (billowing waves pounded the bottom of flat boats until they leaked or came apart). If it too went abroad with cotton, that fact may account for the steamer's presence in the Calcasieu River in 1863 (by then the boat had been confiscated by the Confederacy). The Sabine estuary was permanently blockaded after July, 1862 (except for short intervals), whereas the Calcasieu was seldom blockaded prior to May, 1864, when the U. S. gunboats Wave and Granite City were captured intact in that river.

Although some Confederate customhouse records are available for Sabine Pass, they unfortunately list only the duties collected for cotton exports but give no names of the outgoing vessels. For the first fifteen months of the war, cotton schooners ran in and out of that port at will, and it was Confederate sea captains from Sabine Pass, bragging at Havana about the ease of entry and departure to and from that estuary, who ultimately accounted for the first permanent blockade there by the U. S. S. Hatteras on July 8, 1862, whose commander remarked, "I have come to make the blockade effectual."[137] Although the Sabine customhouse listed no incoming blockade-runners during the first year of the war, the following are recorded as arriving during the period between June 26 and September of 1862, as follows: the British steamer Victoria, importing munitions (and a most virulent form of yellow fever) from Havana; British schooner Rambler from Havana; British schooner Henrietta from Belize; British schooner Tampico (owned by Otto Ruff of Beaumont and Charles Ruff and C. H. Alexander of Sabine Pass), carrying munitions from Tampico, Mexico; British schooner Henry Colthirst from Belize; British schooner Stingray from Kingston, Jamaica; British schooner The Governor from Campeachy, Mexico; and the Confederate States schooner Sara Jordan from Belize, British Honduras.[138] This was the period when the Hatteras was blockading the Sabine estuary at least part of the time. At least six others, including the West Florida, William, Indian No. 2, and Velocity, were captured by the Hatteras or other blockaders as they sought to enter the Sabine Pass. The Velocity was armed and converted to a blockader there soon afterward.

At the outbreak of hostilities, the Union Navy lost many war vessels anchored at naval installations, such as Norfolk, Va., in the southern seaports. And an entire year transpired before the number of new Federal warships was sufficient to enforce a stringent blockade at many of the Gulf ports. However, Galveston was blockaded permanently after July, 1861. During the first year of the war, Confederate troops were ferried by sea along the Texas coast, or from Texas to New Orleans or Morgan City, La., and the old Sabine River steamer, the General Rusk (previously-mentioned), was engaged fulltime in that activity. Despite a usual blockade of five Union ships, the port of Galveston could often be entered or exited with ease, and blockade-runners there sometimes maintained the clock-like frequency of passenger trains.

One of the first Confederate companies to organize in East Texas in April, 1861, and leave for Virginia was Co. F, 1st Texas Regiment, at Woodville, Tyler County. The new recruits then marched to Concord, Hardin County, where the 220-foot Florilda was docked in Pine Island Bayou, north of Beaumont. Like in the upper Sabine River, how this river boat, the largest in Texas, ever succeeded in navigating the twelve miles in the bayou or turning around in a stream that is only from 80 to 100 feet wide, defies belief. Perhaps the stream was at flood stage, or the boat returned to the Neches River in reverse, but the Florilda did carry the new company to Sabine Pass. Upon arrival there, the Woodville troops were welcomed by a newly-mustered Confederate cavalry company at Sabine, commanded by O. M. Marsh, a West Point graduate. Although Capt. Packard of the Florilda offered to take the Tyler County company on to Morgan City, La. (where the Morgan railroad to New Orleans terminated), Captain Henry Scherffius insisted that the Florilda would be "utterly unseaworthy" in the choppy waters offshore, and the recruits eventually were transported to Louisiana on Scherffius' schooner, the Clarinda.

Scherffius was to acquire the most enviable record of any blockade-runner that operated out of the Sabine estuary. For twelve round trips, Scherffius sailed the saucy Clarinda to Tampico, carrying out cotton and returning with gunpowder and munitions. Early in 1864, on his thirteenth voyage, a blockader doggedly pursued him in a storm for three days and eventually ran the Clarinda aground on Padre Island. T. W. House of Houston then gave the captain command of a steam blockade-runner, the new Clarinda (formerly the gunboat Sachem, captured by Lt. Dick Dowling), which made two successful voyages hauling cotton from Sabine Pass. When the war ended, Scherffius was unloading cotton at Havana from his last command, House' newest blockade-runner, the iron-hull steamer Lark.[139]

As early as July, 1861, Captain K. D. Keith of Sabine Pass reported that the Federal war steamer South Carolina blockaded the port of Galveston. But a few days later, Keith, with no apparent fear of capture, ran cannons and other munitions past the blockader at Galveston and into Sabine Pass aboard the schooner Fountainbleau..[140] As late as December, 1861, the Confederate States gunboat Mobile called at Sabine Pass and picked up and delivered to Morgan City, La., a United States naval lieutenant and nine other Federal prisoners-of-war, who had been crewman aboard the Union schooner Annie Taylor which had wrecked near Sabine Pass.[141] But the capture by the Federals of New Orleans, their control of the lower Mississippi River after April, 1862, and afterward, the establishment of the West Gulf Blockading Squadron along the Texas and Louisiana coastlines were to shatter the freedom of offshore movement that the Confederates in Texas had enjoyed during the previous year. Thereafter, the skippers of incoming and outgoing blockade-runners had to employ every wile and stratagem in their "bag of tricks" to avoid capture.

Other factors which soon resulted included the near-isolation of the Trans-Mississippi Department (Texas, Arkansas, Louisiana) from the remainder of the Confederacy, and the establishment of Gen. Richard Taylor's army in Louisiana, charged with containing the Federal Army in and around New Orleans. Often, Taylor's army contained about as many Texas troops as it did from Louisiana. Thereafter until the war ended, much of the food, munitions, and troops for Taylor's army were transported over a number of supply routes from Texas, the southernmost, and perhaps most important, being along the Old Spanish Trail or the Opelousas cattle trail (which formerly crossed the Sabine at Ballew's Fery or Niblett's Bluff, La.) to New Orleans, or along a route from Houston, Texas, to Opelousas, Louisiana. In fact, Niblett's Bluff, La., became the most important quartermaster depot along that route, and it was to become the special assignment of the Sabine River's Confederate transports and tenders to maintain troop and supply movements between that point and the Texas and New Orleans Railroad at Beaumont.

Until September 25, 1862, when the Taylor's Bayou (near present-day Port Arthur) railroad bridge was burned by a Federal raiding party, the tracks of the Eastern Texas Railroad were operational from Beaumont to Sabine Pass. Thereafter the rails and crossties along eight miles of the track south of Taylor's Bayou were removed, probably due to a sunken railroad bed through the marsh, and were ultimately used for military construction needs, principally the building of Fort Griffin. Thereafter, the Confederate Army at Sabine Pass also had to be supplied by steamboats from Beaumont and Orange.[142] Although rails of the Texas and New Orleans Railroad remained operational from Houston to Orange throughout 1862, the line's trackage through the marshlands "east of the Beaumont bridge to Orange" were in a defective and inoperable condition by January, 1863 and remained so until long after the war ended.[143] Some years later, both lines had to be rebuilt completely. From January, 1863, until the war ended, the Beaumont-Niblett's Bluff, La., connection along the southern supply route (as well as Sabine Pass and Johnson's Bayou, La.) had to be maintained entirely by steamboat.

Long before the Orange County trackage failed, the packet Florilda was helping maintain the link, leaving "Niblett's Bluff, La., on Tuesdays, Thursdays, and Saturdays at 3:00 A. M., and arrive at Orange in time to take the cars for Houston at 6:00 A. M."[144] From early in 1862 until at least the end of that year, the single Texas and New Orleans train, which made three round trips weekly, could not begin to carry all of the troops and supplies moving to and from Houston and Gen. Taylor's army in Louisiana, and wagon trains and steamboats had to carry the excess beyond the train's carrying capacity. Both Beaumont and Orange had in storage large quantities of Confederate government-owned cotton and became important quartermasters and transportation depots as well, known as Beaumont Post and Orange Post, along this southern supply line. During May-June, 1862, a Houston "Telegraph" correspondent left three vivid accounts of his rail-steamboat travels as he accompanied Confederate soldiers over this important supply artery, and he described Camp Pleasant, the large and thriving Confederate quartermaster facility at Niblett's Bluff, ten miles north of Orange, Texas.[145] During the frequent measles and dysentery outbreaks among the soldiers, scores of them died at Camp Pleasant and were buried in unmarked graves there. In the summer of 1863, when a Federal army was advancing along the banks of the Bayou Teche and threatening Opelousas, La., Camp Pleasant was for a time the most important Confederate facility in Western Louisiana. In the fall of 1863, when invasion threatened both by land and sea, particularly at Sabine Pass and the Calcasieu River, General John B. Magruder of Houston made Camp Pleasant the headquarters of the First Texas Mounted Rifles Regiment, whose unit commander, Colonel August Buchel, for three months commanded all Confederate forces in Southeast Texas and Southwest Louisiana.

There are a few records, or manuscripts of memoirs, from Orange for those early years of the war. Dr. David C. Hewson, a pioneer physician, wrote of the three Orange infantry companies raised by Captains J. H. Hannah, S. A. Fairchild, and S. F. Baker, who marched away to fight in the Army of Northern Virginia and "none of them ever lived to come back to Orange."[146] In 1911, Robert E. Russell wrote:[147]

> ...During the Civil War, thousands of soldiers passed
> through Orange on steamboats. They were bound for
> Niblett's Bluff. From there they travelled east to join
> the main (Taylor's) army. Everyone would go down
> to the river while the boats were passing, and the
> soldiers would yell, "Goodbye, Joe." I am so sad when
> I think of the many gay and happy soldiers who
> passed here, having left home, and loved ones, never
> to see them again...

It thus becomes clear what activities the old Sabine River steamboats engaged in during the early years of the war, although there are almost no primary source documents of 1861 and 1862 to verify their movements. During those years, none of the steamboats were armed, and their voyages were limited solely to passenger and freight service, troop transport, and on occasion, blockade-running. But for the most of them, carrying cotton abroad, except to Tampico or Matamoros, Mexico, was well-nigh impossible, for choppy seas, often averaging five to eight foot heights, would have pounded unmercifully and eventually torn away the timbers from a flat-bottom river boat.

From September 25 until the end of 1862, Sabine Pass, then in the midst of a severe yellow fever epidemic, fell to a Union invasion fleet, and Sabine Lake was occupied by the Federals principally aboard the steam gunboat Dan and the schooner Velocity, both of them former Confederate vessels. Barges of clam shell sunk on the bars of the two rivers and forts built on both the Sabine and Neches prevented the Federals from ascending successfully either of the rivers. Water communication was severed between Beaumont, Orange, and Sabine Pass for four months. Florilda, Josiah H. Bell and Uncle Ben were all trapped in the Sabine, and no vessel could venture beyond the mouth of the river. Fortunately, the Houston railroad to Orange remained operative throughout that period, which allowed the supply route to Louisiana to remain open. In December, 1862, the U. S. schooner Rachel Seaman, on blockade duty, were sent to Pensacola for repairs, leaving only the Union steamer Dan to guard the Sabine Lake and Pass. During a heavy fog on the night of January 8, 1863, nine Confederate cavalrymen were successful in applying the torch to the Dan, then at anchor at the Sabine lighthouse, leaving it to explode and sink at its anchorage and freeing the lake of Federal occupation. Thereafter the U. S. Navy abandoned the Sabine inland waters, but it quickly stationed the sailing ships Velocity and Morning Light offshore on blockade duty.[148]

On November 29, 1862, Gen. John B. Magruder assumed command of the Confederate forces stationed in Texas, and on New Year's Day, succeeded in driving the Federal occupation forces from Galveston Bay and Island.[149] He also envisioned the capture of the blockade flotilla off Sabine Pass, and he soon ordered that the steamers Uncle Ben and Josiah Bell be armed and converted to cottonclad gunboats at the J. H. Levingston Shipways in Orange. Earlier, the Ben had operated under charter to the Confederate States, but late in 1862, the vessel was purchased outright. However, the Bell remained under charter for the remainder of the war, both vessels being operated by civilian crews with Confederate Army artillerymen aboard to man the guns.

Unfortunately, the general detailed an arrogant and inefficient major, and habitual inebriant named O. M. Watkins, to command the project. The following quote describes Capt. K. D. Keith's (a former cotton merchant at Sabine Pass) first encounter with the major whenever Keith's artillery unit, Co. B of Spaight's 11th Texas Battalion, was transferred from Fort Grigsby at Port Neches to Orange to man the guns on the converted cottonclad gunboat Uncle Ben on January 10, 1863:[150]

> ...We arrived in Orange—very cold, rain and sleet failing. We found two steamboats had been armed. The Josiah Bell was armed with one gun, a 64-pound rifle... The Uncle Ben was armed with two 12-pound guns on ship carriages. Capt. Charles Fowler, architect, and builder of the assignment had mounted the guns on the forecastle of the boat and had piled cotton uncompressed in front of and on either side of the boilers, between two of the wooden bulkheads running up the cabin deck. I immediately proceeded to board the Bell, which being the headquarters of Major O. M. Watkins...My astonishment was great when I discovered our commander was very drunk... He said he would "learn" me to take orders, swearing profusely all the time. I left him as I had found him, leaning heavily on a small table. A candle on the table had burned a large hole on the shoulder of his coat ...

Obviously, the Confederate naval victory offshore from Sabine Pass on January 21, 1863, was accomplished in spite of the major rather than because of any leadership he provided.

On January 20, the two cottonclads steamed from Orange to Sabine Pass, belching upward huge columns of pine knot smoke. Capt. F. Odlum and Lt. Richard "Dick" Dowling of Co. F, 1st Texas Heavy Artillery, had charge of the single gun on the *Josiah Bell*. Other soldiers from Pyron's Regiment and Spaight's Texas Battalion were assigned until the complement on each steamer included about 200 musket sharpshooters in addition to artillerymen and the civilian crew.

Before daylight on the 21st, the cotton clads steamed forth from the Pass, sensing victory in the offing. Their prey, the blockader schooner *Velocity*, with three guns, and the square-rigged ship *Morning Light*, which mounted nine 32-pound guns, immediately hoisted sails in an effort to escape, but the wind was too calm to fill their sails properly. Nevertheless, a 30-mile chase at sea continued before the slow steamboats came within gunnery range. Lt. Dowling's gun crew opened fire at two and one-half miles range, succeeded in striking the *Morning Light* with four explosive shells, and when the musketry from the cottonclads' sharpshooters began peppering the decks as well, the blockaders' commander, John Dillingham, hoisted a white flag.[151]

Many of the old Sabine River steamboatmen participated in that offshore naval battle as either soldier participants or as civilian crew members. Captains William and Napoleon Wiess, who after the Civil War would own and command the Sabine packets *Alamo, Adrianne, James L. Graham, and Albert Gallatin* (No. 2), were detailed as sharpshooters from Co. A Spaight's Battalion. Actually, they both lost whenever straws were drawn to see who would participate, and they then "purchased tickets" at $10 each from two soldiers who had won the right to participate.[152] Sabine River steamboatmen on the *Josiah H. Bell* included Charles Fowler, captain; Green Hall, mate; Theodore Wings, mate; Daniel E. Connor, chief engineer; Israel Clark, engineer; James McKee, engineer; Peter Stockholm, pilot; G. McLean, pilot; Zach Sable, pilot; and Joseph McClelland, carpenter. Crewmen on the Uncle Ben included William Johnson, captain; Silas Greenough, second mate; Antonio Johnson, mate; Sanford Gregory, chief engineer; J. Wildey, second engineer; J. McKnight, third engineer; John Stewart, Charles Burch, and E. Burch, pilots; George Peake, carpenter; and Edward Lynch, night watchman.[153] Several of the old Sabine River skippers, including Stockholm, C. Burch, McLean, Stewart, Hall, and Connor, were sailing at assignments other than captain. Since cotton bales obscured vision in Josiah Bell's wheelhouse, Captain Peter Stockholm had to steer with the assistance of a lookout on the deck. Stockholm once recited a part of the dialogue that transpired between himself and Captain Charles Fowler at the long chase at sea progressed.

"How's the steam holding out, Pete?"

"Fine, Charlie. I got a full head of steam, but it's hotter than Hades here in the wheelhouse!"

"Good. Keep on a-sweatin', Peter, and cut the wheel a mite to starboard!" Fowler answered. Stockholm and Fowler had grown up together in Brooklyn, N. Y., after 1815. Each had apprenticed himself as a ship carpenter, and each ended up as a steamer master on the Texas coast. After the offshore battle, Stockholm obtained a navy cutlass from the Morning Light, which remained a great source of pride until his death at Beaumont, Texas, in 1901.[154]

After the battle, the steamers took the captured blockaders in tow and brought them back to Sabine Pass, but because of the Morning Light's deep, 16-foot draft, she was anchored off the Sabine estuary bar on the major's orders (who had remained intoxicated throughout the fight, leaving actual command up to Fowler). Both Captains Stockholm and Keith pleaded with Major Watkins that the large ship could be kedged through the silty mud of the Sabine bar with the assistance of the steamers, but the major profanely refused them an opportunity to try. Keith always referred to Watkins' profanity as being "unfit to print." Both Stockholm and Keith, although the latter was an artillery company commander, were licensed bar pilots of the Sabine Pass' Texas and Louisiana Channels. Keith and others asked **for** permission to place artillerymen aboard who could man the nine 32-pound guns on the ship and defend it from the attack that was sure to come when the first Union steamers arrived. But again, Watkins profanely refused, allowing only cavalrymen from Company A to remain aboard, and when two Federal warships arrived and opened fire, the *Morning Light* had to be scuttled and set afire to prevent its capture. Watkins' obstinance meant the loss to the Confederacy of nine large guns, 100 tons of shells, gunpowder, and other munitions, 200 barrels of pork and other foodstuffs, and 400 tons of pig iron, which was stowed in the hold as ballast for the ship. After the fight, the Federal gunboats *Cayuga* and *New London* renewed the Union blockade at Sabine Pass.[155] Another report of the battle commended Captain W. W. Word of the transport *Sunflower* and Captain Pamele of the tender *Bertha Roebuck* for "giving the assistance of their respective steamers.[156]

Although the Josiah Bell and the Uncle Ben remained at anchor in the Pass during the winter and spring of 1863, they were up to no particular mischief, moored serenely as they were in the Texas Channel, and they made no further attempt to drive the enemy blockade flotilla away. But they did flaunt their presence in the safety of the Pass, the prow of each cottonclad frowning its figurative defiance, and they certainly enkindled a certain and consuming passion for revenge in Commander Abner Read of the *Cayuga*, who envisioned capturing and using the cottonclads to regain control of Sabine Lake and burn all bridges and ferries on the Sabine and Neches Rivers. The result was the skirmish at Sabine Lighthouse at dawn on April 18, 1863, which ended with the repulse of two whale boats filled with Bluejackets and the death, capture and wounding of several of the participants. Confederate Lt. E. T. Wright and Commander D. A. McDermut, master of the *New London*, were killed in the skirmish; Com. Read had an eye shot out; and James G. Taylor, the Confederate traitor who masterminded the plan, was severely wounded.[156A]

During the year 1863, two mishaps on the *Bell*, not combat related, were to produce the only casualties that the steamers were to suffer throughout the war. In April, a shell exploded in a gun on the cottonclad, killing two men, and the following October, the Bell's boilers exploded, killing four more.[157] In January, 1864, after the Uncle Ben had been disarmed and was running again as a transport, the *Josiah Bell* was the only cottonclad left at Sabine Pass, and the bored crew members were hoping that some offensive action would develop. During the same month, after discovering that the proud Bell had no Rebel emblem to fly at its masthead, Mrs. K. D. Keith, Mrs. R. J. Parsons, and Mrs. Samuel Watson, all of Sabine Pass, sewed together a Confederate flag and presented it to the Bell's new commander, Captain J. T. Cleveland. Cleveland replaced Fowler when the latter was captured at Sabine lighthouse by a Union patrol in April, 1863. (Fowler was imprisoned in New York and eventually paroled to his brother, a Union colonel. He had five brothers in the Union Army).[158]

During the Civil War, the Confederate States "navy" in Texas was known as the Texas Marine Department, an auxiliary arm directly under the commanding general, J. B. Magruder. With the exception of a few captured vessels, such as the Harriet Lane in Galveston Bay and the Sachem and Clifton in Sabine Lake, all of the gunboats, transports, and tenders were old cotton boats. Typically, the crews were civilian employees, whereas the guns on the armed steamers, such as the Bayou City in Galveston Bay, were manned by Confederate Army artillerymen. For instance, in 1863 Captain Keith had to divide his company, placing half of his gunners on Uncle Ben and the other half on a cottonclad gunboat in Matagorda Bay, the John F. Carr. Most of the steamers were chartered, but by 1863, Uncle Ben and a few in Galveston Bay belonged outright to the Confederate States government. The Texas Marine Department was commanded in 1863 by Major (later Colonel) Leon Smith (who was present in the fort at the Battle of Sabine Pass), with the capable assistance of two associates, one of them being one of the earliest Sabine River navigators, Captain John H. Sterrett, serving as Superintendent of Transports, and Major C. M. Mason as Chief of Marine Artillery.[159]

In a report from Houston dated June 24, 1863, the cottonclad gunboat Uncle Ben was reported as:[160]

...engaged in removing obstructions at the mouth of the Sabine River. She is armed with two 12-pounder iron guns, 70 rounds ammunition, in charge of Captain K. D. Keith, Company B, Spaight's Battalion. The J. H. Bell, at Sabine Pass, has one 64-pounder iron gun, 50 rounds ammunition: one 12-pouonder mountain howitzer, under Captain F. H. Odlum, Company F, Cook's Regiment of artillery ... There is not sufficient space on the deck of Uncle Ben to maneuver the two 12-pounder guns to advantage. I

would respectfully request that, if possible, another
gun be substituted; also, if practicable, long range
guns may be ordered for J. H. Bell...

The "obstructions at the mouth of the Sabine River" were, of course, the 80-foot barges of clam shell which had been sunk there in October, 1862, by a Confederate engineer, Major Julius Kellersberg, while the Federals were occupying Sabine Lake and the river forts were being built.[161] The first effort at removing them was done by the Josiah Bell ramming the barges and pushing them out of the way. In June, 1863, with Fort Griffin at Sabine Pass nearing completion and the **river forts soon to be abandoned, the river's bar** obstructions were a menace to river navigation and were no longer needed.

By July, 1863, overland invasion threatened Southeast Texas from the vicinity of Opelousas, Louisiana, and within a month would threaten by sea as well. The general quickly ordered a defense plan formulated for the town and county of Orange, Texas. A month later,[162] Major Smith of the Texas Marine Department urged repairs to the inoperative Texas and New Orleans Railroad tracks in Orange County, adding that 150 slaves could accomplish that assignment in one week and that:[163]

...the steamers in this district (Sabine River) are very
old and more or less out of repair, and liable at any
time to fail, notwithstanding all my exertions to keep
them in good order...

By September 4, 1863, the commanding general had ordered his chief engineer to fortify Sabine Pass "without the least delay," for his intelligence reports indicated that a Federal task force had departed from New Orleans by sea to invade the Texas coast.[164] His informant had been the Galveston "News" correspondent, "Sioux" (W. P. Doran of Hempstead), who had just arrived in Houston following imprisonment in New Orleans and had learned that the large fleet of transports and gunboats collected there were bound for Sabine Pass. Already an unusual number of lights were being observed offshore from Sabine at night.

Nevertheless, General Magruder reduced the land forces at Sabine by transferring some 700 soldiers of Griffin's 21st Texas Battalion, an error that could have proven disastrous, to West Texas. When an invasion fleet arrived at Sabine Pass at daylight on September 8th, only 47 artillerymen, Lieutenant R. W. Dowling's Davis Guards, were present in Fort Griffin to defend the seaport. The detachment of Capt. Keith's Company B, manning two 12-pounder "popguns," were aboard the Uncle Ben in the Pass, and the handful of other military personnel present for duty consisted of a few engineers, quartermaster, and medical personnel, totaling altogether perhaps 150 men. Two companies of Col. W. H. Griffin's 21st Battalion, bound for West Texas, were still at Beaumont, awaiting rail transportation.

At daylight on September 8, nine hours before the Battle of Sabine Pass actually began, Major Leon Smith, having just arrived on the incoming train at Beaumont, heard the distant thunder of cannonading in the direction of Sabine, some 26 shells having been fired by the Union gunboats at Fort Griffin to test its defenses. The range of his guns being much too short, Lt. Dowling did not return the fire. Smith hurriedly ordered Griffin's two companies aboard the Josiah H. Bell, which at that moment was at anchor in the Neches, and then they steamed toward Sabine Pass.[165] For some unknown reason, Smith ordered the Bell's commander to stop at Smith's Bluff (two miles north of Nederland), where Smith debarked, borrowed a horse, and he continued his journey by land, arriving at Fort Griffin while the battle was in progress. In fact, Smith, seeing the Confederate flag shot away, raised it once again over the fort.

Before the battle, the Uncle Ben had made a feint southward in the Pass but retreated inland when fired upon by the U. S. S. Sachem., whose three 135-pound shells from the gunboat's 9-inch rifled cannon passed harmlessly overhead. Hopelessly outgunned and outnumbered, Keith knew it would be suicide for the old cotton clad to face the Union fleet alone with only two small guns, so he ordered the steamer captain to retreat into Sabine Lake. By 3:40 P. M. that afternoon, the artillery duel had ended, the 47 Confederate defenders having fired some 135 rounds from six cannons, most of the time without the minimum precaution of swabbing out the barrels. Actually, only four guns were in use during much of the battle, for one cannon had been knocked off its carriage and a second had had its elevating screw shot away. Several Confederate rounds struck their targets, and two cannon balls struck and exploded the steam drums on the approaching gunboats, the Sachem and Clifton, driving both of them aground and all without a single Confederate casualty. When the battle ended, after which some 19 gunboats and transports turned around and fled from the Pass in panic, the Uncle Ben and Josiah Bell arrived at the fort almost simultaneously, bringing the two companies of men from Beaumont. Shortly afterward the Bertha Roebuck arrived from Orange, carrying three companies of troops from Elmore's Regiment.[166] Ironically, the only person on the Sachem to escape was Clay Smith, the Confederate defector to the Union navy, who had been the owner and master of the T. J. Smith. He was one of three former Sabine Pass ship captains who fought with the Union navy, the others being James G. Taylor and Lt. L. W. Pennington, the latter accepting Sabine Pass' surrender at the end of the war.

After the battle, Uncle Ben accepted the Sachem's surrender and towed the crippled Union gunboat to the Texas side of the Pass. Major Smith immediately began removing its rifled cannons in order to increase the firepower of Fort Griffin.[167] That the Uncle Ben was in bad running order with a broken paddle wheel is evident from the report of one man among the 315 prisoners of war who rode the cottonclad to Beaumont the following day while in route to prison camp at Camp Groce. He reported that:[168]

> ...We were soon transferred to the rickety old
> cottonclad (Uncle Ben) and started for Beaumont ...
> We found the old boat to be a sidewheeler in every
> sense of the word; one of the paddle wheels was
> broken and useless, and they could only keep her on
> course by keeping the helm hard a-starboard...

The following two months were a period of intense excitement and military preparation at Sabine Pass because of Gen. Magruder's haunting and morbid fear of a second invasion attempt, and it never occurred to him that the large Federal fleet might abandon the project and return to its base. He moved his headquarters to Sabine Pass for the next month and transferred troop companies, battalions, and regiments there until troop strength rose to nearly 4,000 men, or 40% of the Confederate troops in Texas. For the remainder of that year, the Sabine steamers received their greatest wartime workout, freighting men and equipment at a time when most of them sorely needed repairs. Soon after, they were also to receive the first major overhaul that some of them had had in five years.

Only ten days after the battle, the captured gunboats Sachem and Clifton were again operational, their steam drums and other damage having already been repaired by four marine engineers, who had been transferred from Galveston, with the strict assignment to get the vessels running again as quickly as possible.[169] General E. Kirby Smith of the Trans-Mississippi Department headquarters in Shreveport received a "blank commission from Richmond" to determine if one or both vessels could be fitted out and put to sea as commerce raiders, and he sent a Lieutenant Wharton to Sabine Pass to inspect them.[170] By October 1, the Uncle Ben had been disarmed, probably while having its paddle wheel repaired, and Captain Keith's company was then transferred to Fort Griffin to man the additional armament that had been installed there. By October 14th, the Clifton, Sachem, and Josiah Bell were the only gunboats at Sabine Pass; "the last two were undergoing repairs; the first was in good condition, manned chiefly by a company of artillery of Cook's Regiment."[171]

Apparently, Lt. Wharton considered the captured steamers' use for commerce raiding as unfeasible (the Clifton was formerly a New York ferry boat), and eventually both were converted to blockade-runners. In March, 1864, while attempting to escape the coast with 700 bales of cotton aboard, the Clifton ran aground on a Texas Point mud flat and had to be burned to avoid its capture. A portion of its superstructure remained visible there until the hurricane of June 26, 1957, and her steel walking beam is encased in concrete in a Beaumont park. The Sachem, renamed the Clarinda, was sold at public auction to T. W. House of Houston, and the packet ran the blockade a couple of times before the war ended. In September, 1864, Clarinda was at Sabine, loaded with cotton and awaiting a favorable opportunity to escape the coast. Soon afterward, the Clarinda was blockaded in port at Tampico by a Union gunboat, and Captain Scherffius changed her registry to English and sold her to a British concern for L8,000 in gold.[172]

On October 27, 1863, Captain John Sterrett, the Superintendent of Transports, gave the following report on the old Sabine River steamers:[173]

> *...Steamer Sunflower (chartered), now undergoing repairs at Beaumont, will soon be in running order, light draught; steamer Grand Bay (chartered), in the engineering department, not in good order, some work to be done to her heaters (boilers), but can run for a short time, very light draught (sic) of water; steamer Uncle Ben (owned by the government), in good order, now running as a transport, but of heavy draft of water, say, 3 feet, light; steamer Roebuck, in very bad order, not in condition to run without undergoing heavy repairs, heavy draught, say 3 feet, light; steamer Jeff Davis (chartered), laid up, broken (paddlewheel) shaft, not of much service; steamer Dime, tender to the gunboats, very small...*

After the battle, the transport Florilda, because of her huge freight capacity and 220-foot length, became the workhorse of the Confederates in Sabine waters. The vessel was in constant movement between Beaumont, Sabine, Orange, and Niblett's Bluff, La., where slaves were impressed at the latter place "to cut wood for the steamers," all of which was transported on the Florilda. On October 1, 1863, Major J. C. Stafford, at Camp Pleasant, Niblett's Bluff, wrote General Magruder at Sabine Pass that he "had about 120 cords (of firewood) cut, but the steamers Roebuck, Grand Bay, and Florilda have used that up." Stafford promised to forward 100 cords on Florilda's next trip, and he added that "government cotton (was) arriving slowly; this steamer (the Florilda) takes all that is here now."[174]

A letter of October 18 reported that the Sachem had been sent to Orange, presumably for conversion to blockade runner; the Florilda was hauling government-owned cotton; the Dime was detailed to ferry cavalrymen and horses to the Louisiana shore at Johnson's Bayou; and the gunboat Bell, while dragging two anchors, had been "blown ashore" during a gale.[175] In a letter of the 24th, it was noted that the transport Jeff Davis was "laid up at Orange with a broken shaft. A new shaft is being made at Houston for her." When not ferrying cavalrymen, who had to patrol the Southwest Louisiana marshes for Jayhawkers and Union infiltrators, the principal assignment of the steamboat Dime and her barge was to haul all of the fresh water used by the troops at Sabine Pass.[176]

On October 28, 1863, Colonel Augustus Buchel of Niblett's Bluff, whose command was so wholly dependent on the Confederate tenders for the movement of men and supplies, wrote that:[177]

> ...The steamboats Florilda and Uncle Ben are not sufficient to supply this post with provisions, forage, etc.; the Sunflower ought by this time to be repaired, the time given for the repairs having expired. As the steam- boats are all in charge of the Marine Department, I respectfully request that an energetic officer be detailed to watch their movements, as I am convinced that much time is lost by the masters of the boats... The steamboat Florilda should be appraised; in three months she will make more from the Government at the rate she charges than she is worth...

During the spring of 1864, all supply routes from Texas to Louisiana were heavily taxed as soldiers and supplies moved eastward to meet a new Texas invasion threat presented by General Nathaniel Banks' army moving northwest along the Red

River, culminating eventually in the Battles of Sabine Crossroads and Pleasant Hill (where Colonel Buchel was killed). In general, the southern supply route was a two-way street. For each Texas unit transferred to Gen. Richard Taylor's army in Central Louisiana, some war-weary unit was shifted back to Texas to help defend the coastline. Buchel's First Texas Mounted Rifles was one of the first units shifted to Northwest Louisiana to counter the threat of invasion. And that constant shifting of men and equipment would leave few idle moments for the Sabine steamers to tie up at the wharves. But such routine movements were seldom the cause for publicity or written communications that have survived as sources of history. One of the last recorded operations involving the steamers Ace and Dime was the movement of 350 Confederates, horses, wagons, and artillery to and from Sabine Pass and Johnson's Bayou, Louisiana, prior to the Battle of Calcasieu Pass, La., on May 6, 1864. The steamers had to navigate ten to fifteen miles inside the bayou in order to reach high land, and on the return trips from that battle, they also transported the 175 Union prisoners-of-war captured aboard the Federal gunboats Wave and Granite City.

Beginning in 1864, a news blackout regarding activities on and around Sabine Lake was to take effect and continue until the war ended. Nothing else is recorded about them during that last year of the war except that Josiah H. Bell was docked at an Orange shipyard, being converted to blockade-runner, and Florilda and Uncle Ben were still plying the Sabine River as of April, 1865. The fate, however, of the steamers Bertha Roebuck, Dime, Grand Bay, Ace, and Jeff Davis remains a mystery to the present day. Nothing else is recorded about them in the 158 volumes of the War of the Rebellion or in the Galveston and Houston newspapers. In the final days of the war, some of them may have run the blockade with cotton. But if that is correct, none of the vessels ever came back or appeared in the post-bellum period, that is under their original names, in the cotton trade of the Sabine, Neches, or Trinity Rivers. Of course, it is highly likely that some of the new vessels on the river beginning in 1867 were simply the old steamers with new names. And too, some of them may have been bought or confiscated by the incoming Federal occupation forces and moved to other ports.

In brief, it can be said with considerable accuracy that the Sabine steamboats served the Confederacy faithfully until the South's demise at Appomattox Courthouse in Virginia in 1865. When the Southeast Texas railroads failed during the early years of the war, the steam packets, despite their age and general lack of maintenance, kept the southern supply routes in motion, which in turn enabled Gen. Taylor's army to crush Gen. Banks' army at the Battle of Sabine Crossroads and to defend much of Louisiana and the eastern boundary of Texas successfully. The saddest moment came at the end of the war when the Josiah Bell and the Florilda met undeserved fates at the bottom of the Sabine River, the former a suicide, scuttled by its own crew in the river's depths, and the latter capsized by the raging hurricane of September, 1865. Only Uncle Ben, the proud old cottonclad of the Sabine fleet, would survive to respond to the call of "King Kotton" once again. And there were others who returned, not the steamers, of course, but the proud old Confederate steamboatmen who, though their heads were bowed in defeat, mounted the gang planks and wheelhouses once again to help revive the only life that they knew or cared for, the Sabine River cotton trade.

Writer's note: The writer's grandfather and three of his brothers were Confederate cannoneers in Co. B, Spaight's 11th Texas Bn., stationed variously on the cottonclad Uncle Ben and in garrison at Forts Grigsby, Griffin, and Manhassett at Port Neches and Sabine Pass.

Endnotes—Chapter 4

[137](Galveston) *Tri-Weekly News*, July 15, 1862; W. T. Block, A HISTORY OF JEFFERSON COUNTY, TEXAS, FROM WILDERNESS TO RECONSTRUCTION (Nederland: Nederland Publishing Co., 1976), 101.

[138]Confederate Customs Records, Port of Sabine Pass, B. F. McDonough, collector, Chap. X, Vol. 268, in the Confederate States Treasury Records, National Archives.

[139]"Biography of Capt. Henry Scherffius," (Galveston) *Daily News*, November 26, 1894; C. K. Ragan, "Tyler County Goes To War," *It's Dogwood Time in Tyler County,* 20-page booklet (Woodville, Tx., 1961), celebrating the Civil War Centennial; W. T. Block, FRONTIER TALES OF THE TEXAS-LOUISIANA BORDERLANDS (Nederland, 1988), 95-96.

[140]K. D. Keith, "Memoirs of Captain Koszciusko D. Keith," edited and compiled by W. T. Block, in *Texas Gulf Historical and Biographical Record,* X (November, 1974), 55.

[141](Galveston) *Tri-Weekly News*, December 19, 1861.

[142]See V. Sulakowski, Chief Engineer, "Map No. 116–Coast From Sabine Pass to Galveston, Texas," Map Z-54-2, in Record Group 77, Confederate Records in the National Archives.

[143]Letter, Leon Smith, August, 1863, in WAR OF THE REBELLION–OFFICIAL RECORDS, ARMIES, Ser. I, Vol. XXVI, Part 2, 209-210.

[144] (Galveston) *Tri-Weekly News*, September 3, 1862.

[145](Houston) *Tri-Weekly Telegraph*, May 23, and June 6, 13, 1862,

[146]MSS, Dr. D. C. Hewson, "History of Orange," Unpublished, circa 1890.

[147]MSS, Robert E. Russell, "A History of Orange, Texas," January 25, 1911, and published in (Beaumont) *Enterprise*, April 23, 1922.

[148]Keith, "Memoirs of Capt. K. D. Keith," pp. 57-59; MSS, "Diary of First Sergeant H. N. Connor," Unpublished Manuscript, p. 5-a, copy owned by the writer. For a detailed account, see W. T.

Block, HISTORY OF JEFFERSON COUNTY, TEXAS (Nederland: 1976), 103-107.

[149](Houston) *Tri-Weekly Telegraph,* December 5, 1862; *Weekly News,* January 7, 1863.

[150]Keith, "Memoirs," p. 60.

[151]*Ibid.,* p. 61; Connor, "Diary," pp. 5-6; OFFICIAL RECORDS, NAVIES IN THE WAR OF THE REBELLION (Washington: 1894-1927), Ser. I, Vol. XIX, 565, 571.

[152]W. T. Block, "From Cotton Bales to Black Gold: A History of the Pioneer Wiess Families of Southeastern Texas," *Texas Gulf Historical and Biographical Record,* VIII (November, 1972), 39-60; W. Wiess, "Captain William Wiess Tells of Forty-Eight Years Ago," (Beaumont) *Enterprise,* January 21, 1912.

[153] Ben C. Stuart, "Stirring Story of Old Sabine," (Beaumont) *Enterprise,* June 1, 1913.

[154](Beaumont) *Journal,* September 26, 1901, being the long obituary of Capt. Peter D. Stockholm; W. T. Block, "Stockholm-Dean of Steamboatmen," (Port Arthur) *News,* December 23, 1973, reprinted in Block, FRONTIER TALES OF THE TEXAS-LOUISIANA BORDERLANDS (Nederland: 1988), 320-323.

[155]Keith, "Memoirs," p. 62.

[156]OFFICIAL RECORDS, NAVIES IN THE WAR OF THE REBELLION (Washington: 1894-1927), Series I Vol. XIX, 566.

[156a]OFFICIAL RECORDS, NAVIES, Series I, Vol. XX, 147-153.

[157](Houston) *Galveston Weekly News,* April 29, and October 7, 1863; (Houston) *Tri-Weekly Telegraph,* October 6, 1863.

[158](Houston) *Tri-Weekly Telegraph,* January 29, 1864; (Houston) *Galveston Weekly News,* January 26, 1864.

[159]OFFICIAL RECORDS, ARMIES, Ser. I, Vol. XXVI, Part 2, pp. 82, 363.

[160]*Ibid,* p. 81

[161]*Ibid.,* Series I, Volume XV, 852-853, 150.

[162]*Ibid.,* Ser. I, Vol XXVI, Part 2, pp. 133-134.

[163]*Ibid.,* p. 210.

[164]OFFICIAL RECORDS, NAVIES, Ser. I, Vol. XX, 555.

[165]J. T. Scharf, HISTORY OF THE CONFEDERATE STATES NAVY (New York: Rogers and Sherwood, 1887), 524.

[166]OFFICIAL RECORDS, NAVIES, Ser. I, Vol. XX, pp. 555-561.

[167]OFFICIAL RECORDS, ARMIES, Ser. I, Vol. XXVI, Part 1, pp. 309-312; Part 2, 218-219.

[168]Henry S. McArthur, "A Yank at Sabine Pass," *Civil War Times Illustrated,* VII (December, 1973), 43.

[169](Houston) *Tri-Weekly Telegraph*, November 2, 1863.

[170]OFFICIAL RECORDS, NAVIES, Ser. I, Vol XX, 840-841.

[171]OFFICIAL RECORDS, ARMIES, Series I, Vol. XXVI, Part 2, p. 321.

[172]OFFICIAL RECORDS, NAVIES, Series I, Volume XXI, 160; (Houston) *Galveston Tri-Weekly News*, May 11, and September 14, 1864.

[173]OFFICIAL RECORDS, ARMIES, Series I, Vol. XXVI, Part 2, p. 362.

[174]OFFICIAL RECORDS, ARMIES, Ser. I, Vol. XXVI, Part 2, pp. 272, 282.

[175]*Ibid.*, p. 336

[176]*Ibid.*, p. 351.

[177]*Ibid.*, p. 367.

Chapter 5—Sabine's Post-Bellum Cotton Trade

If by the antebellum standards of life in the South, the East Texas of April, 1865, appears to have been quite desolate, destitute, and threadbare, one can readily understand why. In Jefferson County, Texas alone, some 85 families, one-half of the 1860 population of that geographic unit, were starving and receiving public assistance in the form of county-owned beef and corn meal.[178] More than 1,000 residents of Sabine Pass had deserted the town, never to return. In neighboring Orange County, where the Sabine River's mouth flows placidly past Pavell's Island (the delta island) and into the lake, the population deficit was equally severe. It would sink even lower in September, 1865, the month that a devastating hurricane destroyed the former bustling county seat of Orange County, adding many more dead and insult to the already sustained injuries of the war. The effects of the prolonged war and coastal blockade were quite apparent on the threadbare garments worn by all and the makeshift household utensils in use. Every town of any size in East Texas was occupied by contingents of Federal troops, and Freedmen's Bureaus for the former slaves were established. The adjective "plenty" could be applied only to the quantities of worthless Confederate currency that everyone had on hand. Some people reputedly used the worthless "shinplasters" to paper the inside walls of houses, and one Orange resident is said to have thrown a large box filled with Confederate money into the Sabine River.

For the many East Texans formerly engaged in the timber manufacturing industries, the outlook for the future was somewhat less pessimistic. The virgin forest adjoining the Sabine still stood, stately and proud, and many of the mills required only the restoking of their boiler fires to resume production. But for the former large-scale cotton planter, who in antebellum days had depended on slave labor to plow and harvest his fields, the outlook was quite dismal. Even the Freedman knew no other way of life than cotton production, but in the summer and fall of 1865, the former slaves manifested no inclination whatsoever for farm employment, most of their sparse needs being provided by the Freedmen's Bureau. And even if their services were available, the planters had no United States currency with which to buy their labor. Out of that chaos would eventually evolve the "sharecropper" or tenant-farmer institution that would continue to plague the Southland, particularly the Negroes, for decades thereafter. It can only be said that the relationship between landowner and laborer did succeed in reviving cotton production on the larger plantations, whereas there were thousands of East Texans, too poor to own slaves, whose previous mode of living consisted of producing only a few bales of cotton annually on their small farms, harvested by family members.

If the plight of East Texans seemed dismal for the local inhabitants, it nonetheless must have had the appearance of plenty for those residents of Georgia, where earlier Sherman's armies had plowed a 60-mile swath of destruction and utter desolation, or of Virginia or the Carolinas, where entire cities had been put to the torch. The East Texas towns had known no such circumstances because the fighting had remained at a remote distance. Hence, the region was soon to experience new migrations from the east that would dwarf those of antebellum days. By 1866, the revived commerce along the Sabine River was only about one-third of its antebellum size, but with the passage of time, would eventually acquire its pre-war stature once more. But personal needs and self-sustenance came first—the production of corn and the rebuilding of the cattle and swine count, much as at the end of the Texas Revolution.

In 1866, the exports at Sabine Pass were as follows: 6,500 bales of cotton (down two-thirds from its pre-war level); 4,760 head of cattle to New Orleans; 855 barrels of rosin; 110 barrels of turpentine; 10,000 beef hides; 3,000,000 feet of lumber; and one million shingles. Within three years, however, the Sabine River trade appeared to have risen again to its antebellum proportions. A Galveston newspaper reported in November, 1869, that cotton exports at Sabine Pass would reach 15,000, "some say 25,000," bales for that year. A week later the same editor added that "not less than 20,000 bales will come down the Sabine River this season," but again the presence of much exaggeration is apparent.[179]

To counteract an earlier statement, the writer has located a record which indeed places the antebellum sternwheeler Kate, owned by Bondies, Roehte and Co., in the Sabine River in May of 1852. Actually, its presence there could be foretold from the fact that the George Bondies and Theodore Roehte owned a half-interest in a cotton brokerage firm at Fredonia, Rusk County. Captain Peter Stockholm had brought the Kate from Sabine Pass in route to Sabinetown, but being trapped by low water in the stream, he tied up at Belgrade, where T. S. McFarland recorded the incident in his acknowledgement book, which in 1971 was still in the possession of a descendant, Mrs. Elizabeth P. Smith of Newton, Texas. McFarland also noted a similar incident involving the steamer Buffalo in 1850.[180]

In 1866 Uncle Ben returned to the Sabine River trade, but the vessel's ownership after 1865 is unknown. As property of the Confederate States government, it was subject to seizure by the Federals, much like the government-owned cotton, as legitimate spoils of war. The steamer most probably was resold at auction under an admiralty court order. On the packet's last voyage to East Hamilton in 1867, it was snagged and foundered, a total wreck, in the Sabine River.[180A]

In 1866, Captains William and Napoleon Wiess of Wiess Bluff, Jasper County, began their careers as steamer masters and owners on the Sabine-Neches waterways, the former until 1875 and Napoleon until his death in March, 1872. Their careers were equally divided between the Sabine and Neches Rivers. Until 1870 Napoleon Wiess plied the rivers aboard the second packet to bear the name Albert Gallatin, after which he became master and owner of a new packet, James L. Graham. One source recorded that:[181]

> *...the steamboat Albert Gallatin, built in Beaumont,*
> *with Captain Napoleon at the helm, sent word ahead*
> *when the river was at flood stage in 1870 that he*
> *would come and get the cotton. The boat docked at*
> *Boone's Ferry for two days and a great ball was held*
> *for two nights on the upper deck, and people from 20*

miles away came—Woodville to Moscow—by ox
wagon ...

The fate of Albert Gallatin is still unknown. If the boat had wrecked, there would surely have been some mention of it in the newspapers, so the writer presumes it was sold and removed from East Texas.

In 1869, a newspaper carried an account of two early post-bellum steamers, "the Alamo and Adrianne, owned by Messrs. Wiess, which ply between the Pass, Bunn's (Bluff), Wiess (Bluff), Beaumont, and Concord."[182] At various times, William Wiess captained both vessels. One source noted that the belt-driven Adrianne, because of its duck-like and unsightly posture on the water, was commonly referred to as the "sitting goose."[183]

In 1910, Mark and William Wiess were leading exponents when the United States Corps of Engineers was considering deep canalization of the Sabine and Neches Rivers in order to open the ports of Orange and Beaumont to deep sea shipping. In the "deep water" edition of the Beaumont Enterprise on September 21, 1910, Captain William Wiess wrote two articles about the early East Texas steamboats that had traveled the two rivers during the course of his lifetime. Wiess recorded that:[184]

> *...I desire to say that I helped to wear out two*
> *steamboats on those rivers, and as I have myself run*
> *a 400-bale boat as high up the Angelina as Pattonia,*
> *to Rockland on the Neches, and Belzora on the*
> *Sabine, I feel I am competent to speak on these*
> *matters ... The steamer J. J. Warren, carrying 1,400*
> *bales, ran as high up the Angelina as Townsend's*
> *Bluff, in the south end of San Augustine County, and*
> *brought out cotton. She also ran in the Sabine River...*

Wiess' and R. E. Russell's statements that J. J. Warren carried cotton on the Sabine River are the only communications found to date which verify that vessel's presence on the Sabine

River. No mention of Warren has ever been found in any of the old newspapers of the post-bellum years.

Captain Wiess also recorded a long list of steamers, including their captains and cotton bale capacities, on the Sabine-Neches waterways that he recalled as sailing during his lifetime, as follows:[185]

Name of Steamer	Bale Capacity	Captain(s)
Juanita	400	D. Brandenberg, Stockholm
Angelina	350	R. and M.L. Patton
Pearl Plant	450	J. Clements
Mary Falvey	450	L. Falvel, Charlie Burch
Sunflower	600 (e)	J. Clements, W. Neyland
Doctor Massie	400	J. Clements, Wolf, J. Dorman
Grand Bay	600	Unknown
J. H. Belle	1,200 (e)	C. Fowler, Cleveland
Uncle Ben	900	R. Patton, Berry, W. Johnson
Adrianne	200	W. Wiess
Stonewall	600	Norris, A. J. Moore
T. J. Emory	200 (e)	Unknown
T. J. Smith	350	H. C. Smith, Anderson
Sabine	450	I. R. Burch
J. L. Webb	450	Unknown
Vickburg	250	P. Bunn, W. Loving
Neches Belle	350 (e)	W. Loving, Allardyce
B. Roebuck	550	P. Stockholm
Kate (2)	75	C. Hausinger
Flora	300	G. Burr, L. King
Comargo	350	Andrew Smyth, Sherwood Burch, and A. Sheffers
Era No. 8	650	G. Burr, J. Snell
Emma	200	Unknown
J. L. Graham	400	N. Wiess, W. E. Rogers
Laura	500	Andrew Smyth
Cora	900	A. F. Gripon
Pearl Rivers	1,200	J. Poitevent, W. Junker

Orleans		Lewis King
Rough and Ready	?	Unknown
Pelican State	?	W. E. Rogers
Florilda	1,200 (e)	Packard, J. Price
J. J. Warren	1,400	J. Poitevent
L. Q. C. Lamar	1,000	J. Poitevent
Tom Parker	100	P. A. Work
Early Bird	800	J. Poitevent

One of the earliest post-bellum packets mentioned by Wiess was the T. J. Emory, but very little is known about that vessel except that it was probably on the Sabine during the 1868 season. It was a 300-bale (Wiess reported 200) packet, which was in the Trinity River trade during the 1866-1867 shipping season, but it abandoned that stream after that year. Its ultimate fate is unknown.[186] In November, 1869, a Galveston editor noted that the steamboat Fleta was plying the Sabine River in the cotton trade, but no other mention of this packet has ever been found. Nothing else is known of its bale capacity, captain, or ultimate fate.[187]

During the 1869-1870 shipping season, two new steamers, the James L. Graham and Orleans, appeared on the river. Shortly afterward, a Galveston newspaper recorded that they were the only boats engaged in the cotton trade on the Sabine River, and they would "not be able to carry all of the cotton at the river landings."[188] A week later, the same editor added that both steamers had sailed from Sabine Pass to Orange but could not ascend the river much farther due to the "low stage of the water."[189]

The Sabine Pass cotton commission firm of Keith and Vaughan had acquired the packet Orleans, captained by Lewis King, from the Trinity River trade in 1869, and for the next two years, the vessel earned a considerable profit for the owners, hauling cotton on the Sabine River. In fact, business was so good during this period when there was a steamer shortage on the river that the Orleans always left some cotton at the landings. When a small hurricane struck the Pass on June 9, 1871, the packet broke loose from her mooring at the company wharf at Sabine Pass, but because of "the exertions of Mr. Niles H. Smith (the Orlean's pilot), she weathered the gale sustaining but little damage."[190] In a history of the K. D. Keith family written by 1907, Sumpter Keith recorded that the Orleans capsized and sank during the hurricane of September, 1871. The storm destroyed everything the old cotton merchant and ex-Confederate owned except his and his family's lives, forcing Capt. Keith to go to Galveston with only one dollar in his jeans and find work as a clerk with D. Theo Ayers and Co., cotton merchants of Galveston in order to survive.[191]

In November, 1869, the James L. Graham was purchased "by Messrs. Hadnot and Pry of Jasper for the Neches trade," but the steamer promptly entered the Sabine trade, where it enjoyed a lucrative stay for much of the next five or six years.[192] In the meantime, Capt. Napoleon Wiess disposed of the Gallatin (No. 2) and purchased the Graham which he owned until his death in March, 1872. The owners, Hadnot and Pry and later, Capt. Wiess, lived on or near the Neches River, so the sternwheeler may have plied equally as much in that stream. For many years, Graham's principal competition on the Sabine River was Captain G. B. Burr's packet, the Era No. 8.

In the course of its voyages on the Sabine-Neches waterways, the Graham was undoubtedly the fastest of the antebellum steamboats in Southeast Texas. When the storm struck Sabine Pass in June, 1871, there was considerable fear for the Graham's safety, for the packet had just steamed north into Sabine Lake in route to Beaumont. However, it outran the gale with ease. Only a week earlier, the steamer had just set a new record of four hours and thirty minutes for the fifty mile voyage between Beaumont and Sabine Pass. The editor of the Sabine Pass Beacon was soon bemoaning the fact that patrons had to tolerate "a contemptible pony mail to Beaumont" when such excellent mail service by boat could be substituted.[193]

Notwithstanding an alarming number of steamboat explosions on the western rivers, especially while racing, during the mid-nineteenth century, steamboat racing continued in East Texas, and some Sabine River skippers were not beyond venting their own sporting instincts via that dangerous practice. Between 1840 and 1852 (the year that safety and inspection legislation was enacted), 209 steamboats on western rivers had exploded with 1,440 people killed and 838 injured. In 1841, the first Albert Gallatin had blown up in Galveston Bay for that reason, with a loss of fifteen killed and scalded.[194] One must recall as well that almost no steam safety devices existed during the 1850's. In March, 1853, the packets Farmer and Neptune were racing in Galveston Bay. Not content with feeding a steady stream of pine knots into the Farmer's furnaces, the boiler fireman began breaking open hogsheads of bacon, tossing the slabs of fat onto the fire until the furnace interior was a solid cauldron of flaming grease. Thirty persons died when the Farmer exploded.[195]

A similar incident involving Captain W. E. Rogers of Graham and his archrival, Captain G. B. Burr of the Era No. 8, occurred on Sabine waters in 1873. Fortunately, no accident occurred, as the following quote reveals:[196]

> ... J. L. Graham and Era No. 8 are having lots of fun racing with each other. On Thursday about 4:00 P. M., the puffing steam admonishes us of the approach of the rival boats. First, we discern the dense black smoke of the Era and in a short time that of Graham. As they passed up the reach below town, the Era was between one and 200 yards ahead and the citizens of the place crowded the banks of the upper landing to watch the result ...The black smoke rose in perfect clouds indicating an unrestricted use of pine knots. The two boats were nearly abreast when they left the landing ...In the race from Sabine Pass, the Era left about 56 minutes ahead of the Graham, and the latter boat made one landing on the route, which gave the Era an hour advantage over the Graham. We suppose, however, the Era will not give it up yet, and we will have the pleasure of seeing a little more of the fun ourselves ...

Obviously, the captains were aided and abetted in promoting that unsafe practice by the public at large.

Over a long period of years, the many ads of James L. Graham in the Sabine Pass Beacon, the Neches Valley News, and the Beaumont News-Beacon all place the steamer on a regular run from Sabine to Beaumont, Bunn's Bluff, Concord, and Wiess Bluff. But the ads notwithstanding, numerous writeups in the Galveston papers place Graham in the Sabine River on numerous occasions. One can only surmise that the packet traveled wherever the cotton was available or wherever its cargo billings and freight consignments required. In March, 1873, the Graham was near at hand when the ill-fated sternwheeler Ida Reese was snagged and sank in the Sabine River, a few miles north of Stark's Landing, with a full cargo of cotton aboard. Graham managed to salvage and complete its load with 209 bales of Reese's cargo removed from the river's murky depths and deliver the water-soaked cotton to the Vaughan and Kyle commission firm in Sabine Pass.[197]

The best account of J. L. Graham appeared in the Beaumont News-Beacon in 1873, as follows:[198]

> *... The steamer Graham has for several days past been on the way at this place, and during that time has had strong new timbers placed in her bow, and also has been dressed out in a new coat of paint. Graham has always borne the name as the fastest steamer in these parts, and with the thorough overhauling just given her, we expect soon to hear of her making "lightning time" to and from the cotton country above. The officers of the Graham are too well known in this country to require special mention from us, for more deservedly popular gentlemen than her captain, W. E. Rogers; her clerk, G. W. Hawley, cannot be found. The pilot, Capt. Clark; the engineer, Capt. S. Gregory; and the mate, Mr. Wm. Lapham, are also well known as capable, efficient officers ...*

The J. L. Graham was apparently sold by its owners in 1875, and writer's last two records placed the fast packet in the Brazos to Galveston trade in February, 1876. The packet sank near Redfish Reef in Galveston Bay the following May.[199]

Over a ten-year span from 1870 to 1880, Era No. 8 probably became the most lucrative and best documented steamer ever to ply the Sabine River. When Capt. G. B. Burr acquired the packet in the fall of 1870, he was already a well-known cotton merchant of Burr's Ferry, Louisiana. In 1874, he became a partner of David R. Wingate in a new commission and general mercantile firm at Orange, where he also owned a steam grist mill.[200] In the winter of 1871, the Era carried cotton on both the Trinity and Sabine rivers, but remained on the Neches-Sabine waterways thereafter.[201] By 1877, Burr had acquired a new steamboat, the Flora, and he apparently sold the Era No. 8 to Captain J. J. Snell, a cotton merchant of Toledo.[202] In November, 1880, the Beaumont Enterprise reported that the "steamer Era No. 8 lies at the bottom of the river." The sale may have had something to do with the condemnation of the steamer by Captain L. C. Hershberger of the Steamboat Inspection Service in 1877, but obviously the packet was placed back in service since it continued to haul cotton for three more years. Later, the Era was raised, dismantled, and the hull was converted into a barge.[203]

Throughout the decade of the 1870's, there were many records of the Era No. 8 sailing forth from Orange, heavily loaded with freight and merchandise for Pendleton, Hamilton, and intermediate points, or arriving at Orange with cargoes of cotton. In March, 1871, the packet came "down the Sabine with 309 bales of cotton;" 220 more bales in March, 1875; 551 bales in January, 1876; 519 bales in February, 1977; and 513 and 523 bales on two voyages in January 1978. On a subsequent trip in 1878, the packet carried cotton, 88 bales of hides and deer skins, and 279 hand-hewn railroad crossties, the latter also becoming an important commercial item at the landings along the Sabine.[204]

It is not entirely clear why Capt. Burr chose to replace the Era with the Flora, except that the latter was perhaps a newer vessel, and the hull of the Era was becoming unseaworthy. In 1877, the year that he changed steamers, Burr moved to Orange, where he also built a planing mill and a "portable house factory," and his newly-acquired lumber interests may have dictated his decision to change. In the same year, he transferred the Flora, momentarily captained by Lewis King of Sabine Pass, to the Neches. But the following year, Burr was back as master of the new packet, making his regular trips once again to Pendleton and East Hamilton. The Flora sank at Orange during the devasting hurricane of August 22, 1879, at which time Era No. 8 also lost its smokestacks and pilot house.[205] Captain Snell, however, continued to haul cotton on the Era until the packet sank in 1880.

Another well-documented Sabine River steamer was the Comargo. Purchased at Galveston in 1869 by Captain Andrew Smyth, the steamboat was soon in the Neches River trade, but the captain quickly discovered that the sternwheeler was hard to steer and virtually unmanageable during the swirling river freshets. In his book, Texas Riverman, Dr. William Seale described the steamer as a "stubby, square-nosed boat with one cramped cabin, a pilot house, a stern wheel, and a vast open deck."[206] After he decided to buy a better boat, Smyth and his partners sold the Comargo in 1872 to Charles H. Alexander of Sabine, who promptly put the "scow steamer" in the Sabine River trade under Captain Aaron Sheffers (a brother of Captain Henry Scherffius, the blockade-runner, who had altered his name). The Comargo, however, was tied up for several months at Sabine Pass following Alexander's death in June, 1872.

In February, 1873, Alexander's estate sold the packet to Crain and Griffith of Johnson's Bayou, Louisiana, and the Comargo was promptly returned to the Sabine River trade under Captain Sherwood Burch, the former pilot of the steamboat Sabine.[207] During the same month, the sternwheeler "passed up the Sabine with a large cargo of merchandise."[208] The steamer remained on the River during most of 1873 but was transferred back to the Neches at the beginning of the following shipping season. In January, 1874, while descending from Pattonia on the Angelina, the Comargo struck a sunken log near Townsend's Ferry and sank, a total wreck, with 202 bales of cotton aboard.[209]

In January, 1872, a Galveston editor announced that "the Neches has a new steamboat called the Laura."[210] Today it can likely be said that no other early Texas steamer has become the subject of an entire book, Texas Riverman , which also contains the biography of her captain and co-owner (also a Texas Army veteran), Andrew Smyth.[211] It may also seem strange that the writer would introduce into this treatise a packet so thoroughly associated with the Neches River, but by his own definition, a record of any single voyage on the Sabine River qualifies the vessel for inclusion. Actually, proof of a steamer sailing in the Neches should suffice, for any vessel sailing there probably sailed in the Sabine as well. And in 1880, the Galveston Weekly News recorded that:[212]

> ...the Laura arrived {in Beaumont} this evening with
> 27 bales of cotton and a few hides, all for Galveston.
> Captain Smyth says there is plenty of freight up both
> rivers, but he could only get to Bevilport, on the
> Angelina, and to Bondies, on the Sabine River, on
> account of the low stage of water...

For the cotton steamboat enthusiast, the writer recommends Dr. Seale's history of the Laura, and her genial master as "must" reading.

There were three new steamboats that arrived on the Neches to compete with the Laura between 1877 and 1881, but only one of them with certainty can also place in the Sabine River. In 1877, the Busy Bee, under Captain Baxter, was a new 500-bale steamer that had just been built at Pattonia, Nacogdoches County, and it made a number of successful voyages with full cargoes that year, discharging each at Beaumont. At the same time, the packet D. Van Buskirk arrived on the Sabine River and brought out a number of cargoes, averaging from 300 to 500 bales on each trip. For three years, the Buskirk disappeared from the local scene, but was back in 1881 to compete with Laura and bring out a number of large Neches River cargoes. One article noted that the Van Buskirk left Beaumont on Tuesday "with full freight" for Town Bluff and was back the following Sunday with a load of cotton, the fastest voyage ever to that point. In 1880, the steamer General Hooker made a number of successful voyages while competing with Laura, also remaining only one season. Both the Hooker and the Buskirk disappeared from the Sabine area after 1881.

One incident of 1880 leads the writer to conclude that whenever a surplus of cotton existed on the Sabine beyond available transportation's ability to bring it to market, steamer captains or merchants telegraphed Houston or Galveston for help. In March, 1880, the 1,400 bale steamboat Lizzie belonged to the Houston Direct Navigation Company and had been in the Galveston Bay trade continuously for four years. Suddenly Lizzie made a 1,000 mile round trip from Galveston to Hamilton on the Sabine River, and her master, Captain Joe Boddaker claimed it was the fastest voyage of record between those points, his time from Sabine to Galveston being only six hours. The Lizzie made only the single voyage to the Sabine, bringing out 1,156 bales, before it returned to the bay trade.[212A]

In 1871 a weekly passenger and freight service via the steamer Stonewall connected the Sabine and Neches Rivers with Galveston. Like the Liberty before it, the packet was actually a low pressure deep sea steamship, both square-rigged and sidewheel-paddled, with an iron hull. Owned by Norris and Co. of Galveston, the steamer sailed as high up the Sabine River as Orange and to Bunn's Bluff, ten miles north of Beaumont on the Neches, on its weekly round trips.[213] In February, 1873, a Galveston editor reported that the "Stonewall arrived at Galveston with 298 bales of cotton from the Sabine and Neches Rivers." Commenting on the same voyage, a Beaumont newspaperman added that "on the 13th instant, the Era No. 8 passed down the Sabine well freighted with cotton. On the 15th the Stonewall and the Ida Reese came in at Orange, and during the past week the Tobe Hurt, our mail packet, paid us a couple of visits."[214]

In a letter written in January, 1873, Judge Seymour White of Jasper reported quite favorably about his voyage from Galveston to the Neches on the Stonewall and of the value of the vessel's weekly services to the Jasper County merchants and to the traveling public. He closed his letter with this statement:[215]

> ...before leaving the boat at Bunn's Bluff, I looked over her freight list for the trip and it footed up to 1,572 barrels and 18 packages, not counting 17 of {Isaiah E.} Kellie's pets (?), babies, and six deck passengers. All the babies were bound for Tyler County ...

On one of its voyages to Galveston, the Stonewall "carried out 75 bales of cotton, 50 bundles of hides, and 500,000 shingles," the latter presumably from Orange, since it was the only town in the Sabine area producing such large quantities of shingles as of 1873.[216]Apparently the packet discontinued its weekly service to the Neches and Sabine Rivers around 1874, and its subsequent history is unknown. The Stonewall probably returned to coastwise service between the Gulf ports.

One of the oddities of Texas inland river boat history is that the cotton trades should end so abruptly and quickly on both the Trinity and Brazos Rivers but lingered on for two decades on the Sabine and Neches. The answer, of course, was the railroads and the timber industries. The railroads intersected the Trinity and Brazos rivers much more often than they did the Sabine, and in the case of the Trinity, the post-bellum packets belonged to the planters, who basically were not in the transport business and owned steamboats only as long as there was no other means for getting their cotton to market. The Trinity trade peaked around 1871, when some 28,000 bales of the total amount of cotton exported, went by steamer to Galveston, but by 1878, that figure had been reduced to less than 1,000 bales. J. Poitevent, who name appears in an earlier list of steamboat masters, was one of those Navarro County planters, who was more than eager to tie up his steamers as soon as he had a railroad available for his and his neighbors' cotton. The pattern on the Brazos was somewhat similar. Early in 1873, an over-supply of cotton boats, some seventeen altogether, on the Trinity River soon resulted in two steamboats, the Tobe Hurt and the Ida Reese, being transferred to the Sabine River. It was a regrettable decision on the part of each steamer captain, for each vessel soon met an untimely fate and an ignominious end within the depths of the Sabine River.

In 1872, Captain J. H. Maratta, who owned the Tobe Hurt, had won the Galveston-Liberty mail contract, and he kept the packet in the Trinity River, where he freighted small quantities of cotton, from landings south of Liberty, as well. Early in 1873, he won the Orange-Sabine Pass mail contract also, and he moved the Hurt to the Sabine River, making two round trips weekly to deliver mail to Orange and neighboring communities. On the night of April 23, while moored at its wharf in Orange, the steamer caught fire and was "entirely consumed" by flames, burning to the water line within a very few minutes. The fire claimed the life of a night watchman who was asleep on board, but Capt. Maratta, his wife, and another watchman managed to jump overboard and escape.[217]

The steamboat Ida Reese, following its purchase by David R. Wingate of Belgrade, Newton County, left the Trinity River when the shipping season there ended rather abruptly early in February, 1873, and its arrival at Orange on the Sabine on the 15th was recorded in the Beaumont News-Beacon of February 22, 1873. The Reese, a 1,000-bale packet, ascended the Sabine all the way to Hamilton, but had only 385 bales aboard when it started downriver on the return journey. On February 28, at a point "15 miles above Stark's Landing," the sternwheeler struck some underwater obstruction, ripping out its bottom, and the vessel quickly sank, "a total loss." Fortunately, James L. Graham was also plying the river a short distance behind, and it arrived at the scene while the Reese was sinking. Graham salvaged 209 bales from the wreck, which filled it to capacity, and delivered the cargo to Vaughan and Kyle, cotton merchants of Sabine Pass.[218]

After the Reese' hulk had lain submerged for four years, D. R. Wingate, the owner, hired a marine salvage crew, under Captain A. T. Skinner, to recover whatever metal paraphernalia that was salvageable. After laboring for 24 days, the crew managed to remove the Reese' engine, boilers, "doctor," shaft, piping, and other machinery, which Wingate subsequently utilized in his Orange sawmilling operations. Wingate was the same person who bought the Pearl Plant in 1862, loaded it with cotton in an attempt to run the blockade, and then had to burn the steamer when it ran on a mud flat at Texas Point.[219]

Captain Jules Poitevent, who brought the steamers Early Bird, J. J. Warren, Pearl Rivers, and L. Q. C. Lamar to Sabine-Neches waterways, was a well-to-do planter of Navarro County, whose cotton acreage was on the Trinity River. He and his brother, Captain Adolph Poitevent, entered Trinity steam boating primarily as a means of getting theirs and their neighbors' commodities to market. In 1868, the former bought the Early Bird, a 600-bale packet, in Louisiana, and for four years, brought the steamboat to the Sabine River trade only after all the cotton had been removed from the Trinity landings. In 1873, J. Poitevent tied up the Early Bird at his plantation at Parker's Bluff, Navarro County, and removed the packet's engine and boilers to power his cotton gin and grist mill.[220] Between 1879 and 1881, Poitevent brought two more steamers to the Sabine River, so his dismantling of the Early Bird and his discontinuance of cotton-hauling on the Trinity River had nothing to do with his love of steam boating. Hence, the writer presumes the Early Bird was an old, leaky vessel, the hull of which was probably unseaworthy and needed to be scrapped.

So little is known about J. J. Warren, except for William Wiess and R. E. Russell's statements, that the writer is hesitant to speculate about it. Not a single newspaper account of the 1860's-1870's had been found which connects that steamboat with the Sabine River. Poitevant tended to own and operate only one steamboat at a time. Since he owned the Early Bird from 1868 until 1873 and did not buy the Pearl Rivers until 1879, it would seem logical that he owned the J. J. Warren sometime between 1873 and 1879. But there are too many surviving newspapers that most certainly would have recorded something about Warren during those years and did not. Since there are virtually no surviving papers for the year 1869, the writer feels that was probably the year, and also, that Warren probably made no more than two or three voyages, all in the same season.

It is likewise odd that the name J. J. Warren was never connected at any time with the Trinity River cotton trade (at least under that name), a strange coincidence indeed since Trinity was normally the Poitevent brothers' base of operations. However, in 1872, they did bring another packet to the Trinity trade, the W. J. Poitevent, commanded by Captain Adolph Poitevent, and named for their father, who was a wealthy industrialist of the Pearl River region of Mississippi. Could that also account for the name of the Pearl Rivers, which Jules Poitevent also owned? And could the old J. J. Warren have been the new W. J. Poitevent of the Trinity River trade, renamed to honor their father? Their bale capacities tended to match, but most likely, the East Texas steamboat historians will never know for certain. The careers of the steamboats Pearl Rivers and L. Q. C. Lamar will appear in Chapter 6 of this treatise.

A contemporary of the Flora and Era No. 8, the Pelican State, under Captain W. E. Rogers, was on the Sabine during the middle 1870's, but very little is known of the steamer, except for the information furnished by William Wiess. And what little is known connects it with the timber trade rather than the cotton trade. In September, 1877, after Rogers had signed a contract with the Beaumont Lumber Company to remove sunken logs, "snags and sawyers" between Yellow Bluff and Wiess Bluff, the Pelican State was preparing to transfer to the Neches River when it was wrecked in a hurricane at Sabine Pass early in October, 1877. A Galveston editor recorded that the steamboat, "which plied between Sabine Pass and the upper landings, was wrecked in the late storm at the Pass. Her boilers went overboard, and she was driven into the marshes beyond recovery."[221] Most likely, the vessel's engine and other metal apparatus were installed in some other boat.

The Cora and Rough and Ready, except for information furnished by both Wiess and Russell, are also unmentioned in the old surviving newspapers of Beaumont, Orange, Sabine Pass, or Galveston. Captain Wiess, whose memory was usually superb, could not recall who had captained the Rough and Ready; hence, the writer believes that steamer to have been on the Sabine for only a brief season, perhaps also in 1869 and probably for only one or two voyages. The Cora was a 900-bale packet captain by A. F. Gripon of Sabine Pass and very likely was a contemporary of the Rough and Ready. The fate of either vessel is unknown, and there is no record that either of them ever sailed in the Brazos or Trinity Rivers.[222] (There was no A. F. Gripon listed in the 1870 Sabine Pass census. There was a Theodore Gripon, a merchant, living there in that year, but he died soon after. Perhaps Wiess got an initial in the name wrong.)

Late in 1877, the steamer Wren, the last of the old cotton boats of the once fabulous Trinity River cotton trade, came to the Sabine. In April, 1872, Captain James Roach had purchased the Wren at public auction from the United States marshal for $3,882, and when Roach abandoned the river, the Wren could have carried all of the cotton moving along the Trinity to Galveston on a single voyage.[223] In December, 1877, Roach sold the steamer to Davis, Call and Co. of Orange, and the Orange Tribune reported that "Captain Selby left (Orange) Tuesday morning for Galveston and will return with the steamer Wren."[224]

In September, 1879, a large party of Orange revelers made a two-day excursion voyage aboard the Wren to Beaumont and Sabine Pass, and a three column account of that voyage in the Orange Tribune certainly deserve mention, although not verbatim, for it is one of the best for either the lower Sabine River or the Neches during the decline of the steamboat epoch. It occurred immediately following the bad hurricane of that year, and upon reaching Sabine Pass, the excursionists soon found the waterfront heavily damaged. The packet Vicksburg was blown out of the water, "entirely stripped of her upper appurtenances and said to be a total wreck." As Chapter 6 of this treatise will later reveal, that early assumption was erroneous. Captain Smyth's steamer, the Laura, was also at the Pass during that storm and sustained moderate damage, including the loss of stacks **and** pilot house.[225]

By 1870 it appears that all steam navigation to the upper Sabine River around Belzora had ceased entirely, and Captain

William Wiess, aboard his "sitting goose" packet, the Adrianne, may well have made the last voyage inland to Smith County to haul out cotton. In February, 1880, a Galveston editor recounted that:[226]

> *... the Sabine River has been navigated during high water a distance of 900 miles above Orange, but of late years, owing to the crossing of railroads, the river is navigated only about 500 miles, or to East Hamilton. There are now on the river the steamboat Wren, steamboat Vicksburg, the steamer Lark, tug S. V. Stowe, steamer Fannie, and other boats ...*

Two weeks later, another account related that "there are 4 steamboats on the Sabine River after cotton. The steamer Wren arrived down the Sabine yesterday, bringing 654 bales of cotton and 92 bales of hides." On April 20, 1880, the Wren struck a snag and sank, "a total wreck," near Sudduth's Bluff, but the steamer Lark managed to salvage and deliver most of her freight, which was insured.[227]

The arrival in 1877 of the steamboat Fannie marks a turning point in the history of the Sabine River trade, but not necessarily a decline. Prior to 1877, the primary attention of the steamers was turned toward cotton-freighting in the winter and spring months, and mail contracts, excursions, and freight service on the lower river during the summer and fall. Boats not so employed were quickly tied up by May or June of each year somewhere in the tidewater region and were usually out of service until the following December when upriver water levels began to rise. Actually, the Sabine River cotton-carrying trade did not peak until 1881, when six steamers were engaged full-time, and freighting cotton remained a primary function in season until around 1895. But after 1877, cotton boats often had to "pole" or feel their way through miles of floating logs, gently pushing them aside in the stream, which slowed the forward progress of the steamers to as little as one mile per hour. In April, 1881, after its return from the Brazos to the Neches River, the D. Van Buskirk made one voyage in the Sabine during which it had to "pole" its way through the Sabine River at a turtle's pace.

In 1877 a newspaper account observed that "J. C. Fichnor reached Orange Tuesday night with the Fannie. Captain T. J. Davis purchased her several weeks ago and will be used in the Sabine for towing logs {log rafts}." A few weeks later, the same source added that "Capt. Wilson and Mr. Fichnor returned with the Fannie from Belgrade this week and report the Narrows {of the Sabine River} almost choked with pine and cypress timber."[228] The Fannie was engaged in logging pursuits for many years thereafter, either towing rafts, or towing barges of finished lumber for export to Sabine Pass or hauling supplies and corn for oxen and mules to the tram companies that dumped logs into the river. As an example of the many difficulties of steam boating through floating logs, one needs only to read the following quote from the year 1878: "the largest run of timber ever brought down the river was turned loose Wednesday by Rufus Wingate ... It is two miles long."[229]

From the time of the Texas Revolution, Orange, Texas, had had some small sawmill industry; and by 1851 was a milling center of some note, but until 1876 there had been little cause for releasing large quantities of logs into the stream. Thirty billion feet of virgin pine and cypress lumber still stood on both sides of the Sabine River, and a billion feet of that was within five miles of the city. After the war and devastating hurricane of September, 1865, there had actually been some retrogression of the sawmilling industry, the storm having laid flat several square miles of tall timber in Orange County. Yet as late as 1873, there were only three small saw and shingle mills, belonging to W. B. Black, Eberle Swinford and R. B. Russell and Son, slicing up timber in Orange.

Beginning with the rebuilding and reopening of the Texas and New Orleans Railroad from Houston to Orange in 1876, however, the timber industry there expanded at an unparalleled pace. Within two years, several industrialists, among them H. J. Lutcher, G. Bedell Moore, David R. Wingate, C. H. Moore and Swinford, Alexander Gilmer, Norris and Bancroft, and John McKinnon, built huge mills there that soon consumed a half-million feet of saw logs daily and became nicknamed "Texas' big log eaters." As far north as Belgrade, logging crews and tram roads probed ever deeper into the forests in order to supply the unquenchable appetites of the huge band saws. Among the bigger log suppliers were the Sabine Tram Co. at Laurel and Cow Creek Tram Co. at Sudduth's Bluff, both on the west side of the Sabine. And on the east side was the Lutcher and Moore Tram, which utilized ten locomotives, 130 logging cars, and 100 miles of railroad in its 500 square miles of forest and dropped 300,000 feet of saw logs into the river daily. Every log had to be branded like cattle in order for ownership to be established later. At the peak of the logging season, some of the rafts eventually reached 14 miles in length. Several shingle machines at Orange could cut 80,000 shingles daily from cypress logs by 1879, and the 22-gang saw at Lutcher-Moore's sawmill could drop twenty-two 1" by 12" boards, each 20 feet long, every thirty seconds, or 100,000 feet daily by 1880. By 1890 Lutcher's Upper and Lower mills were EACH cutting 150,000 feet daily. In summary, the Orange timber industries greatly hampered the movements of the Sabine River steamboats, but because of that industry, their use on the stream was to continue for two or three decades after river steam boating had effectively ceased on all the other (except the Neches) Texas rivers. And in part because no rail lines ran parallel to the river and only two rail heads intersected it at Logansport, La., and Orange, some 400 river miles apart, five steamers were engaged still in hauling cotton on the river until 1895. No other river even came close to that record.

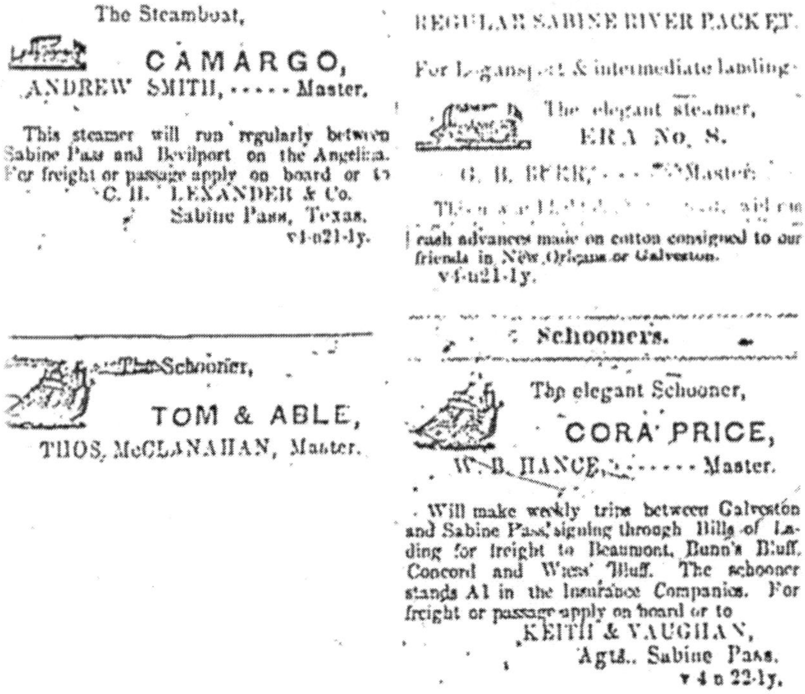

The Steamboat,

CAMARGO,

ANDREW SMITH, ····· Master.

This steamer will run regularly between Sabine Pass and Bevilport on the Angelina. For freight or passage apply on board or to
C. H. LEXANDER & Co.
Sabine Pass, Texas.
v4-n21-1y.

REGULAR SABINE RIVER PACKET.

For Logansport & intermediate landings

The elegant steamer,
ERA No. 8.
G. B. BURR, ···· Master.

cash advances made on cotton consigned to our friends in New Orleans or Galveston.
v4-n21-1y.

The Schooner,

TOM & ABLE,

THOS. McCLANAHAN, Master.

Schooners.

The elegant Schooner,

CORA PRICE,

W. B. HANCE, ······ Master.

Will make weekly trips between Galveston and Sabine Pass, signing through Bills of Lading for freight to Beaumont, Bunn's Bluff, Concord and Wiess' Bluff. The schooner stands A1 in the Insurance Companies. For freight or passage apply on board or to
KEITH & VAUGHAN,
Agts., Sabine Pass.
v4 n 22-1y.

Figure 2 - Ads for Schooners

Endnotes—Chapter 5

[178]Vol. C, pp. 185-188, Commissioners' Court Minutes, Jefferson County, Texas, Archives.

[179](Galveston) *Tri-Weekly News*, November 10, 17, 1869.

[180](Beaumont) *Enterprise,* October 5, 1971.

[180a] (Port Arthur) *News*, September 5, 1971; (Beaumont) *Enterprise*, October 24, 1974, as reprinted in W. T. Block, FRONTIER TALES OF THE TEXAS-LOUISIANA BORDERLANDS (Nederland, Tx.: 1988), 129-131.

[181] J. P. Landers, "Valentine Burch," *Texana,* III (Summer, 1965), 109-110.

[182](Galveston) *Tri-Weekly News*, November 10, 1869.

[183]T. C. Richardson, EAST TEXAS: ITS HISTORY AND ITS MAKERS, III (New York: Lewis Publishing Co., 1940), 941.

[184]W. Wiess, "Some Reminiscences and Suggestions Concerning The Sabine-Neches Project," (Beaumont) *Enterprise,* September 21, 1910, p. 11.

[185]*Ibid*., pp. 11, 21. The letter 'e' beside bale capacity of a vessel indicates an error as known to the writer, Capt. Wiess having underestimated considerably in some instances. Either by his actual or a typographical error, he listed the *Florilda* as the *Florida,* and other writers have picked up that error. He also listed its bale capacity as 1,200 when actually it was 2,500, although the boat was involved in railroad construction instead of carrying cotton. No river steamer named *Florida* was ever known to ply the Sabine prior to 1900.

[186](Galveston) *Tri-Weekly News*, April 4, and May 9, 1866; (Beaumont) *Enterprise,* September 21, 1910.

[187]*Tri-Weekly News*, November 10, 1869.

[188]*Ibid.*, February 11, 1870.

[189]*Ibid.,* February 23, 1870.

[190](Sabine Pass) *Beacon*, June 10, 1871, p. 4.

[191]MSS, Sumpter Keith, "History of the K. D. Keith Family," Unpublished Manuscript, 1907.

[192](Galveston) *Tri-Weekly News,* November 10, 1869.

[193](Sabine Pass) *Beacon,* June 10, 1871.

[194]*Telegraph and Texas Register*, December 19, 1841; July 30, 1852.

[195]John A. Caplen, "Early Steamboat Days," (Galveston) *Daily News,* January 7, 1900*;* (Nacogdoches) *Chronicle*, April 5, 1853.

[196](Beaumont) *News-Beacon*, May 31, 1873.

[197]*Tri-Weekly News*, March 14, 1873. See also issues of March 27 and June 12, 1871.

[198](Beaumont) *News-Beacon*, January 11, 1873.

[199](Galveston) *Weekly News*, February 14, and June 1, 1876.

[200](Orange, Tx.) *Weekly Tribune*, February 22, 1884.

[201]*Tri-Weekly News*, April 24, 1871.

[202](Galveston) *Weekly News*, October 8, 29, 1877; January 24, 1878, quoting the Beaumont *Lumberman.*

[203](Beaumont) *Enterprise*, November 6, 1880.

[204](Galveston) *Tri-Weekly News*, March 27, 1871; *Weekly News,* March 1, 1875; January 24, 1876, January 24, and April 1, 1878; (Galveston) *Daily News*, February 24, 1877, and January 1, 1878.

[205]*Weekly News*, October 8, 29, and November 19, 1877; June 24 and July 22, 1878; (Galveston) *Daily News*, August 24, 1878.

[206]William Seale, TEXAS RIVERMAN: THE LIFE AND TIMES OF CAPT. ANDREW SMYTH (Austin: 1966), 142.

[207]File 45-B, Estate of C. H. Alexander, Probate Records, Jefferson County, Texas, Archives.

[208](Beaumont) *News-Beacon*, February 22, 1873.

[209](Galveston) *Weekly News*, February 2, 1874.

[210]*Tri-Weekly News*, January 5, 1872.

[211]For that steamer's lengthy history, see bibliography in footnote 206.

[212]*Weekly News*, April 22, 1880, quoting the *Beaumont Lumberman*; see also W. T. Block, EMERALD OF THE NECHES: THE CHRONICLES OF BEAUMONT, TEXAS FROM RECONSTRUCTION TO SPINDLETOP (Nederland, Tx., 1980), 180, 190.

[212a](Galveston) *Daily News,* January 25, February 1, 18, 22, 1877; March 25, 1880; also Block, EMERALD OF THE NECHES, 149, 173, 180, 198, 239.

[213](Sabine Pass) *Beacon*, June 10, 1871; *Tri-Weekly News*, September 10, 1873.

[214]*Tri-Weekly News*, February 19, 1873; (Beaumont) *News-Beacon*, February 22, 1873.

[215]*News-Beacon*, January 11, 1873.

[216]*Ibid.*

[217](Galveston) *Tri-Weekly News*, December 11, 1872; and *Weekly News*, April 28, 1873.

[218]*Tri-Weekly News*, March 14, 1873; (Beaumont) *News-Beacon*, February 22, 1873.

[219](Galveston) *Weekly News*, November 5, 1877.

[220](Beaumont) *Enterprise*, September 21, 1910; (Galveston) *Daily News*, April 23, 1893.

[221](Galveston) *Weekly News*, September 17, and October 8, 1877, quoting the (Beaumont) *Lumberman*; (Beaumont) *Enterprise*, September 21, 1910.

[222]*Enterprise,* September 21, 1910 and April 23, 1922; MSS, Russell, "History of Orange, Texas," p. 3.

[223](Galveston) *Tri-Weekly News*, April 24, 1872.

[224](Galveston) *Weekly News*, December 3, 1877, quoting the (Orange) *Tribune;* (Orange, Tx.) *Weekly Tribune*, September 12, 1879.

[225](Orange) *Weekly Tribune*, September 12, 1879.

[226](Galveston) *Daily News*, February 7, 1880.

[227]*Daily News*, February 25, and April 27, 1880

[228](Galveston) *Weekly News*, December 3, 1877; May 13, 1878, both quoting Orange *Tribune*; W. T. Block, EMERALD OF THE NECHES, 196.

[229]*Weekly News,* August 12, 1878.

Chapter 6—Decline of the Sabine River Steamboat Trade

In a strictly numerical sense, the use of the word 'decline' is a misnomer, the trade of the Sabine River declining more in quality rather than quantity. With the launching of the steamboat Dura at Orange in June, 1893, there were still seven cotton-carrying sternwheelers on the river, one more than in 1881, whereas two or three smaller steamers (such as the S. V. Stowe or J. V. Guillote), the forerunners of the modern tugboats, were engaged full-time in towing barged lumber to Sabine Pass for export or in other lumber trade assignments. After 1895, the long cotton-freighting voyages to Orange and Logansport ended. Four packets had been hauling cotton on the lower river to Orange, and three packets hauled cotton on the upper river to the railhead at Logansport, Louisiana.

The geography of the river was certainly enlarged somewhat, during the first part of the twentieth century, with the deepening of the Sabine River to Orange, Texas, which admitted ocean-going ships to the Port of Orange. This was accomplished when the Port Arthur Ship Canal was extended along the shore of Sabine Lake to the mouth of the Neches River, and thence some five miles farther to the mouth of the Sabine River. About the same time, the Intercoastal Canal, connecting New Orleans with Texas, was dug across the northern sector of Cameron Parish, Louisiana, until it intersected the Sabine River. From that point, the Intercoastal Canal extends through several miles of the lower Sabine River, thence into the Port Arthur Ship Canal and to a point south of the Port Arthur refineries, where the Intercoastal Canal begins anew in route to Galveston Bay and points to the Southwest. Until World War II days, when the lower Calcasieu River channelization was deepened and jetties completed, that portion of the Intercoastal Canal connecting the Sabine River with the Calcasieu River in Louisiana was a part of the Port of Lake Charles deep sea shipping channel.

With the passage of time, the old Sabine River cotton steamboat has certainly changed from its former flat bottom and stern wheel status to become the present-day Diesel-engine tugboat with its screw propeller. And certainly, the cargoes have changed as well, first from cotton and farm commodities to timber products, and eventually to every conceivable manufacture of mankind that moves in the inland river traffic of today, dominated, of course, by the petrochemical industries which currently abound in Southeast Texas and Southwest Louisiana. In essence, the old cotton bale-bedecked river steamer did not pass away entirely. The first tow boats on the river were old sternwheelers pulling cotton or lumber barges or towing rafts of logs. Between 1846 and 1861, cotton steamers earned extra money by pulling rafts of chained logs down the Sabine River from Belgrade and across Sabine Lake to the sawmill at Sabine Pass. But the passage of time would eradicate all evidence of the old cotton and logging industries. The old cotton steamer simply evolved, or better, it was phased out, to be replaced by other cargoes and marine vessels, and its modern-day counterpart, the screw-propulsion "pusher" tug with its long tow of barges, is visible in every mile of the lower Sabine River and the Intercoastal Canal every day. And this evolvement or phasing-out, at first brought about by the giant sawmills built at Orange, resulted in the decline of Sabine River cotton trade after 1880. By 1930, even the era of floating logs had ended, until today, the only boats that travel on the river north of Orange are those of pleasure seekers or fishing expeditions. But before the story of the cotton trade ends, there are still a score or more of old steamboats to be introduced into it.

On September 4, 1879, the Orange business community petitioned the Secretary of War in Washington, D. C., to cut through and deepen the Blue Buck bar, located at Blue Buck Point, the northeastern terminus of the Sabine Pass, or southern exit of Sabine Lake. A Corps of Engineers survey to determine the cost and feasibility of the project had been completed four years earlier, and legislation to fund it was enacted. Having become bound up in bureaucracy and "red tape," however, no further action had developed, and the shallow bar was stunting Orange' industrial growth by limiting the size of barged lumber cargoes that could pass over it.[230]

As might be expected, the petition bore the signatures of all the principal merchants and sawmill operators of Orange, but those of the shipping interests are also worthy of note. In addition to those of many schooner owners and captains, the following Sabine River steamboatmen signed it, as follows: G. B. Burr, steamboat owner; G. B. Moore, master, steamer Fannie; Stephen Chenault, lawyer and master, steamboat Bonnie, Davis, Call and Son, owners, steamer Wren, and T. J. Davis, owner, steamers Lark and Fannie.

This is the one of only two records ever found which places the steamboat Bonnie on the Sabine River, but the vessel was probably there for no more than two shipping seasons. Chenault was a well-known lawyer of Orange during the 1870's, and it may surprise the reader to learn of a lawyer who also owned and captained a steamboat. Financially, law and medicine, as lucrative as those pursuits may be today, were quite unrewarding, especially after the Civil War, on the sparsely-settled East Texas frontier, and there were few physicians and attorneys of those days who did not engage in a sideline occupation, usually land speculation and even merchandising. Even steamboaters had to have a sideline occupation to pursue during the six-month off-season when no cotton was on the river. But steamboat ownership or a career as steamer master or crewman was equally lucrative between December and May, providing the highest wages to be found in frontier East Texas. The only other reference found so far to the steamer Bonnie appeared on the same date that Captain L. C. Hershberger of the Steamer Inspection Service condemned the sternwheeler Era No. 8. He also inspected the Bonnie and passed it as being seaworthy and up to required standards.

During 1879 the rails of the present Southern Pacific route were pushing westward toward Orange from Lake Charles, La., and were then known as the Louisiana Western Railroad. Captain J. Poitevent brought the 1,200-bale steamer Pearl Rivers, then under contract to the railroad, to the Sabine River. In April, 1881, the rails finally linked up at Orange with those of Texas and New Orleans, providing Houston with its first 'through service' to New Orleans and the lower Sabine River with a new route to market. The first record of the Pearl Rivers appeared in September, 1879, which then noted that the steamer was in route to Orange from the Calcasieu River with a load of railroad iron.[231]

Poitevent soon sold the Pearl Rivers to Wilson A Junker of Orange, who became the vessel's new master, and in turn Poitevent was soon to return to the Sabine River with a new packet from the Mississippi River trade, the 1,000-bale L. Q. C. Lamar. During its eight year career on the Sabine, the Pearl Rivers carried cotton, railway construction materials, freight for the tram roads at Laurel and Sudduth's Bluff, as well as work on the Sabine Pass jetties and other government contracts. In November, 1880, a Beaumont editor observed that the Pearl Rivers, Capt. W. A. Junker, has been repaired in Captain McClanahan's Shipways at Sabine Pass and will soon return to the Sabine River trade."[232]

At the beginning of the 1881 cotton season, one newspaper recounted that:[233]

> ...Five steamers are doing a lively business in the Sabine River. The Bertha, a new boat just received from New Orleans, the Pearl Rivers, the Vicksburg, Lark, Call, and Davis. A new boat, the L. Q. C. Lamar, is expected to start soon...

The prospect of seven boats on the river speaks well and attests to the fact that the Sabine River trade, despite the handicap of floating logs during the winter months, was still attractive to shippers and still could lure packets from rivers elsewhere. The writer speculates that the Sabine River cotton trade peaked in 1881, the year that seven steamers were hauling cotton. As noted elsewhere, only four packets were hauling in the cotton trade in 1880, and the Lizzie came from Houston and picked up 1,156 bales on its only voyage in the Sabine. Hence, the writer believes that much cotton was left at the landings until very late in the season for lack of transportation.

The career of the sternwheeler Bertha, however, was to prove both short and disastrous, and early in February, 1881, less than three months after its arrival and probably on its second or third voyage, it caught fire as the following article recounts:[234]

*...the steamboat Bertha burned last night on the
Sabine River above the Narrows. The boat and cargo
are a total loss...The value of the cargo is variously
estimated at from $25,000 to $100,000. ...The
steamer Pearl Rivers arrived yesterday with 680
bales of cotton...*

In March, 1881, the Rivers left the Sabine River to go to Galveston and complete a government contract for jetty construction, but it returned to the Sabine the following season. Late in January, 1883, Captain Junker and the Pearl Rivers were again involved in government contract work, moving "mats" made of poles from the Sabine River to be used in the construction of the Sabine Pass jetties. The "mats" were sunk in the mud at the bottom of the jetties to form a cushion for the rock, quarried in the East Texas counties, and the Pearl Rivers' many years in jetty construction was probably the steamer's greatest contribution.[236] In January, 1884, Isaiah E. Kellie, a former editor of the Orange Tribune and founder of the Jasper Newsboy, rode the steamer Pearl Rivers, by then captained by Will O. Loving, to Belgrade while the packet was ascending the Sabine with freight and in search of a cargo of cotton. Two years later, on January 22, 1886, the steamboat arrived at Orange from upriver with a mixed cargo of commodities and passengers, a part of which consisted of 393 bales of cotton. Hence, despite its government jetty and railroad contracts, which probably only engaged the steamer for a half-season, the Pearl Rivers also traveled to the upper river in search of the fluffy, white commodity. According to another source, the Pearl Rivers sank in the Sabine in 1886 with 21 carloads of uninsured freight aboard, but it was quickly raised and repaired.[237]

Nothing else is known about the steamboat Dennis Call as well, except that the packet plied the river throughout the season of 1881. Even though its ownership is unknown, it certainly belonged to either of two companies that its namesake was the owner of or a partner in. One of Orange's oldest commission merchants, Dennis Call, Sr. founded Dennis Call and Son many years before the Civil War, probably about 1847, and he organized the shipping firm of

Call, Davis, and Company, in partnership with Capt. Tom Davis, when the partners brought the steamer Wren from the Trinity River trade.

The large sternwheeler L. Q. C. Lamar enjoyed a number of profitable seasons on the Sabine River. Between January 23 and February 14, 1882, the vessel made two successful cotton voyages, bringing down cargoes of 677 and 408 bales to Orange, respectively. During the summer of 1882, the packet carried excursion parties to and from Orange, Beaumont, and Sabine Pass.[238] In December, 1883, upon arriving at Orange with 782 bales of cotton and three passengers aboard, the master of the steamer reported that the water was extremely low in the river all the way to Hamilton for that normally-rainy season of the year.[239] In February, 1884, the editor of the Orange Weekly Tribune noted that "the steamer L. Q. C. Lamar, Capt. H. T. Davis, master, arrived Sunday with 214 bales of cotton. She made an exceedingly quick trip..." A month later the cotton boat brought down 111 bales on a second voyage.[240]

On October 12, 1886, when a massive hurricane destroyed Johnson Bayou, La. and Sabine Pass, Texas, drowning 200 persons, the Lamar was the first of two Orange packets to arrive at Sabine, bringing a relief party and supplies to succor the stricken storm victims. On its return voyage to Orange, the steamer carried a load of several hundred destitute and often incoherent refugees, who had to be fed and housed in Orange for several weeks afterward.[241] About 1888, the Lamar left the Sabine River and went to the Brazos where it hauled cotton for two seasons. During the summer of 1891, the unfortunate Lamar became the last known steamboat victim to join the Trinity River's large graveyard of ships. While ascending that river on its first voyage there for the lumber industry, the old cotton boat struck a large underwater snag and foundered nine miles south of Liberty, Texas. During the next nine months, there were three unsuccessful attempts made to raise the Lamar. The third effort, in March, 1892, ended in another disaster, resulting in the death of a Galveston diver when his air lines failed, and thereafter, the salvage pursuit was abandoned.[242]

Captains Will O. Loving and Pearl Bunn brought the 250-bale packet Vicksburg to Sabine from the Trinity River in 1879. Although blown ashore at Sabine Pass and stripped of its "upper appurtenances" during the hurricane of August 22, 1879, damage that some predicted would prove fatal to the old cotton boat, the Vicksburg was soon refloated, repaired, and put back in service on the Sabine River.[243] An earlier article indicated that the Vicksburg was one of the seven packets hauling cotton on the Sabine during the 1881 season. From the moment of its first voyage on the river, the old riverboat had developed a leaky and unseaworthy hull, and upon assuming command of the Rivers in 1884, Captain Loving tied up his old steamer. In 1890, whenever he and Capt. Bunn launched the hull of the new Neches Belle on the banks of Brake's Bayou at Beaumont, the engine, boiler, piping, and other metal paraphernalia on the Vicksburg were removed and were installed on the Neches Belle.[244]

In 1883, the steamer Emily P., the second Texas steamboat to bear that name, was built at Orange and soon joined the Sabine River cotton fleet. Its namesake predecessor, a Trinity River veteran, sank at anchor in Galveston with a load of cotton aboard during the hurricane of June 9, 1871.[245] In February, 1884, the Emily P., commanded by Capt. W. D. Bettis, left Orange with a load of freight for all points on the upper river. In January, 1885, the steamer, by then commanded by Capt. Lancaster, brought down 150 bales of cotton and 20 bundles of hides from Hamilton.[246] In October, 1886, the Emily P. was the second Orange steamboat to arrive at storm-devastated Sabine Pass and Johnson Bayou, La., with aid for the terror-stricken survivors.[247] It is not known what exact year the packet left the Sabine River, but it was not listed among the Sabine River's cotton fleet of 1888. The packet spent its last years in the Brazos River cotton trade, because in 1898, the Emily P. was recorded as being one of several Brazos River cotton steamers, which lay half-submerged, decaying, and abandoned, engines and boilers removed, in a "steamboat graveyard" at West Columbia, Texas.[248]

Two other cotton boats, the steamers Lark and Extra, seem to have enjoyed profitable careers on the Sabine during the decade of the 1880's. The first record of the former appeared in the Orange Tribune in 1879, when the Lark belonged to Capt. Tom Davis. During the 1881 season, the packet made a number of successful voyages.[249] As late as 1888, one account observed "that the river is in good boating order, and that the Lark and Extra continue to make regular trips to the upper river..." Late in January, 1888, the Extra carried a load of freight upriver and returned to Orange with a full cargo of cotton.[250] In February, 1888, a correspondent reported that:[251]

> ...the steamer Lark, owned and run by Captain
> Joshua Griffith, careened, and filled with water last
> night. She had a full cargo and valuable merchandise
> for points between this and Stark's Landing. All will
> be saved but it is badly damaged. Nearly all of the
> cargo is insured...Her larboard side rests on the
> bottom in about five feet of water...

Within a week, the Daily News recounted that the *Lark*, "reportedly sunk on the 15th", was raised and pumped out yesterday by Davis and Adams. She suffered very little damage and will soon resume her regular trips." Less than a month later, the packet was reported as having "arrived today from Stark's landing with cotton."[252] No further record of the Lark on the Sabine River was ever located after 1889.

The sidewheel steamboat Extra came to the Sabine River under Captain J. M. Liles in 1883, and ten years later, she was still plying the river's upper reaches. She was certainly one of the larger packets to carry cotton along the stream during the decline of the steamboat epic. In February, 1884, the Daily News noted that the Extra had left Orange "on her regular trip up the river" in search of cotton, adding that, as of February 1, "5,000 bales have been shipped from Orange this season."[253] On March 1, 1884, the steamer:[254]

> ... Extra arrived with 122 bales of cotton consigned to
> New Orleans, 25 to Houston and 98 to

*Galveston...The Emily P. brought down 60 bales and
a number of passengers.*

During the first week of January, 1886, the packet Extra, "with the first cargo of cotton this season, arrived yesterday" at Orange with 282 bales aboard. Later that month, another account recorded that "the steamer Extra, on her second trip up the river, arrived yesterday with 330 bales." Only two weeks later, at the end of its third voyage that season, the sidewheeler was back at her Orange berth with another 340 bales.[255]

In 1888, the Lark and the Extra were still the principal cotton carriers left on the river, and each made a number of successful voyages again that season. Late in January, the Extra was reported as arriving "today with 171 bales of cotton for Houston, 106 bales for Galveston and 63 bales for New Orleans (total, 340). She left Hamilton Friday (21st) and found the river rising all the way down. The Lark will leave with a full cargo for the upper river tomorrow, and the Extra will start for Hamilton in a few days."[256]

On January 2, 1893, the Extra, by then captained by J. M. Allardyce, was loaded with freight at Orange and preparing to "leave for Hamilton and intermediate landings."[257] As of the year 1892, its voyages to Orange had become rather infrequent, for the Extra was one of three packets based at Logansport, Louisiana. The steamers normally travelled south on the Sabine to Pendleton and East Hamilton in pursuit of cotton and then returned, transshipping their cotton cargoes via rail to Shreveport. The smart steamer skippers thus avoided the slow movement through the masses of floating logs on the lower river, but they also risked, even in wintertime, a quick drop in water level on the upper stretches of the stream that might cause them to have to tie up and wait for a rise. One account of 1892 recounted that:[258]

*...the steamers Maude Howell and Ada are making
weekly trips to points on the lower river, bringing
back barrel staves and cotton. The steamer Extra is
lying at this point {Logansport, La.} awaiting a rise in*

*the river as the water is too low for large boats to
run...*

The last record of the Extra appeared in print in 1893, the
year that the packet sank near the railroad bridge in Logansport,
La., a spot that eventually became a "steamboat boneyard" much
like the one at West Columbia, Texas, on the Brazos.

If the river's cotton trade was already in a state of decline, it
was not apparent from one of the records left in 1893. One
correspondent reported during that shipping season that:[259]

> *...steamboats are utilizing the Sabine River for all it is
> worth. There are three boats running from
> Logansport down as far as East Pendleton and
> carrying cotton up to Logansport, and four others are
> making regular trips from this place (Orange) to East
> Hamilton and below, carrying assorted merchandise
> up and bringing cotton down...*

The Maude Howell was a small 250-bale boat which plied
the upper reaches around Logansport during the early 1890's.
However, like the Extra, the steamer infrequently travelled the entire
distance to *Orange as the following account reveals:[260]

> *...Captain H. F. S. Martin of the steamboat Maude
> Howell, who came down today, reports that on the
> 7th one of the piston rods knocked out a cylinder
> head of the main engine ... forcing him to tie up ten
> miles above Sudduth's Bluff ... His boat left
> Logansport on the 5th and is loaded to guards with
> cotton. There are about 800 bales at Hamilton yet...*

The Maude Howell may have remained on the upper river
for a number of years, but no later record in the Daily News has
been located by the writer to date; and no other area newspaper,
except the Vindicator, has survived. Likewise, nothing else is known
about the small steamer Ada, except that it was one of the three
Logansport packets during the early 1890's. Of the four or five

packets that ended up in the Logansport "steamboat boneyard" during the late 1890's, the Extra and the Neches Belle are two of them and it is probable that the Maude Howell and Ada are there also.

Along with the Lamar, Pearl Rivers, and Extra, the Neches Belle was one of the stream's largest and most lucrative steamers during the declining years of the river trade, and Sabine's undisputed "river queen" after 1892. For all of its years spent in the Sabine, it's a shame the packet wasn't named the "Sabine Belle," but it was named for the river at Beaumont where the Belle was built. During the 79th year of his life, its builder and first captain-owner, Will O. Loving of Bunn's Bluff, left a complete record of the steamboat's origin. In 1870 Loving had begun his river career as a deckhand on the old Neches River packet Kate, under Capt. Charlie Hausinger. In time he graduated to pilot on the steamboat A. Van Buskirk of the Neches River trade, and eventually as master of the Vicksburg, Pearl Rivers, and Neches Belle in the Sabine River trade.

In 1933, the veteran steamboatman, who still lived in retirement beside the banks of the Neches, revealed that the old Neches Belle had been:[261]

> ...built (in Beaumont) in 1890 right close to the
> mouth of the (Brake's) Bayou where the Southern
> Pacific bridge stands today. My brother-in-law, Pearl
> Bunn, and I built 'er. We bought the lumber from the
> old Reliance Sawmill, and I knew every board that
> went into that boat...We used the machinery from
> our old boat, the Vicksburg. We built the Neches
> Belle on dry land, then put 'er on rollers, and lowered
> her into the water. She cost us $3,000, not counting
> the machinery that we took from Vicksburg...

Only a few months after the new packet was afloat, Bunn and Loving sold the capacious steamer to Captain S. G. Allardyce for $4,500 and thereafter the sternwheeler plied the Sabine River until it was tied up in 1897 in Logansport, La., where it eventually sank. Continuing the old river boatman's history of the Belle, Loving added that:[262]

> *... River steam boating was dying ... We had taken*
> *her up the Sabine River with a load of freight. The*
> *water fell and we were disheartened enough to*
> *accept the offer that Allardyce had made us. Like the*
> *Laura that sank in the Neches at Beaumont for want*
> *of care, the Neches Belle lies at the bottom of the*
> *river at Logansport ...*

With its excellent cuisine and spacious accommodations, the Neches Belle was to play a significant role during the off-season as an excursion steamer, a role that strengthened and abetted the sparse social life and primitive pioneer entertainment then to be found on an otherwise harsh and unfriendly frontier. One article of the year 1892 recounts that:[263]

> *...The First Regiment band gave a moonlight*
> *excursion on the steamer Neches Belle Thursday*
> *night. The music, moonlight, and cool breeze were*
> *enjoyed by about 125 people who were loath to*
> *leave the boat when shores were reached...*

In February, 1893, the Belle reached Orange with 210 bales of cotton and 6,000 oak barrel staves for the wine industry of France. A month later, the steamboat returned there from Logansport with 118 bales for New Orleans and another 6,000 barrel staves for trans-shipment to France.[264] In May, 1893, the Neches Belle's "owners have the contract for cleaning snags and sawyers out of the Sabine River as high as Belgrade," and for the remainder of that summer, the packet was occupied fulfilling that obligation.[265]

Apparently, the steamboat was engaged for several summers in clearing the lower river of navigation impediments. In November, 1895, another newspaper article observed that:[266]

*...the steamer Neches Belle came down yesterday
evening from the Narrows, having completed her
contract for removing obstructions in that reach of
the river between Morgan's Bluff and — (name
omitted, racial epithet). General J. B. Slaughter was
the inspector for the United States Government, and
he feels that a very satisfactory amount of work has
been accomplished ...*

The year 1893 appears to have been the last significant year of the Sabine cotton trade, and although five smaller steamers may have found full cargoes along the river, the small quantities carried by the Neches Belle never amounted to more than about 20 percent of the packet's bale capacity. "King Kotton's" heyday when 500 or 600 bale cargoes were common along the river had long since passed. Cotton production along the lower river had consistently declined as hundreds of farmers, both black and white, deserted the fields for the flourishing lumber and logging camps, thus insuring monthly or semi-monthly pay days for themselves. Today, it is difficult to look at large areas of timberlands in Jasper and Newton Counties and realize that these were once cotton farms of a century ago that have returned to forest.

In addition, other alternative routes to market for cotton developed after 1880 as two main rail lines were built parallel to the Sabine River, and elsewhere several short logging tram roads, which carried cotton and freight as well as logs, linked up with the railroads. In 1895 the Kirbyville, Beaumont and Gulf Railroad was built from Kirbyville to Beaumont, and the Cow Creek Tram Co., which ran all the way to the Sabine River, intersected that line at Call Junction, Texas. Rails of the Yellow Bluff Tram Co. on the Neches River intersected the same line at Buna, Texas, which was founded as one of its logging camps. In 1895, rails of the Kansas City Southern Railroad were laid parallel to the Sabine River. Beginning at Dequincy, La., that line retraced the path of the Lutcher-Moore Lumber Company's tram road, through its logging camp at Starks, La., and on to the river. And rails of the Sabine

Tram Company intersected the Kirbyville line at Evadale, Jasper County, Texas, providing another route to the Sabine River.

There was still plenty of freight to be carried north on the Sabine River to supply some shorter tram roads and independent logging camps, but it's doubtful if any steamer as large as the Neches Belle could have realized a profit in a one-way trade. On the packet's last trip to Logansport in 1897 with a load of rail construction material, the Belle was tied up and its title was impounded in court litigation. Much like the Washington of a half-century earlier, the Belle's timbers dried out as it lay on a sand bar during a low water season, and its leaking hull filled up on the next river freshet, leaving the once proud steamboat berthed in its final watery grave.[267]

In an article undeniably prophetic of the changing times, a Galveston editor revealed in 1893 that:[268]

> *...the steamboat Neches Belle ... is now being*
> *equipped with electric lights and will be the first boat*
> *on the Sabine River to carry a strong search light ...*

Hence, the transition from cotton bales, steam, and kerosene for lamps to Diesel tugs, screw propellers, and two-way radio for communications was already in progress.

Four new packets, the Una, the Dura, the Robert E. Lee, and the Charles Lee, would mark the final decade of the Sabine River steamboat trade, and three of them, all except the Charles Lee, would linger on into the twentieth century. But it was the commerce of the logging tram roads and logging camps, not the cotton trade, that would account for their prosperity. The Sabine Tram Company had rail lines and log skids into the river at Salem, Sudduth's Bluff and Laurel, and it belonged to George W. and J. B. Smyth. The tram utilized dozens of oxen and mules in addition to locomotive and cars, and its 500 employees dumped around 200,000 board feet of logs into the Sabine River daily. The Cow Creek Tram ran between Belgrade and Call Junction on the Kirbyville line, and it belonged to Dennis Call, Jr., and others of Orange.[269] Its manpower, number of oxen and mules, and production statistics were about the same. Most trams operated from two to four locomotives, 50 to 75 logging cars and employed from 100 to 500 loggers in the forests and lumberjacks on the river. Lutcher and Moore's Gulf, Sabine, and Red River Tram Company of Calcasieu Parish, La., owned ten locomotives, 130 log cars, 100 miles of track and employed 1,000 loggers and lumberjacks to dump 300,000 to 500,000 feet of logs daily into the river. Collectively, these firms dumped close to one million board feet of logs daily in their heyday. There were other small logging tram companies and scores of small, independent log contractors, including Beckham's Brothers Tram Company and the Newton County Tram Company, which intersected the river at Stark's Landing. Lutcher and Moore had one Texas tram for logging in north Orange County, and today its tracks, now the Orange and Northwestern Railroad, connect Orange with Buna, Texas.

The steamboats Una and Robert E. Lee entered the Sabine River trade in 1892, and their activities in the commerce of the lower river are recorded on a daily basis in the Galveston News until well after 1900. Although intended primarily for the tram supply trade, each vessel, if loaded with cotton, had a capacity of about 200 bales and measured about 65 or 70 feet long. Captain Tom J. Davis was owner and master of the Una until June, 1893, when he launched his new steamer, the Dura, after which Captain Wiley Phillips commanded the Una. On return voyages, their cargoes usually consisted of a few bales of cotton and sundry hides and farm produce, but on the upriver trips, the steamers carried every conceivable item used by the tram roads, from hardware and merchandise to rails, locomotives, livestock, and grain for the oxen and mules. The bigger trams also operated company stores and post offices or allowed private merchants to do so.

On its first trip in 1893, the Una left Orange for Salem with a full cargo of merchandise and towing a heavily-loaded barge, an indication that business was booming. On two downriver voyages in February, the packet arrived at Orange with cotton and hides from Belgrade and Sudduth's Bluff. In March, the steamer was making "tri-weekly trips" to Sudduth's Bluff, carrying lumber for the Sabine Tram Co.[270] In May and June, 1893, the sternwheeler made a number of voyages all the way to Logansport, and by July, when Captain Davis transferred to the Dura, the Una received its new master, Captain Wiley Phillips. In August, the packet carried a complete load of corn and fodder in sacks to Sudduth's Bluff for the log-hauling oxen and mules of the Sabine Tram Co.[271]

In September, 1896, an Orange correspondent of the Galveston Daily News recounted that the Una had:[272]

> *...returned light from Sudduth's Bluff...The new hull being built here for the Una is nearly ready to launch and will be put in the water within a few days. The machinery will be transferred to it and the old hull will be converted into a barge...*

During the next year, it appears that the new steamer was engaged full-time hauling supplies for the Sabine Tram Company at Salem and Sudduth's Bluff. There was still some cotton moving along the river, for as late as January 5, 1898, the Una had a number of bales aboard when it reached Orange from its return voyage to Salem.[273]

By March, 1898, the Una was hauling lumberjacks and supplies for some of the newer tram roads which were beginning to line both banks of the Sabine River. During the same month, an article reported that the Una had left Orange "loaded to the guards with raftsmen and their supplies, bound for Whitman's Ferry." In December, 1898, the Galveston News added that the sternwheeler had left Orange "for Beckham's Bluff today, loaded with supplies for the Beckham's Bluff Tram Company." Between January and April, 1899, the destination of the steamboat's upriver trips was Stark's Landing, indicating that the Una was engaged full-time by a different logging firm. In March, one account recorded that the boat "was loading and will leave tomorrow for Stark's Landing with a full load of merchandise for the Newton County Tram Company."[274] In 1900, the year that the writer's research and the official time period of this treatise ended, the veteran steamer was still plying the lower stretches of the river to supply the tram roads.

One could almost classify the Robert E. Lee as being the 'sister ship' of the Una, its size, tenure, and type of service on the Sabine River having so closely paralleled that of the latter. Owned and captained by J. J. Jordan, the steamboat spent all of 1893 and much time thereafter supplying the Cow Creek Tram Company. In January, 1893, Captain Jordan arrived at Orange from Belgrade, his steamer having "brought down cotton and hides." In the course of that year, there are many records of the R. E. Lee making round trips with full cargoes, and in March of that year, one account noted that the packet was "taking on board log cars for the Cow Creek Tram."[275] During 1896, the voyages of the Robert E. Lee were hampered often by low water and miles of floating logs.[276]

In September, 1896, the Lee was hauled out on the way at Snoad's Shipyard at Orange, and its machinery and hull were thoroughly repaired from stem to stern. After its relaunching, the vessel's hull and boilers were inspected by Captains L. C. Hershberger and R. G. Murray, who were employed as United States steamboat inspectors. Hershberger was best known as one of the famed and last surviving steamboat captains from the heyday of the Trinity River cotton trade after the Civil War.[277]

In November, 1896, Robert E. Lee made a trip upriver to "Brice's timber landing, where she delivered a cargo of supplies for the camps."[278] While upriver, the packet was trapped by low water and had to tie up for one month at Droddy's Shoals. While docked there, one well-recorded incident observed that not all of the dangers and pitfalls of Sabine River steam boating were related to the river. One night, Robert Jordan, the 14-year-old son of the captain, heard dogs baying along the neighboring riverbank. Grabbing a rifle, the youth went ashore in the moonlight at the very moment when some unknown dark object sprang upward into a nearby cypress tree. With only the limited vision offered by a bright moon, young Robert fired at what appeared to be a large cat up in the tree, and a full-grown black panther fell to the ground, momentarily stunned. As the barking hounds gathered around, the panther was recovering and in the process of defending itself with fang and claw, when the lad grabbed a large pine knot on the ground and struck the wounded panther on the head, thus ending the battle. He brought the carcass back to Orange, where he had it skinned, stuffed, and mounted by a taxidermist as a trophy for his father's steamboat.[279]

In February, 1898, R. E. Lee arrived at Orange "from Knight's Landing with less than half a load of cotton". The sternwheeler was one of the few steamers still navigating the Sabine River at the dawning of the twentieth century, and since no further research was conducted after 1900, the ultimate fate of Lee is unknown to the author.[280]

Throughout the latter half of the nineteenth century, the veteran pilot and steamboat owner-master, Captain Tom J. Davis, emerges as the last "dean of steamboatmen" of the Sabine River, a rather honorary appellation or position of respect, based on years of river service, granted previously by the author only to Captains Peter Stockholm and John Clements. As far back as 1861, Davis had built and sailed the old Confederate tender, the Dime, which had been the Orange-to-Sabine Pass mail packet. During the 1880's-1890's, other members of his family stood equally erect beside him as veteran navigators and skippers, the first being Captain H. T. Davis of the L. Q. C. Lamar, and finally Captain Charles Davis of the sternwheeler Charles Lee.

The origin of Charles Lee is likewise unknown to the writer. In 1893-1894, the vessel, then captained by Aaron Sheffers, was in the Neches River trade, making weekly voyages to Wiess Bluff to haul out cotton.[281] About 1895, Davis replaced Sheffers as master, and the vessel was then transferred to the Sabine River. Thereafter, the ownership of the Charles Lee is likewise uncertain. It may have belonged to Davis or to the Lutcher and Moore Lumber Company, in which log-towing, lumber-freighting and tram supply service the packet usually remained.

In May, 1896, the Charles Lee left Orange for Niblett's Bluff "with a full cargo of stores and feedstuff, consigned to Craddock and Arbogast," who were log camp operators at Field, Louisiana on the Gulf, Sabine, and Red River Railroad, which was a rather fancy name for Lutcher and Moore's tram road. In July and August, the steamboat towed rafts of logs for Lutcher and Moore. In November and December, 1896, the sternwheeler was again hauling cargoes to Niblett's Bluff, consigned once more to Craddock and Arbogast, who supplied logs for Lutcher and Moore's sawmills. When the latter discontinued their own logging in 1894, Craddock and Arbogast were the first prime contractors who employed from 500 to 1,000 men in their logging camps, on the Gulf, Sabine, and Red River Railroad, and as lumberjacks riding the log rafts down the river.[282]

Also in November, the Charles Lee was hauled out at an Orange shipyard for a major overhaul of her hull but was soon relaunched "to resume her place in the trade." Afterward the steamer made a number of voyages to Sudduth's Bluff, and in February, 1897, "brought down a second shipment of wood oil, turpentine, and wood acid from the {turpentine} still at Stockholm, Louisiana." During the same month, the packet's owner signed a contract with the Kansas City, Pittsburgh, and Gulf Railroad (now the Kansas City Southern) to haul 1,000 cubic yards of clam shell and 1,000 barrels of cement for the pillars of a new railroad bridge across the Sabine River, which was at that time under construction at Deweyville, Texas, north of Orange.[283]

In 1898, its machinery apparently worn out beyond repair, the Charles Lee was stripped of its engine, boilers and other machinery, and the hull was converted into a barge, which was then towed by the steam tugboat George Sealy. In January, 1899, the Sealy, with the barge Charles Lee in tow, was still plying the river between Orange and Sudduth's Bluff. The barge and tow boat were still on the river in 1900.[284]

During the winter of 1893, the flourishing trade of the Sabine River prompted Captain Tom Davis to build a larger steamer, the Dura, its origins being quite extensively preserved in the Galveston Daily News, as follows:[285]

> ...Capt. Tom J. Davis has the keel laid for a new
> steamboat that he will build here {Orange} to run on
> the Sabine River. She will be after the model of the
> steamer Una, though much larger and wider. The

*increase in trade on the lower river calls for larger
boats and she is being constructed to accommodate
this demand...*

In May, 1893, there were "nearly 100 ship carpenters now employed, at work on the four barges and on Capt. Davis' new steamboat, besides several who are engaged at the repair ways at William Snoad's shipyard."[286] On June 15, another article recounted that:[287]

*...Capt. Davis launched his new boat yesterday and
christened her the Dura. She is 72 feet long and has a
sixteen foot beam, flat-bottom and square bow, and
stern. The machinery and cabin will be put in as
quickly as the work can be done...*

Two months later, Davis and the Dura left on the new steamer's "maiden voyage for the upper river," but by September 5, the Dura was tied up at Belgrade, plagued by that frequent scourge of the Sabine River steamboatmen, low water, and a correspondent noted that "a few 100 yards below the Dura, the water in the river is less than one foot deep."[288]

Another account of the following December suitably recalls the perils of Sabine River steam boating, observing that the Dura had left Orange:[289]

*...for Belgrade on the 29th of August. Her trip was
made in average time, but while unloading at
Belgrade, the water ran out of the river, and there
has not been a time until about four weeks ago when
she could get out. She left Belgrade on the 16th of
November, and soon overtook the jam of pine logs
that for a month has cut off navigation on the
Sabine...The captain put on an extra crew. and with
pike poles, levers, cant hooks, and plenty of muscle,
he broke his way through...The Dura brought several
"first bales" for the different merchants along the*

*Sabine River. The bales should have been in
Galveston as early as the 8th of September last...*

The Dura's fortunes improved considerably during the next two years, and the new packet earned considerable profits for her owner. By 1896, Tom Davis had placed Captain George Wolford in command of the steamer, and a newspaperman in March of that year recorded that the Dura had "shipped her new engine, completed connections, tried her machinery, and was taking on cargo" at Orange.[290] During the summer of 1896, the vessel experienced again many of the same low water problems that had created such an ordeal for her in 1893.[291]

In April, 1899, the Daily News reported that the steamboat had just arrived at Orange:[292]

*...from Logansport with 66 bales of cotton. She
formerly belonged to the lower river, but last spring
she left for Logansport and since then has been
engaged in that trade. This is the first time she has
touched here since May 18, 1898...*

As late as 1901, the Dura was mentioned as still sailing the Sabine River, having just arrived "from Klondyke," 125 miles by the river, and reports ... the first 50 miles full of floating pine logs." In truth, the times were changing rapidly, but the boating conditions for the steamer crews remained the same.[293]

Throughout the 1890's, there were a few other packets also navigating the Sabine, but a sparsity of accounts in the News leads one to believe that they were present in the Sabine River only for brief periods or perhaps for a single voyage. One of these was the steamboat Minna, the keel for which was laid sometime late in 1897. In February, 1898, the Galveston newspaper recorded that "Captain George Wolford has been engaged to take command of the new steamboat Minna, recently launched at Logansport, La... He will load her there with oak staves for delivery to Sabine Pass." The sternwheeler apparently remained in the Sabine River for at least two years, for in May, 1899, a newspaper article recounted that:[294]

> ...the steamboat Minna, owned and operated by the
> Austro-American Stave Co. of Shreveport, La., has
> reached here {Orange} from the upper river with
> another load of staves {for the French wine-making
> industry} ...and left for Sabine Pass...

In April, 1899, a single voyage in the river was made by the 113-foot steamboat, H. A. Harvey, Jr., which was reported as arriving at Orange from Sabine Pass and "on Sunday will take an excursion party to Port Arthur."[295] At that moment, the packet was normally engaged in the late lumber trade of the Neches River. The Harvey had been built in 1891 as a snag boat for the Calcasieu River, and still equipped with her special channel-clearing machinery, was the same Harvey which made the second and last voyage over the entire distance of the Trinity River {even removing sections of railroad bridges temporarily} between Galveston and Dallas in 1893. At that moment, there was a movement in effect for the canalization of that river, which came to naught.[296]

Throughout the 1890's, there were a number of steam tow boats on the lower Sabine, and although other writers have already elevated some of these to 'steamboat' status, the writer remains reluctant to dignify them with that appellation, at least, in the same sense as he applies it to the majestic, old cotton carriers of the river. The earliest ones of them, however, were steam-driven, although quite small, and propelled by a single, stern paddle wheel. But again, indicative of the changing times, Nellie and a few others were exceptions, being powered already with internal-combustion, naphtha-burning engines. Even so, Nellie still deserves some attention. In December, 1893, the News revealed that the "towboat Nellie, Capt. Lee Rosenbaum, came in {to Orange} today from Wiess Bluff by way of Johnson's Bayou. She had in tow the barge Maude M., loaded with cotton."[297] Hence, the Nellie sounds very similar to the Neches River steamer Kate of the 1870's which also towed a barge loaded with cotton. In February, 1898, Nellie "brought the barge Welcome from Bland's rice farm on Cow Bayou today with 864 sacks, totaling 135,260 pounds of rough rice." In 1896, the Nellie and the Charles Lee were both engaged in towing log rafts from Niblett's Bluff to the Lutcher and Moore log booms at Orange.[298] For the reader's benefit, a "boom" was a floating corral, made of logs connected together with chains or cables, for storing one sawmills logs prior to milling, and between 1850 and 1910, there were several of them in both rivers at Beaumont and Orange.

Johnson's Bayou, Louisiana, located near Sabine Lake, had two post offices, Radford, and Johnson's Bayou, and about 800 residents until the storm of October, 1886, drowned 110 of them and drove hundreds of the survivors away. Nevertheless, enough of them remained to rebuild the place. Being cut off from the world except by water, Johnson's Bayou became entirely dependent upon Orange for its supplies and markets, and usually the steamboat which held the mail contract would average two to three round trips a week between the towns. After the sawmills came to Orange in 1877, that town became wholly dependent upon Johnson's Bayou for farm produce and even cattle for the meat markets, all of which was brought in on the mail steamer. Emily P. was the steamer engaged in the Johnson's Bayou trade when the storm hit. By 1880, Johnson's Bayou was producing annually about 900 bales of cotton on 600 acres of land; it also had 100 acres of bearing satsuma orange trees and grew about 500 acres of sugar cane for its three cotton gins and three sugar mills. After the storm hit, the bayou never rebuilt sufficiently to require the full-time use of a steamer again. It remained cut off from the world except by water until the causeway bridge was built over Sabine Lake during the 1960's

Throughout the 1890's, the best known tugboat on the lower Sabine River was the large J. V. Guillote, captained by L. L. Bettis. Its daily burden was a long tow of lumber-laden barges, bound for the export docks at Sabine Pass. In 1899, another account related that "the steamer J. C. Griffith brought a barge load of cattle from Johnson's Bayou to this place {Orange}." Also in 1899, the steam tow boat Ava, "belonging to the Port Arthur Fish Oil and Fertilizer Company," was reported as "hauled out at Weaver and Levingston Shipyard" at Orange.[299] During the summer of 1896, the Fannie, which was a 50-foot steamer, but was occasionally referred to as a tugboat, was still making excursion voyages along the lower river, where it first arrived in 1877. In 1901, the Fannie was sold to the Atlantic Rice Milling Company of Beaumont, and it was used thereafter to tow barges filled with rough rice from Cow Bayou, a tributary of the Sabine, Taylor's Bayou near Port Arthur, and Beaumont, where the mill was located. Also in 1901, Wesley Block of Orange sold his tow boat Ideal to the Nicaragua Banana Company. His tug was one year old, was an oil burner, and had been built at Orange.[300] These early Sabine River tugboats are worthy of mention only as far as they were a party in the transition of the Sabine River steamer from a cotton carrier to the long Diesel tows of petrochemicals that have long since replaced them.

Three other late Neches River steamers, the Caprice, the John H. Kirby, and the W. P. Rabb, most assuredly made at least single voyages in the Sabine River between 1890 and 1905, if for no other reason than excursion voyages during the hot summer months, but the writer has no confirmation of that. The packets were all based at Beaumont, and all of them belonging to the sawmills; they pulled log rafts during the winter months whenever the water levels were high enough. The latter, named for its long-time captain, W. P. Rabb, was purchased by the Port Arthur Townsite and Land Company in 1896, and ended its days afloat as an excursion steamer and a tow boat for lumber schooners crossing Sabine Lake.[301] Another "single voyage" in the Sabine River occurred in May, 1897, when the steamboat Henrietta went up the river to the site of the new Kansas City, Pittsburgh, and Gulf Railroad bridge, "loaded with stringers and ties." No other reference to that steamer has ever been found.[302]

To the dawn of the twentieth century and beyond, the trade of the Sabine River remained as colorful, even if perhaps less profitable, as in the heyday of the old cotton boats. Those were changing times, indeed, during the declining years of the cotton trade, and integral parts of that change were a vast influx of population and improved transportation methods, both ashore and afloat. The export lumber schooners quickly passed from the local scene, giving way to the deep sea steamers which soon began docking at Orange following the deep canalization of the lower Sabine River. In time, long tows of barges began travelling the lower Sabine River while in route from New Orleans to Galveston Bay via the Intercoastal Canal. In 1900 passenger trains were already commonplace at Orange and Beaumont, and would soon be augmented by trucks, passenger buses and automobiles. The river steamer, as an instrument for passengers and freight on the Sabine River, had bowed once again to its successors, but for the frontier traveler, it provided the best, and often the quickest and most comfortable conveyance for the traveling public. The old cotton boat was phased out, but with its passing, a certain nostalgia of the quieter and friendlier days of the frontier prevailed. And perhaps too, there still survived to the discerning ear the distant and faint echoes from that moment when the steamboat's shrill whistle shattered the ominous silence below the horseshoe bend in the Sabine River.

Endnotes—Chapter 6

[230]Navigation Petition, Orange Board of Trade to G. W. McCreary, Secretary of War, reprinted in (Orange) *Weekly Tribune*, September 12, 1879.

[231]*Ibid.*

[232](Beaumont) *Enterprise*, November 6, 1880.

[233]*Ibid.*, December 18, 1880.

[234](Galveston) *Weekly News*, February 10, 1881.

[235]*Ibid.*, March 17, 1882; (Galveston) *Daily News*, February 2, 1882.

[236]*Daily News*, January 14, 1883.

[237](Orange) *Weekly Tribune,* February 22, 1884; *Daily News*, January 24, 1886; and (Beaumont) *Enterprise*, January 8, 1933.

[238](Galveston) *Daily News,* January 24, February 14, and July 18, 1882.

[239]*Ibid.*, December 12, 1883.

[240]*Weekly Tribune*, February 22, 1884; *Daily News*, March 20, 1884.

[241](Galveston) *Daily News*, October 15, 16, 1886.

[242](Liberty, Tx.) *Vindicator*, March 18, 1892.

[243](Beaumont) *Enterprise*, December 18, 1880, and September 21, 1910; (Orange) *Weekly Tribune*, September 12, 1879.

[244]*Enterprise*, January 8, 1933.

[245](Sabine Pass) *Beacon,* June 10, 1871; (Galveston) *Weekly News*, June 19, 1871.

[246](Orange) *Tribune*, February 22, 1884; *Weekly News*, January 8, 1885.

[247](Galveston) *Daily News*, October 15, 16, 1886; (Newton, Tx.) *Newton County Record*, September 17, 1884.

[248]*Daily News*, January 9, 1898.

[249](Orange) *Weekly Tribune*, September 12, 1879; (Beaumont) *Enterprise*, December 18, 1880.

[250]*Daily News*, January 26, and April 12, 1888.

[251]*Ibid.*, February 17, 1888.

[252]*Daily News,* February 23, and March 11, 1888.

[253]*Ibid.*, February 19, 23, 1884.

[254]*Ibid.*, March 1, 1884.

[255]*Ibid.*, January 9, 23, and February 5, 1886.

[256]*Daily News*, January 26, 1888.

[257]*Ibid.,* January 3, 1893.

[258]*Ibid.*, November 26, 1892.

[259]*Ibid.*, January 11, 1893.

[260]*Ibid.*

[261]"Captain Loving Who Built *Neches Bell* in Beaumont Recalls Steamboat Days," (Beaumont) *Enterprise*, January 8, 1933.

[262]*Ibid.*

[263](Galveston) *Daily News*, May 15, 1892.

[264]*Ibid.*, February 26 and March 28, 1893.

[265]*Ibid.*, May 21, July 16, and August 6, 1893.

[266]*Ibid.*, November 3, 1895.

[267](Beaumont) *Enterprise*, January 8, 1933.

[268](Galveston) Daily News, December 18, 1893.

[269]See "Biography of Dennis Call, Jr." in John H. Brown, INDIAN WARS AND PIONEERS OF TEXAS (Austin: 1897); also "The History of the Lutcher-Moore Lumber Co.," (Beaumont) *Enterprise*, October 15, 1905.

[270](Galveston) *Daily News*, January 11, February 19, 26, and March 7, 1893.

[271]*Ibid.*, May 14, June 16, 20; August 6, 13, 1893.

[272]*Ibid.*, September 8, 1896.

[273]*Ibid.*, December 10, 17, 1896; January 11, 1897; January 6 and February 28, 1898.

[274](Galveston) *Daily News*, March 7, and December 28, 1898; January 29, March 2, and April 4, 1899.

[275]*Ibid.*, January 11, February 26, March 7, 30, April 4, 24, and May 14, 21, 1893.

[276]*Ibid.,* May 25, June 21, and July 4, 1896.

[277]*Daily News*, September 8, 24, 1896.

[278]*Ibid.,* November 25, 1896.

[279]*Ibid.,* January 11, 1897.

[280]*Ibid.,* February 17, 1898.

[281]*Ibid.,* November 13, 1893 and January 4, 1894.

[282]*Daily News*, July 4, August 30, November 30, and December 10, 1896.

[283]*Ibid.,* January 1, 11, 18 and February 6, 21, 1897.

[284]*Ibid.,* January 29 and February 11, 1899.

[285]*Ibid.,* April 23, 1893.

[286]*Daily News*, May 14, 1893.

[287]*Ibid.,* June 16, 1893.

[288]*Ibid.,* August 13 and September 3, 8, 1893.

[289]*Ibid.,* December 15, 1893.

[290]*Ibid.,* March 21 and May 25, 1896.

[291](Galveston) *Daily News*, June 21, July 4, and August 1, 1896.

[292]*Ibid.,* April 21, 1899

[293]*Ibid.,* March 31, 190

[294]*Ibid.,* February 20, 1898; May 24, 1899.

[295]*Ibid.,* April 15, 1899.

[296](Liberty, Tx.) *Vindicator*, March 24, 1893.

[297](Galveston) *Daily News*, December 18, 1893.

[298]*Ibid.,* August 30, 1896; February 28, 1898.

[299]*Ibid.,* March 10 and May 17, 1899.

[300](Galveston) *Daily News*, April 6, and August 30, 1896; September 1 and December 25, 1901.

[301]*Ibid.,* March 7, 1896.

[302]*Ibid.,* May 14, 1897.

Chapter 7—Sabine River Trade Conclusions

Today, upon viewing any part of Sabine's sluggish lower reaches, one can still lose himself momentarily in somber quietude and antebellum nostalgia if one so yearns. But some distant air whistle would quickly awaken and remind one that the river's brisk trade of yesteryear is neither dormant nor dead. It has evolved, indeed, but the large ocean-going vessels and cargo tonnages moving on that stream today would dwarf any figures of earlier decades. In fact, many decades ago, the lower stretches of the stream became a part of our Intercoastal Canal System in an area between New Orleans and Houston, where daily hundreds of barge tows can be observed moving chemical products in both directions. And only an old-timer such as the writer might recall when the Sabine River and Intercoastal Canal was the route for large deep-sea steamers reaching the Port of Lake Charles, Louisiana, the lower Calcasieu River channelization not being completed until World War II days. And the lower Sabine River's placid flow can also deny those moments in the past when the furies of the river's flood waters formed a sea six miles wide in the Louisiana marshes opposite Orange and threatened to engulf large residential additions in the lower-lying areas. As recently as 1953, the writer is reminded of a wearisome 24 hours that he spent filling sandbags in what was to prove a futile effort to curb the turbulent tides which spilled over Sabine's west bank.

The threat of Sabine River flooding has now been lessened considerably. During the 1960's, the Corps of Engineers completed the Toledo Bend dam and reservoir, creating a lake 110 miles long, in places ten miles wide, leaving wide nooks and corridors where such creeks as Palo Gaucho, Patroon, and San Patricio formerly flowed. In recent times, the lake has become a year-round playground for the pleasure-seeking residents of East Texas and Western Louisiana, but of even far greater worth, the reservoir's storage capacity, measured in millions of acre-feet, can supply the fresh water demands of an expanding regional population and its industries for decades, perhaps even centuries, to come. And the dam's floodgates now possess the muscle needed to control the worst passions of the river and contain its raging tides, which oftentimes inundated the lowlands below the dam.

Over a span of sixty years, some 85 steamboats, ranging from the Velocipede of the 1830's to the Dura of the 1890's, participated in the cotton trade of the matchless Sabine River. In lieu of a more accurate figure, the writer estimates that at least a half-million bales of cotton were floated south on the keelboats and steamers, and perhaps a much greater quantity of the river's cotton bale potential went to market via the railroads or the Red River. In later years, a probable thirty billion board feet of saw logs were floated downriver to appease the ravenous appetites of the Orange sawmills—Texas' "big log eaters." But those figures only represent a fraction of the story that begins to unfold. How many barrels of freight, thousands of barrel staves, bundles of hides, fodder to feed the log oxen and mules, or bushels of corn, tobacco, beans, potatoes, and other commodities moved along its surface during that same sixty-year span of time are secrets that only the mute river could reveal if it had a tongue and speech. Directly, the river provided livelihoods for thousands of keelboatmen, steamboatmen, lumberjacks, loggers, and trappers, and indirectly for the sawmillers, laborers, cotton brokers, railroaders, retailers, and many others who depended wholly on the river's movement of cotton, logs, freight, and other commodities of the Sabine River trade. Over the long span of years, some steamers burned or sank in the river, but its mortality rate at no time equaled or even approached that of the Trinity River, and perhaps the Brazos as well.

The foregoing, especially the cotton statistics, is not intended to imply that the Sabine River trade could be considered as record-setting. If any unequaled record were established there, and the writer believes there was one, it could only have been in the large quantities of logs that constantly moved downstream over a span of eighty years. Lutcher and Moore logged on the river from 1877 until 1930. And many other sawmills preceded that mammoth log-slicing concern. If the volume of cotton bales which floated along its surface ever equaled that of the Trinity River, it was only because the cotton trade of the latter lasted only half as long as that on the Sabine.

Even today, the river, in its own way, continues to bestow its blessings on the City of Orange, Texas, through the benevolence of Lutcher and Stark foundations. A hospital and a domed, red granite Presbyterian Church were endowed by the Lutcher family in decades long past, and only in recent years has the Stark Foundation added the beautiful Stark home, the beautiful Lutcher Theatre, and the magnificent Lutcher Art Museum. And all of it was made possible because the matchless Sabine River floated the philanthropists' logs to market.

Like the Trinity River, whenever and wherever the author views the cypress-studded and moss-draped Sabine, river scenery intermixed with cypress knees, bulrushes, and marsh sea cane and so typical of many areas of Southeast Texas and Southwest Louisiana, he makes no effort to prevent his thoughts from escaping into the last century. The steamers Graham and Era No. 8 race past him again and the pine knot smoke floats heavenward. Elsewhere other sternwheelers meander gracefully around the serpentine bends of the river. Such are fleeting fantasies, the writer admits, but the realities of daily living will stifle such nostalgia posthaste. But somehow, the writer predicts that the matchless Sabine River's verdant beauty and placid surface will survive forever. And hopefully, its colorful history will also emerge unscathed and survive for all time as one of those romantic episodes which has so often characterized the chronicles of frontier Texas.

Riverboat Ads and Photos

GALVEST'N & HOUSTON STEAM PACKETS.

ALBERT GALLATIN.—STERRET, *Master.*
DAYTON.—JENKINS, *Master.*
THE above named, last running, light draught steamers will ply between the above ports, touching at all intermediate landings. These boats have been entirely over hauled and fitted up in handsome style for the accommodation of passengers. For freight or passage, apply on board, or to
GEO. GAZLEY.
dec6;tf   SHEPHERD & CRAWFORD

Figure 3 - Steamboat Ads for the Albert Gallatin and Dayton

In April-May, 1840, The Albert Gallatin, Capt. John Sterrett, carried the Republic of Texas-United States boundary commission up the Sabine River, where the engineers took celestial bearings at various river ports and tributaries and mounted boundary markers. One of the civilian engineers on that voyage, a graduate of West Point, was George Gordon Meade, later commander, Army of the

Potomac, at the Battle of Gettysburg. Daily Galvestonian, Dec. 6,1841.

Figure 4 - Steamboat Ad. Galvestonian April 1840.

MARINE ADS.

Steamships.

MORGAN LINE

U. S. Mail Steamships.

For Galveston and Indiano'a.

The following, new low-pressure iron steamships form this line.

W. G. Hews, I. C Harris, Austin
St. Mary, Agnes, Harlan,
Alabama, City of Norfolk, Morgan,
Josephine, Matagorda, Clinton,
Hutchinson, Whitney,

Steamboats.

FOR GALVESTON, SABINE PASS AND LAKE CHARLES.

The A1 Steamer,

STONEWALL,

A. J. MOORE.............Master.

Will make regular weekly trips to the above named points. For freight or passage apply on board or to

NORRIS & CO.,
Galveston, Texas.

n-21-6m.

Galveston, S bine Pass and Calcasieu.

Regular Weekly Packet,

The staunch iron steamer,

S. J. LEE,

CHAS. BROCKWAY,......Master
E J. KENNEDY..........Clerk.

Will make regular weekly trips from Galveston to Calcasieu via Sabine Pass. The steamer has her Insurance Papers.
v4-n21-6m.

Beaumont, Concord and Bunn's Bluff.

Regular Weekly Packet,
Jas. L. GRAHAM,
N. WEISS, ...Master.

Freights shipped by this line will be handled with despatch, and may, if necessary, be covered by Open Policy of Insurance to all points above named.

For freight or passage apply on board.
v4-n21-1y.

REGULAR SABINE RIVER PACKET

For Logansport & intermediate landings.

The elegant steamer,

ERA No. 8.

G. B. BECK, ...Master.

The usual facilities will be given, and run cash advances made on cotton consigned to our friends in New Orleans or Galveston.
v4-n21-1y.

Figure 5 - Steamboat Ads. Sabine Beacon, June 13, 1871.

Figure 6 - Captain Andrew F. Smyth

Figure 7 - Captain William Wiess 1881. Master Sabine steamboats Alamo & Adrianne. He often took the Alamo all the way to Belzora, Smith County, for cotton.

Figure 8 - Sabine Riverrat Houseboats ca. 1920 (Courtesy Dr. Howard Williams Collection, Orange, Texas).

Figure 9 - Sabine Riverrat Houseboats ca. 1920 (Courtesy Dr. Howard Williams Collection, Orange, Texas)

Figure 10 - Sabine Pass whale, captured March 1910 and towed alive to Port Arthur, Texas for exhibition.

Figure 11 - Sabine pilot boat Florida captured and towed the whale. Captain H. C. Plummer.

Figure 12 - Circle Booms ca. 1900. Being towed down the Sabine River to Orange, Texas (courtesy Dr. Howard Williams Collection, Orange, Texas).

Figure 13 - The H. A. Harvey made the trip from Anahuac to Dallas in 1893. It had hinged stacks which could be lowered in order to pass under railroad bridges. (Courtesy of the C. W. Fisher, Jr. Collection, Sam Houston Regional Lib. and Research Ctr., Liberty, TX)

Figure 14 - Steamboat Lucy. Hauled mail, cotton, produce, cattle from Johnson's Bayou, LA to Orange, TX 1905-1915.

Figure 15 - Steamer Horatio 1894 (Courtesy of the C. W. Fisher, Jr. Collection, Sam Houston Regional Lib. and Research Ctr., Liberty, TX).

Figure 16 - Steamboat Henrietta ca. 1898 docked at Orange, Texas (courtesy Dr. Howard Williams Collection, Orange, Texas).

Figure 17 - Steamboat Laura 1870-80 Captain Andy Smyth. Hauled cotton from Bevilport to Sabine Pass and also plied the Sabine.

Figure 18 - Snagboat Dallas 1899 (Courtesy of the C. W. Fisher, Jr. Collection, Sam Houston Regional Lib. and Research Ctr., Liberty, TX).

Figure 19 - Snagboat Trinity 1911 (Courtesy of the C. W. Fisher, Jr. Collection, Sam Houston Regional Lib. and Research Ctr., Liberty, TX).

Figure 20 - Steamboat John Henry Kirby on an excursion voyage to Orange, Texas in 1900.

Figure 21 - Steamboat Boreallis Rex 1905-1920 sailed Lake Charles to Cameron on the Calcasieu River.

Figure 22 - Lumber Schooners at the Wingate Sawmill ca. 1898 (courtesy Dr. Howard Williams Collection, Orange, Texas).

Figure 23 - T. Bancroft & Son Sawmill Employees ca. 1885.

Figure 24 - Small Steamboat Dura ca. 1895 used to supply log camps.

Figure 25 - Houseboat in which lumberjacks slept ca. 1920 (courtesy Dr. Howard Williams Collection, Orange, Texas).

Figure 26 - Gasoway Log Removal Barge operated on the Sabine River.

Figure 27 - Steamboat Virginia (Courtesy of the C. W. Fisher, Jr. Collection, Sam Houston Regional Lib. and Research Ctr., Liberty, TX).

Figure 28 - Towboats: Guillote, Leonore, and Alamo ca. 1898 (courtesy Dr. Howard Williams Collection, Orange, Texas).

Figure 29 - Bark Amphitrite 1898 Sabine Pass lumber dock Slip #1.

Part 2—Trinity River Trade

Chapter 8—Trinity River's Physical and Historical Background

Easily one of the three most important Texas watercourses of the nineteenth century, The Trinity River enters Galveston Bay near Anahuac, providing a water route that is readily accessible to both Galveston and Houston. While traversing a thousand river miles inland to its source in Archer County, southwest of Wichita Falls, the winding stream drains the coastal meadows and thickets of the Gulf Prairie, the bottomlands and barrens, the vast pine forests of East Texas, until it enters the vast rolling uplands, containing some of the best cotton lands in the South.

In the course of carving its path to the sea, the river slices through the black soil of the prairie lands, geologically known as the Beaumont Clay, the sandy loam of the pine forests, and alternate rock and coal formations. The Trinity River's course is marked by frequent high bluffs or banks, but as the stream meanders through Liberty and Chambers Counties, its flood plain and bottomland thickets widen considerably, to about five miles in some places. The low banks in that region betray the river's susceptibility to flooding during the upriver rainy seasons, and centuries of such inundations have deposited rich layers of silt over the adjacent farmlands.

Many early writers have left vivid descriptions of the Trinity River, its early river ports, and adjacent soil surface. Although some early travelers considered the alluvial plantations along the Red, San Bernard, and Brazos Rivers as comprising the richest cotton lands in the State of Texas, Victor Bracht, a German immigrant, wrote in 1848 that the farms adjacent to the Trinity were "the very best in Texas."[1]

Writing about the river in 1840, William Kennedy, the British consul at Galveston, observed that:[2]

*...the Trinity, a few miles above its mouth, runs
through a low marshy country, with heavily-timbered
bottoms, the soil of which is well-suited to the
cultivation of sugar, cotton, or Indian corn, and
affords an unbounded range for cattle. The country,
for ninety-miles above the bay, is generally low
prairie, with occasional patches of woodland; the
bottoms are wide and fertile, and well-timbered
...Immediately above the town of Liberty commences
a series of beautiful undulations, diversified by
woodland and prairie, which stretches out to the San
Jacinto (River). Above the San Antonio Road, the
lands on both sides of the Trinity are rich, well-
timbered, and watered to its source...*

In 1840 George Bonnell, an Austin publisher, gave the following account of the river's principal tributaries. He reported that Old River, which was probably the main river stream or a mainstream of its delta at one time, entered the Trinity from the west at a point three miles from the delta, followed by Oak, Coushatta, Bedias, Bear, and Richland creeks and the West Fork of the river. The Trinity River's eastern tributaries included Kettle, Milton, Kickapoo, and Hurricane creeks and the river's East Fork.[3]

Describing the stream's other characteristics, Bonnell added that:[4]

*...When the country on the Trinity shall become
settled, it must be the outlet of a rich and extensive
commerce ...By the meanderings of the of the river it
is more than six hundred and fifty miles in length,
and has been navigated by steamboats two hundred
and fifty miles ...The land is rich and well-adapted to
the cultivation of sugar, cotton, or corn, and affords
an unbounded range for cattle ...Several fine salt
springs have been discovered from which the Indians
have been in the habit of manufacturing
considerable quantities of salt...*

In the early days, navigation of the upper Trinity River was greatly impeded by a series of shallows or shoal waters, sometimes characterized by underwater rocks, and known by such names as White Rock, Cannonball, Ryan's Ferry, Beaver, and Kickapoo Shoals. At the beginning of the shoal waters around Lockridge's Bluff, 600 river miles from the sea, were considered the head of navigation. After the Civil War, Captain Jules Poitevent, whose family became large-scale planters in Navarro County, removed "some of the most formidable rocks at all of these shoals."[5] By 1868, Job Boat No. 1, an 85-foot steamboat or snag boat especially outfitted for clearing logjams, shoals, snags, overhanging trees, and underwater obstacles navigated the entire 830 river miles to Dallas after a tedious voyage which consumed six months.[6] Virtually every mile of the upper river contained a raft, logjam or other obstruction, and the overhanging limbs of trees, as well as those eroded trees fixing to fall into the river, had to be cleared away as well.

As was the mode of settlement of the Anglo-American pioneers, each set of high bluffs along the Trinity River was soon occupied by log cabins, and often the first settler started a ferry and added his name to the early geography of the river. Many of them built wharves and warehouses along the banks for the storage and shipping of cotton, and that pursuit, along with ferry operation, supplemented their meager incomes. A few pioneers surveyed townsites along the Trinity River, but gradually each of them receded to ghost towns, largely after the river traffic plummeted and the railroads were built. Of the many villages which at one time or another acquired some fame as bustling river ports during the antebellum era, only the city of Liberty survives today as the Trinity River's lone community of any significance. And it survived principally because Liberty was also an antebellum railhead, a point where the river intersected the Texas and New Orleans Railroad, and thus became a major cotton-shipping and storage facility as well.

Before the Civil War, the Trinity River ports included Wallisville, Liberty, Smithfield, Swarthout, Sebastopol, Newport, Cincinnati, Cairo, Alabama, Magnolia, Marianna, and West Point. Some acquired early populations perhaps numbering in the hundreds, but in each instance, nothing, with the possible exception of a state historical marker, is left today to mark their former locations.

In 1844, an Englishman named William Bollaert ascended the river on the steamer Ellen Frankland, and his diary survives as the best account of an early-day Trinity River voyage. On his upriver passage from Cincinnati, the traveler described the "coal beds" near the newly-surveyed town of "Osceola," which, Bollaert noted, contained none of the chemical properties of the coal fields of Pennsylvania or England.[7]

Ellen Frankland ascended the river as far as Magnolia. On the return voyage, the steamer stopped at all of the landings to load cotton, but apparently it acquired most of its cargo at Cincinnati. Bollaert observed that the river had an average depth of forty feet, which sometimes increased to sixty during the river freshets of the winter and spring. Of the various river ports that he depicted in prose, only Swarthout appeared to be "a considerable village" in 1844.[8] Above Swarthout, which was about eighty miles north of Liberty, Bollaert also found two villages of the Alabama-Coushatta Indian tribe.

The traveler also noted the abundance of game and fish along the stream, and huge alligators basked everywhere on the sand bars. Because the Ellen Frankland has to lighten much of its cotton cargo over the Trinity River's three-foot depth of bar at its mouth and many days would be so consumed, Bollaert transferred there to the steamer Vesta for the remainder of his journey to Galveston. He predicted that the Trinity River trade would prove unprofitable and could not foresee the season when seventeen steamers would be engaged in hauling the river's 28,000 cotton bales as well as other commodities.[9]

Following the Trinity River's serpentine meanders, the mileages between the landings were more than double the airline distances, and many old Trinity pilots have left some records. From Anahuac at the mouth of the river, the mileages are as follows: to Liberty, 50 miles; to Smithfield, 150 miles; to Patrick's Landing, 175 miles; Swarthout, 200; Carolina, 245; Robbins' Ferry, 330; Cairo,

360: Alabama, 385; Hall's Bluff, 435; Navarro, 443; Magnolia, 485; Parker's Bluff, 510; Jones' Bluff, 570; Buffalo Bluff, 620; Porter's Bluff (or Taos), 646 miles; and Dallas, 745 miles.[10]

In 1869, two old Trinity pilots, Dugal Williams and J. W. Whitfield, prepared the following table of distances between Galveston and Lockridge's Landing, which at that time was considered the head of steam navigation:[11]

Landing	Miles	Landing	Miles	Landing	Miles
Anahuac	50	Stubbs	73	Gordon's	98
Wallisville	58	Bryan's	77	Dugat's	99
McManus	68	Moss Bluff	79	Duncan's	104
Geary's	69	Moore's Bluff	91	Day's	105
Kilgore's	72	Swelley's	94	Cole's	111
Pruitt's	112	Frisbee's Landing	324	Stell's	445
Liberty	113	Sublett's Landing	329	Hall's Bluff	456
Green's Mill	121	McDonald's	334	Barrow's	458
Hardin's Bluff	143	Thomas'	335	Hog Pen	460
Robinson's Bluff	167	Newport	337	Taylor's	461
Davis' Landing	177	Stubblefield's	342	Major Smith's	469
Farrior's Landing	185	Harrison's	343	Andrews'	472
Nichols' Landing	190	Cincinnati	361	Mitchell's	478
Nevil's Landing	208	Tuscaloosa	363	Navarro	485
Ellis or Long's	209	Calhoun's	371	Bannaman's	488
Smithfield	229	Wright's Bluff	374	Wallace's	492
Washington's	232	Randolph's	377	Dailey's	498
Drew's Landing	236	Hyde's	374	Fields'	500
McCandle's	245	Robbins' Ferry	400	Magnolia	512
Smith's	247	McKinsey's	401	Blackshear's	522
Cedar Landing	251	Boseman's	406	Bonner's Ferry	535

Landing		Landing		Landing	
Swarthout	260	Haley's	410	Sulphur	538
Johnson's Bluff	298	Cairo	416	Parker's Bluff	543
Wheeler's Landing	305	Warren's	428	West Point	558
Woods'	306	Alabama	434	Pine Bluff	575
Patrick's Ferry	308	Rayburn's	436	Jackson's Bluff	595
Ryan's Ferry	310	Adair's	438	Lockridge's Landing	600
Chalk Bluff	321	General Smith's	443	Wild Cat	640
Sebastopol	322	Brookfield	444		

In 1893, Charles N. Eley of Smith's Point completed the list of river mileage from Wild Cat to Dallas. Between 1867 and 1873, Eley had served as agent for thirty-six steamboats engaged in the Trinity River trade, and there were many others that he did not represent. The distances from Galveston to these upper landings were as follows:[12]

Landing	Miles	Landing	Miles	Landing	Miles
Spivey's Ferry	665	Trinity City	807	Dowdey's Ferry	855
Burton's Bluff	687	East Fork	808	Clark's Mill	863
Baggett's Ferry	702	Pruitt's Mills	815	Eley's Bluff	873
Buffalo	722	Big Slough	830	Miller's Ferry	882
Porter's Bluff or Taos	754	Big Old Raft	845	Tubbeville	888
Tellico	782	Mac's Pass	850	Dallas	893

The writer is also indebted to Eley for a list of the ten largest merchants and cotton traders on the river. They were as follows: A. G. Van Pradelles, whose store and large plantation were at Wallisville; Proctor Brothers at Moss Bluff; J. D. Skinner and Brother, Joseph Richardson, and Henry Steinhoff of Liberty; John F. Carr of Smithfield, who was a steamboat builder, captain, and plantation owner as well; F. M. Samson of Drew's Landing, also known as Marianna; Dr. J. A. Smith of Cincinnati; W. A. Hagood of Magnolia; and Joseph Weiner of Newport.[13]

From 1838, the year that the Branch T. Archer, the first steamer of record, entered the river, until 1878, the year that the Trinity River commerce dropped to an insignificant level and was no longer recorded, one can envision the majestic scenery which must have greeted the early Trinity travelers. The primeval forests appeared to be still untouched by human hands, for what few Indians there were, tiptoeing about for their game and with no greed for gold, left the forest exactly as they had found it. From the river's serene delta near Anahuac to the turbulent waters of the upper shoal rapids, the Trinity River, its banks teeming with deer and alligators and sheltered by towering pines and hardwoods, meandered through the heartland of East Texas. Many of the felled monarchs of the forest would eventually become beams, ship timbers, masts and spars for the many schooners and steamboats that were built along the shores of the stream. And a like number of vessels, snagged and sunk in the river's depths, were left to rot and waterlog in its graveyard of ships. That staggering record of losses is the one blemish on an otherwise spotless and colorful history of the Trinity River, its sternwheelers, and the record-breaking volume of cotton bales that they carried to market.

Endnotes—Chapter 8

[1]Viktor Bracht, *Texas in 1848,* translated by C. F. Schmidt (San Antonio: Naylor Co., 1941), p. 8.

[2]William Kennedy, *Texas; The Rise, Progress, and Prospects of the Republic of Texas* (Reprint: Fort Worth: Molyneaux Craftsmen, Inc., 1925), p. 144.

[3]George W. Bonnell, *Topographical Description of Texas To Which Is Added An Account of The Indian Tribes* (Reprint; Waco: Texian Press, 1964), 22-24.

[4]*Ibid.,* 21-25.

[5](Galveston) *Daily News,* June 11, 1893.

[6]*Ibid.,* April 23, 1893.

[7]W. E. Hollen and Ruth L. Butler (eds.), *William Bollaert's Texas* (Norman; University of Oklahoma Press, 1956), p. 311.

[8]*Ibid.,* p. 315.

[9]Hollen and Butler (eds.), *William Bollaert's Texas,* 311-318.

[10](Houston) *Telegraph and Texas Register,* May 4, 1848.

[11](Galveston) *Daily News,* April 23, 1893.

[12]*Ibid.,* April 26, 1893.

[13]*Ibid.*

Chapter 9—The Trinity River

Its Ships of Wood and Crewmen of Steel

Between 1838 and 1893, at least one hundred steamboats navigated the Trinity River at one time or another. Some made only one trip, whereas others were engaged in the cotton trade of the Trinity over a long period of years. During the antebellum era, there were never sufficient packets during any one season to carry the volume of cotton which reached the steamboat landings, particularly those on the upper river. The acute need for transportation spurred the construction of the railroads, and by 1860 the rails of the Texas and New Orleans line had already been extended to Liberty, Texas, and by 1862 reached the Sabine River at Orange. During the Reconstruction years, rails of the Houston East and West Texas Railroad would be built to Shreveport, Louisiana, intersecting the river near Livingston and other lines, principally the Houston and Great Northern, would crisscross East Texas, connecting such towns as Huntsville, Palestine, Madisonville, Trinity, Crockett, Corsicana, and Athens, all of them in the proximity of the river.

As late as 1855, much of the cotton trade of Henderson, Cherokee, and Nacogdoches counties was still going to New Orleans via the Red River, and in some locations, the shipping costs, which included wagon freighting costs to Natchitoches, Louisiana, exceeded $10.00 a bale. On one occasion, it was recorded in 1843 that cotton wagons from 130 miles to the west, or from about the vicinity of Palestine and beyond, were passing through San Augustine, in route to the Red River at Natchitoches.[14] Whenever wagon freight was available, the shipping cost from Palestine to Houston was $1.75 per hundred weight or $8.75 for a 500-pound bale.[15] In 1841, shipping costs via the Red River were $6.50 to $7.00 per bale from Sabinetown, on the Sabine River, to New Orleans. In 1850, it cost $8.75 a bale to ship via the Red River from Nacogdoches to New Orleans.[16]

The high costs and general lack of transportation facilities from many East Texas counties soon resulted in cotton shipments on the Trinity River via flatboat or keelboat. While information on that mode of movement is unsure, a flatboat, much as the name implies, was crudely constructed of rough timbers, and designed to float with the river currents during the rainy season. Lacking conventional power and steering equipment, such vessels were "poled" around the curves and sand bars, and the least miscalculation could result in the flatboat going aground and disgorging its cotton cargo into the river.

Much more advanced in design, keelboats often had the appearance of box-like barges but were usually propelled and steered in the same manner as flatboats. While flatboats were usually dismantled and sold as construction timbers at the journey's end, some keelboats were substantially-built to include pilot house and crew's quarters, and after reaching their destinations, were sailed, towed, or "poled" back to the points of origin.[17] One such vessel was the Thomas J. Rusk, which plied the Angeline-Neches watercourse in 1844.[18] In 1843, the keelboat of J. Heald on the Colorado River was "propelled a great part of the distance up the river by sails."[19]

Keelboaters experienced two extremes on the Trinity River, the first and most hazardous being the swift rapids of the shoal regions, and the second upon reaching south Liberty and Chambers counties, where the rapid currents subsided entirely and the waters of the placid stream were too deep, sometimes as much as 90 feet, for "poling." The White Rock Shoals upstream soon became known as the "terror of steamboatmen."[20] One account noted that at "one of the rapids near Cincinnati, she (the steamboat T. F. McKinney) was unable to move half a mile in three hours; the current of this river is so rapid that steamers with very powerful engines are required to navigate it during a freshet."[21]

Texas keel boating probably dates from about 1824-1825— or within a short time after the arrival of Stephen F. Austin's colony on the Brazos River. Keelboats were probably in use on the Trinity River by 1830 and were certainly in use on the Angelina-Neches watercourse in that year.[22] Since flatboats and keelboats could not navigate in Galveston Bay, it was necessary that they anchor near the river's mouth and lighten their cargoes to the steamboats and schooners that were anchored there and were bound for New Orleans.

In January, 1844, William Bollaert, while descending the river, encountered the flatboat of "Messrs Jones and Company full of cotton." The steamer Ellen Frankland took the flatboat in tow to Brown's Pass at the mouth of the Trinity River.[23] In 1855 a traveler observed a keelboat, "loaded with cotton, peltries, etc.," at Taos (or Porter's Bluff), which was near Kerens, 50 miles southeast of Dallas. The vessel was awaiting a river freshet before challenging the shoal rapids below.[24]

In February, 1856, the Trinity flatboat Tom Wooten wrecked as a result of striking the rocks at Evans' Gin (location unknown). Of the 407 bales of cotton aboard, 250 bales were loaded aboard the sternwheeler Grapeshot, whose captain then delivered them to Galveston at the exorbitant rate of $8.00 freight per bale (which had been offered by the flatboat's master).[25] Despite four steamboats which operated on the Trinity River during that season and a large volume of cotton moved by keelboat as well, there were an estimated 20,000 bales of cotton of the 1855 crop still at the landings as of March, 1856.[26]

In May of that year, Captain J. Reynolds' keelboat, the Mount Prairie, arrived at Wallisville with 294 bales aboard. The vessel had spent two weeks floating down from Parker's Bluff, after which she lightened her cargo aboard the steamer Dr. W. R. Smith. During the same month, the keelboat Major Lea reached Wallisville from Porter's Bluff, 754 river miles inland from Galveston, with 390 bales aboard. Another flatboat belonging to "General Beaver and Colonel Long of Crockett" arrived with 200 bales–altogether, 884 bales for the three boats. An additional 5,000 bales were due to arrive aboard the four steamers which were upriver during that month.[27]

In 1893 Charles N. Eley of Smith's Point prepared a list of ninety-seven Trinity steamers, some 35 of which he had acted as agent for between 1867 and 1873. His list appears as follows, along with a few overlooked by Eley, which the writer has added. The list is still incomplete, as some names which will subsequently appear in the text will indicate. It should also be noted that the names of many of the vessels which follow were also associated with navigation on the other Texas rivers:[28]

Author	Galveston	Ogden
Arizona	Guadalupe	Orleans
Alice S. Ruthven	Gen. Harrison	Orizaba
Alice M.	Grapeshot	Pathfinder
Anne S.	James L. Graham	Rufus Putnam
Branch T. Archer	H. A. Harvey	Rob Roy
Brownsville	H. F. Matthews	Reliance
Billow	Henry A. Jones	Royal Arch
Bay City	Indian No. 2	Swan
Bay State	Ida Reese	Star State
Beardstown	Jack Hays	San Nicolas
Belle of Texas	Josiah H. Bell	S. J. Lee
Belle Sulphur	John F. Carr	Shreveport
Betty Powell	Justice	St. Patrick
Black Cloud	Job Boat No. 1	Stonewall
Caddo	J. D. Hines	Sam M. Williams
Cleona	Kate (No. 1)	San Antonio
Colonel D. S. Cage	Kate (No. 2)	Thomas F. McKinney
Colonel Stell	Laura	Texas
Correo	Lafayette	T. J. Emory
C. K. Hall	Leonora	Tennessee
Cash	Lone Star	Tobe Hurt
C. B. Lee	Lucy Bell	Uncle Ben
Dallas	Lucy Gwin	Vesta
Dr. Wm. R. Smith	Lurline	Como
Ellen Frankland	L. Q. C. Lamar	Vicksburg
E. M. Pease	McLean	Warsaw
Early Bird	Matamoras	William Penn
Era No. 12	Mary Conley	W. J. Poitevent
Era No. 13	Mary Hill	Wren
Emily P.	Mollie Hambleton	Wyoming
Friend	Mustang	J. H. Sellers
Fannin	Nick Hill	Camorgo
Fort Henry	Ned Burleson	Fleta

While preparing the list of Trinity steamers, C. N. Eley also listed the numerous steamboatmen—captains, pilots, engineers, clerks (or supercargoes), and other crewmen—whose acquaintance he had made over the years. Some of his list could be equally applied to the Sabine and Brazos Rivers or the Galveston Bay trade and reflects the early steam boatman's inclination to seek out the most profitable avenues of commerce. Some of the captains, who were also the owners of the steamers, owned stores, and plantations along the banks of the Trinity River as well, and steam boating very often became a necessary "sideline" occupation for exporting one's own and one's neighbors' cotton and other commodities.

The list includes men whose careers spanned thirty years or more on the Texas rivers. Captain John H. Sterrett, who during the Civil War was Superintendent of Transports and executive officer to Colonel Leon Smith of the Texas Marine Department, probably brought more steamboats to Texas than any other man. Correspondingly, he probably lost more vessels to snags, fires, and explosions in the Brazos, Trinity, and Sabine Rivers than any other person. James H. Havilland, an early mayor of Galveston, became captain of several McKinney-Williams and Co. steamers, and as a Texas naval lieutenant, he was vice-commander of the makeshift Galveston war squadron which put to sea in search of Mexican men-of-war during the invasion scare of March, 1842. Captain T. J. Stubblefield was murdered on his packet in the Trinity River in 1870 and became a celebrated murder case. Charles Fowler, master of the Confederate gunboat Josiah Bell, was captain of the Port of Galveston for the Morgan line and was captured by the Federals at Sabine Lighthouse in 1863. A list of the best known Trinity skippers would have to include S. W. Tichenor, Wash Rose, L. C. Hershberger. H. L. and D. E. Connor, Tom Peacock, Joe Boddeker, Jules Poitevent, James McGarvey, William Jenkins, and many others.

As compiled by Eley as well as others known to the writer, the roster of known Trinity River steamboatmen is as follows:[29]

| W. A. Andrews | Joe Baldwin | James Cook | Charles Calloway |

Walter Ansell	William Bristol	William N. Cook	B. Collins
Charles Atkins	– Blakeley	A. St. Clair	Wash Clark
Ben Allen	Sam Burk	Pat Christian	William Chase
F. Bailey	R. A. Burney	W. J. Crozier	William Christy
George Bondies	Caesar Burgess	B. F. Cameron	John Connell
Ned Brown	J. M. Cooper	John Curley	John Clark
H. A. Budman	B. P. Cooper	Phil Carey	Robert Dickey
C. Blakeman	D. E. Connor	Doc Collins	William Dwyer
Joseph Boddeker	H. L. Connor	Barney Collums	Sebastian Drouet
Frank Boddeker	Pat Connor	John F. Carr	A. Dunberry
J. M. Briggs	Bud Clough	Eugene Crane	– Douglass
John Bone	Israel Clark	A. B. Crane	William Everett
W. A. Bowen	Israel Clark, Jr.	William Cruse	A. B. Elliott
T. W. English	J. H. Havilland	Peter Menard	James Reese
Joseph Evelt	L. Hershberger	James McGarvey	Joseph Rogers
George Evelt	T. Hopkins	John McConnell	W. J. Rogers
Ed Evans	C. M. Hausinger	M. McConnell	Martin Reese
William Enloe	William Hibbert	John Morrison	Dick Rolles
John Elliott	Steve Havilland	James McKee	Dennis Riley
William Eggert	Sam Havilland	George	Macomber R. Roach
L. A. Falvel	Nelson Henry	James Minters	James Ransom
Luke Falvel	Doc Hailand	Charles Marston	J. Remfrey
Charles Fowler	Green Hall	A. McKee	Capt. Rose
James Forth	Ed Hemmingway	Alf Menard	John N. Reed
John Flynn	Harry Irvin	R. Murray	John H. Sterrett
William Fulton	Ed. L. Jones	Arthur Magill	N. Port Spears
James Ferguson	William Jenkins	Geo. McDonald	Charles Spears
Ed Foulke	William Johnson	J. E. Mayhew	P. Speckernagle
George Fallon	N. N. John	Bob Mercer	J.M. Swift
James H. Forbes	Steve Johnson	John J. Moore	Bill Sangster
Lee Ferguson	Jim Johnson	James Miller	John T. Smith
George Gordon	Sam Johnson	Steve J. Nagle	Sam Shoemaker
Ed Graves	John Kieff	John Nagle	T. C. Sweeney
Byrd M. Grace	John King	Dick Nagle	T. J. Stubblefield
– Gilliman	John Kountze	W. A. Pettit	Leon Smith
A. C. Green	John Kerman	Thomas Peacock	Frank D. Shaw
Charles Gainey	Edward Lynch	John Payne	Charles Settle
Frank Gainey	Oliver Lampton	Jules Poitevent	John Summers

Matt Gayle	John Lewis	Adolph Poitevent	Jessie Stagg
William Guinard	A. LeClerc	V. B. Poole	George Snowden
John Grisham	S. R. LePeyre	John Price	R. V. Tompkins
James Graham	Peter LaPeyre	W. A. Pettit, Jr.	S. W. Tichenor
William Gifford	John Lynch	Tom Pritchard	Joe Taylor
T. Gripon	Munson Lewis	William Perkins	James Taylor
James Gray	M. McLean	George Pattillo	Ed Taylor
Sanford Gregory	James Montgomery	Henry Quick	D. Vanderventer
J. H. Getty	William Mauke	John Roach	– Vandergriffe
A. H. Gulley	Tom Miller	Shed Roach	James Words
J. S. Gibson	Frank Maratta	James Roach	W.D. Williams
Jeff Garrity	James Maratta	Wash Rose	D. H. Weekes
– Gamble	John Menard	John Redman	M. D. White
John Westrop	Thomas Webb	Carter Walker	George Wilson

Except for some records maintained in Galveston, there seems to be no accurate information obtainable concerning the cotton exports of the Trinity River. During the 1850's, the volume was variously computed at from 25,000 to 50,000 bales annually, but the reliability of such estimates is questionable. Probably half or more of the river's cotton output was carried to Houston by freight wagon, and the volume of cotton exported directly to New Orleans aboard waiting schooners anchored in Galveston Bay at the mouth of the river is likewise unknown. Schooners frequently waited there to buy from the keelboat masters who could not sail into Galveston Bay because their crude vessels lacked steering equipment.

The following figures reflect the amount of Trinity River cotton that reached Galveston between 1865 and 1878. By the latter year, the Trinity cotton trade had receded to such a negligible level that record keeping was discontinued. However, the following figures from the Daily News may prove grossly unreliable when compared to another set of figures which will appear in Chapter 12:[30]

Season	Bales	Season	Bales
1865-1866	7,420	1872-1873	2,500
1866-1867	6,415	1873-1874	1,732

1867-1868	11,450	1874-1875	4,023
1868-1869	15,425	1875-1876	5,554
1869-1870	7,584	1876-1877	2,034
1870-1871	5,440	1877-1878	979
1871-1872	3,211		

In like manner, the exact cause for the abrupt demise of the Trinity River steamboat trade during the 1870's is uncertain. While it is generally conceded that the advent of the railroads throughout East Texas ended the river-carrying trade, that theory concerning the Trinity may be only a half-truth. Although railroads crossed the lower Trinity in three or four places by 1880, they had also reached the Neches River at Beaumont, Rockland, and Diboll and the Sabine River at Orange and Logansport, Louisiana. Nevertheless, a heavy cotton-carrying trade continued on the latter two rivers throughout the 1880's and well into the 1890's, and that despite the fact that, after 1875, both rivers were frequently choked with logs, bound for the Beaumont and Orange sawmills, at the precise moments of the river freshets when the cotton steamers needed to move upstream or downstream. And often the cotton steamers on the latter streams could move forward no more than one mile and hour while they were "poling" their way through miles of floating logs. During the 1892-1893 shipping season, the Sabine steamers Maude Howell, Ada, Extra, Neches Belle, and Robert E. Lee were engaged full-time in the cotton trade of that river.[31]

For the many intermediate planters along the Trinity River, the wagon-freighting of cotton to the nearest railroad was often a costly and tedious operation, even if the primitive roads were dry, and very likely, almost as expensive as shipping by steamboat. And sometimes, planters complained about the exorbitant freight rates charged by the railroads. So, in many instances, the arrival of a sternwheeler to carry away the cotton would have been more than welcomed.

During an interview in June, 1893, William A. Bowen, a journalist who had formerly been a Trinity River steamboatman, may have pinpointed the actual cause, or at least a principal cause. He stated that the Trinity cotton carriers of the 1870's were plantation owners, to whom steam boating was only a sideline occupation for the accommodation of theirs and their neighbors' commodities. When they were successful in obtaining railheads at or near their own plantations, they tied up their boats and abandoned the river trade. Bowen noted further that:[32]

> ...All of the boats I have mentioned except the (Josiah) Bell were owned by men having interests in large plantations, and they abandoned the river because railroads came near or through their plantations. Somehow or other the stopping of the boats seems to have been taken as evidence that Trinity navigation did not pay, and no one else ventured to try it. Nearly all the boats stopped at the same time, because railroads penetrated the regions of the owners who operated the boats...

Although subsequent attempts were made to revive the cotton trade on the river, including an elaborate plan in 1893 to connect Dallas with the Gulf of Mexico via canalization and a series of twenty locks, all efforts proved fruitless. The Trinity River steamboat cotton trade remained a corpse, which soon signaled the demise of the river ports. Most of them were soon abandoned and/or moved to the nearest railhead, and very quickly such names as Swarthout, Smithfield, and Cincinnati were soon forgotten. The pleasant and welcomed blast of the Trinity steamer's whistle, which also shattered the ominous silence of the forests, became only a dim memory to those who cherished it the most.

Endnotes—Chapter 9

[14](Galveston) *Weekly News,* May 1, 1855; (Houston) *Telegraph and Texas Register*, October 4, 1843.

[15]*Weekly News,* September 4, 1854.

[16](Houston) *Morning Star*, August 14, 1841; (Nacogdoches) *Chronicle*, November 6, 1852; (Houston) *Telegraph and Texas Register*, October 4, 1843.

[17]Cleo F. Burns, "Transportation in Early Texas" (M. A. Thesis: San Antonio: St. Mary's University, 1940), 13-14.

[18](San Augustine) *Redlander*, January 6, 20 and March 23, 1844; Lois F. Blount, "The Story of Old Pattonia," *East Texas Historical Journal*, V (March, 1967), 13-14.

[19](Houston) *Telegraph and Texas Register*, June 21, 1843.

[20](Galveston) *Weekly News,* May 1, 1855.

[21](Houston) *Telegraph and Texas Register*, June 1, 1848.

[22]A W. Williams and E. C. Barker (eds.), *The Writings of Sam Houston, 1813-1863*, IV (8 volumes; Austin: Pemberton Press, 1970), 32-34.

[23]Hollen and Butler (eds.), *William Bollaert's Texas*, p. 317.

[24](Galveston) *Weekly News*, May 1, 1855.

[25]*Ibid.*, February 26, 1856.

[26]*Ibid.*, March 11, 1856.

[27](Galveston) *Weekly News,* May 20, 1856.

[28](Galveston) *Daily News*, April 26, 1893.

[29]*Ibid.*

[30](Galveston) *Daily News*, April 23, 1893. The *Daily News* figures as indicated may prove grossly unreliable and understated. See Chapter 12 for the 1869-1871 figures as reported in the *Weekly News.*

Chapter 10—The Earliest Trinity River Steamboats

While it cannot be said with absolute certainty that no steamboat entered the Trinity River prior to 1838, there is no record of such an event. Steamers of McKinney-Williams and Company were in the Brazos River trade by 1835 and were navigating Buffalo Bayou by 1837. The writer can readily understand, however, that as of 1835, the only concentration of cotton-growing plantation owners would have been members of Stephen F. Austin's colony situated along the banks of the Brazos. Yet it seems inconceivable that neither Laura nor Yellowstone would have made any attempt to make an exploratory voyage in the deep and beckoning Trinity, at least as far inland as Liberty, where many settlers and some merchants already resided.

Late in May, 1838, Captain John E. Ross took the steamer *Branch T. Archer* on a 400-mile exploratory voyage up the Trinity. One account noted that the *Archer* "ascended that river as far as the Coushatta village (north of Swarthout) and will probably proceed still farther, as the late rains have swollen the stream ..."[33] After returning to Houston, Captain Ross reported that he had sailed the *Archer* to a point eight miles above Cincinnati (near present-day Onalaska) before turning around, but that he could have gone much farther.[34]

Only three weeks after the Archer entered the river, Captain Motley sailed Wyoming up the Trinity as far as Liberty but chose to go no farther "as the water was quite low and the river was failing rapidly." This was Wyoming's first river voyage in Texas, other than navigating in Buffalo Bayou. Upon reaching Houston, the *Telegraph* reported that the *Wyoming* had just arrived from St. Louis by way of the Bayou Placquemine Brule in Louisiana.[35]

There is no record that either the *Wyoming* or the *Branch T. Archer* made a second voyage up the Trinity, and apparently both captains were discouraged as to the prospect of profitable commerce. The latter vessel spent some time in the Galveston Bay trade, and there is no record that either boat ever entered the Brazos or Sabine River trade. Nor was there any mention of cotton cargoes carried to Houston or Galveston, but as late as the month of June, any cotton produced along the Trinity River probably had already been freighted south by either wagon or flatboat.

Actually, there was very little cotton production anywhere in East Texas during the first two years following the Texas Revolution. The events of the spring of 1836 had thoroughly depleted the food supply and the livestock herds, and thereafter top priority was given to corn production until the shortages of food for both man and beast were alleviated. Under the Texas Republic, the early settlers of Liberty County were principally stockmen and subsistence farmers, but by 1859, cotton production there had increased to 1,565 bales annually.[36] Nevertheless, the cotton production of either Liberty or Chambers County was only a minute percentage of that elsewhere in the Trinity River counties.

The steamer *Warsaw* reached Liberty in the fall of 1838, thus becoming the third packet to probe the Trinity's depths in that year, and her master, Captain Lawrence, seemed equally unimpressed with the river's commercial prospects. Warsaw had reached Houston the previous July and, at that time, was the largest sternwheeler running in Buffalo Bayou. One account noted that Warsaw had a pleasing appearance, "her machinery in good order (and) her cabin remarkably neat, elegant, and commodious."[37]

Too large for Buffalo Bayou, the Warsaw had the dubious distinction of becoming one of Galveston's earliest (and undoubtedly its only maritime) hotels. Located at the foot of Sixteenth Street, the vessel was owned by a Dr. Worcester who was subsequently killed at Vera Cruz during the Mexican War. How long Warsaw served as a hotel is uncertain, but it is believed to have been destroyed by a savage hurricane that struck Galveston Island in 1842. In January, 1839, the Galveston *Commercial Intelligencer* reported that:[38]

...The fine, large, and commodious steamer Warsaw,
being too large for the profitable navigation of
Buffalo Bayou, has been permanently laid up at
Galveston Island and converted into a receiving ship

for goods and merchandise...Her accommodations,
being spacious, will be converted into a marine hotel,
with everything that sea and land can furnish will be
served. A few staterooms for families and ladies. A
fine yawl boat, sail, and rowboat will be kept for
fishing and pleasure parties. Arrangements will be
made for comfortable sea bathing for ladies and
gentlemen, and no pains spared to render the
establishment a desirable one to the man of business
and pleasure.

During 1839 and 1840 a number of steamboats entered the Trinity River, but again, these were usually single voyages to test the river's navigation and commercial possibilities. All of the vessels were regularly engaged in the Buffalo Bayou and bay trade between Houston and Galveston, which trips were short and remunerative because of the passenger traffic. In November, 1840, a Houston newspaper observed that three steamboats were at that moment:[39]

...now running on our bayou and the fourth, we
understand, is expected soon ...The fact that this city
can support through the dull season of the year at
least two boats and for nine months can give full
employment to four or five, while a steamboat
running to any other inland town of Texas is sure of
decay and death after two or three trips, speaks
volumes on the growing importance and proud
destiny of Houston ...

The next steamer known to have entered the Trinity River was the Galveston Bay packet *Correo*. On April 18, 1839, Captain Ferguson returned to Galveston, having sailed the *Correo* all the way to Carolina Landing, and reported the "navigation as being easy as far as that point."[40] This account did not mention a cargo of cotton aboard. The *Correo*, a small boat of perhaps 300 bales capacity, entered the bay trade in 1838 and soon garnered the round-trip record, 40 hours, between Galveston and Houston. The vessel's ads reported that she would depart from landings "at precisely one-half hour after the firing of her gun."[41] The *Correo* made at least one other voyage to Cincinnati on the Trinity River in March, 1840.[42]

Captain John Sterrett brought the steamer *Rufus Putnam* to the Galveston Bay trade in 1839 and made at least one attempt to ply the Trinity River. The steamboat's advertisements noted that she was "provided with chain wheel ropes in case of fire."[43] In January, 1840, having contracted to bring 3,000 bales of cotton to the coast from Sabinetown, Texas, Sterrett sailed the *Putnam* to the Sabine River, but he snagged and sank the packet near Belgrade, shortly after entering the river. The location of the *Rufus Putnam's* wreckage was marked and identified on the Texas-United States Boundary Commission map of that year.[44]

During 1840, there was a significant increase of interest in Trinity River navigation, with four vessels making or planning voyages in addition to the *Correo*. Two of the steamers were destined to ply the stream for some time thereafter, although the ill-fated Vesta encountered disaster during her first attempt. In March, 1840, Sterrett advertised that he would sail the sternwheeler *Brighton* from Houston "on the 18th instant" for Alabama landing on the Trinity. Misfortune, however, stalked the captain again, and while descending Buffalo Bayou on the departure date, Sterrett rammed a snag and sank the *Brighton* two miles below Houston in Buffalo Bayou.[45]

The small steamer *Friend* was another vessel that entered the Galveston Bay trade in 1838, but by 1840 was exploring commercial possibilities elsewhere. Owned by Captains Ferguson and Wheeler, she was variously under the command of Captains N. H. Andrews and J. C. Wheeler. While engaged in the bay trade, the Friend made three round-trips weekly between Houston and Galveston, connecting with the New Orleans steam packet Columbia, which sailed from Galveston on the 8th and 22nd of each month.[46]

In January, 1840, the Friend made an experimental voyage to the Brazos "to test and ascertain to what extent that river is navigable," but apparently the ship's master was not impressed with the remunerative possibilities of that stream.[47] In July, 1840, the steamer ascended the Trinity River as far as Liberty, but was "unable to return on account of the shallowness of the water ...Navigation is almost if not entirely obstructed."[48] That particular account does not state how long the packet was detained in the river. It is likewise unclear as to why the steamers Branch T. Archer, Wyoming, and Friend would attempt to test the Trinity River's navigation during the months of June and July, which were normally low water months on all the Texas rivers and at the very end of the cotton-shipping season, but such are the records left to historians by the old newspapers.

On her first voyage to the Trinity River in December, 1840, the sternwheeler Vesta sank near Liberty, but was subsequently raised as shipping statistics of a later period indicate. A month later, while the boat was still lying in the murky depths of the stream, the Vesta's advertisements continued to tout the advantages of the Trinity packet as a "new and light-draft steamboat ...having been purchased by Captain Gould expressly for the above trade."[49]

In April, 1840, the Galveston Weekly News noted that the new steamer Trinity was "now running from Alabama on the Trinity to Galveston."[50] A month earlier, Howell, Myers and Company, cotton merchants of Galveston, had commissioned Captain Gould to take the new packet on the longest Trinity River voyage ever made up until that date. Soon afterward, the Galveston newspapers reported that:[51]

> ...the steamboat Trinity has just returned from a trip
> up that river. She went up as far as Alabama, about
> 500 miles, and found the navigation uninterrupted,
> and could have gone much farther if it had been
> desired. The upper Trinity (river) country is rapidly
> settling, and some neighborhoods are already pretty
> densely populated, embracing a good variety of
> substantial farmers, many of whom will plant cotton

upon a pretty extensive scale during the coming year
...

Although surely the packet did not return to Galveston empty of cargo, no mention was made of any cotton aboard, and a precedent was established, nevertheless. Both the Vesta and the Trinity remained in the Trinity River trade and would subsequently bring down many cargoes during the succeeding seasons.

Beginning with the Vesta and Trinity, a practice was instituted by the steamboatmen of Galveston Bay and vicinity which adds to the confusion regarding the steamers of that locality–in fact, on all of the Texas rivers. Even the multitude of primary accounts in the old newspapers have not enabled the writer to maintain complete accuracy or lessened the perplexity in each case. In brief, it can be stated that there are instances where the same Trinity River steamboat is known by two different names, whereas in other instances, the same name was carried by two different vessels. Possibly a riverboat superstition accounted for one instance, and perhaps others of similar circumstance. The writer noted that, when a steamer sank and was later refloated and repaired, the vessel's name was sometimes changed. The first case noted was that of Brighton which, when refloated and repaired from its murky berth at the bottom of Buffalo Bayou, was renamed the Sam Houston.[52]

Sometimes an owner was partial to a steamer's name and transferred it from an old boat to a newly-acquired vessel. This was true in the case of Captain Sterrett, and for a time two of his packets bore the name Lady Byron. There are many instances of duplicated names. Two East Texas steamboats carried the name Albert Gallatin, although thirty years apart. The packet Mustang, which in 1842 sailed in the Trinity River, but sank in the Brazos in 1843, was not the same Mustang which foundered in the Trinity many years later. The Kate which sank in the Trinity, an irretrievable wreck, in 1856 was a sternwheeler, whereas the Kate which foundered there in 1873 was a screw propeller packet. Both vessels named Kate came to Trinity from the Neches River Trade.

On its first voyage in Buffalo Bayou in August, 1842, the steamer Mustang arrived on the scene at the same moment that the sternwheeler Edward Burleson struck a snag and sank. The Mustang picked up the Burleson's passengers before proceeding on to Houston. The Telegraph and Texas Register noted that Captain Sterrett's new boat was "now lying at our landing ...and although not yet finished ...she will be one of the most staunch and commodious vessels."[53]

The Mustang's lone voyage of record in the Trinity River occurred in November, 1842, when the vessel was observed ascending the river at Brace's Ferry.[54] The following month, the packet went to the Brazos River trade where it remained for the next ten months. In October, the Mustang was "snagged" near Brazoria and had to "put back" to Velasco for repairs. A month later, however, the steamer, with 230 bales aboard, went to the bottom of the Brazos near San Felipe for all time.[55]

Between 1840 and 1852, the Trinity and bay steamers were often observed racing in Galveston Bay, a practice which was recognized as extremely hazardous and was frowned upon. Between 1815 and 1851, an era when high-pressure engines and virtually no safety steam-control devices were in use, 209 of the 576 steamboats lost on the western rivers had exploded. Explosions accounted for 1,440 of the 4,180 lives lost and another 838 were injured.[56] The first accident (which killed five and injured nine) attributed to that cause in Galveston Bay occurred on December 21, 1841, when the Albert Gallatin exploded.[57]

In 1848, the Houston Telegraph noted that the "steamboats Billow and McLean" had a trial of speed on the 27th (May) instant, which fortunately resulted in no disaster. Long columns of dense black smoke were seen streaming from the chimneys." The packets raced to Redfish Bar, after which they parted, the Billow going to the Trinity and the McLean to Houston."[58] In January, 1853, the new steamers Neptune and Farmer were observed racing in Galveston Bay, and the Telegraph's editor vehemently suggested that the captains satisfy their sporting instincts in a safer manner. His advice, however, was so many echoes cast to the wind, for the

Farmer exploded in the Bay two months later with a loss of fifteen killed and ten persons scalded. According to one source, the fireman on the Farmer was not content to pour into the boiler furnace a steady stream of pine knots. Eventually, he began breaking barrels of fat bacon, and he tossed the slabs into the furnace until it became a sizzling cauldron of flaming grease.[59]

Beginning in October, 1841, the advertisements of the steamer Trinity noted that the vessel had been renamed the Lady Byron, and was still navigating the Trinity River, where it remained until December, 1843.[60] At that time, Captains Sterrett and S. W. Tichenor, who were the joint owners, sold the packet and it was transferred to the Brazos River "to supply the loss of the Mustang."[61] The Byron ascended the river as far as Washington-on-the-Brazos, but sank on the return voyage, south of Richmond, Texas, with 300 bales aboard. In August, 1842, Captain Sterrett acquired a new steamboat, which he also named Lady Byron. Apparently, he had intended to change the name of the old Lady Byron, but did not do so, nor did the new owner before the old packet sank near Richmond. As of November, 1844, the new Lady Byron was one of only six cotton steamboats still flying the Texas flag, several others having sunk or otherwise been disposed of during the previous year.[62]

Late in 1840, Sterrett brought a steamer named Dayton, commanded by S. B. Eves, to the Galveston Bay trade. By February, 1842, the packet had been purchased by Captain John O'Brien of Anahuac, who advertised that he would sail from Galveston on March 1st, stopping at all the landings along the Trinity's banks as far upriver as Magnolia in Burnet County. O'Brien soon changed the vessel's name to General Sam Houston, but it appears that the packet resumed using its original name at some point thereafter. To complicate identification further, Captains S. W. Tichenor and D. S. Kelsey brought a new steamer named Dayton to the Galveston Bay trade in May, 1842.

At the outbreak of the Mexican War, the United States army chartered Captains Tichenor and Kelsey's steamer Dayton to lighter troops ashore at Corpus Christi. Soon afterward the packet exploded with the loss of seventeen lives, nine of whom were soldiers. It is worth noting as well that in April, 1845, months before Kelsey's Dayton left for Corpus Christi, the engine, and boilers of "the steamer Dayton" were installed in the new steamboat built by Captains Sterrett and Tichenor at Cincinnati on the Trinity River. The equipment was apparently from the older Dayton, or Sam Houston, the hull of which evidently had become unseaworthy.[63]

In 1842, the sternwheeler Pioneer made at least one voyage on the Trinity River, ascending as far as Cincinnati. A year later, the vessel was transferred to the Sabine River, where its crew mutinied on the second voyage in that stream. Following their trial in Galveston's admiralty court and a court decree ordering the steamer's sale at public auction, the new owners sent the Pioneer to the Matagorda Bay trade, but the packet sprang a leak and wrecked on the coast near Pass Cavallo while in route.[64]

During the years 1839 and 1840, emigration to East Texas increased sharply, resulting in a corresponding and significant increment in cotton production. Between 1840 and 1841, cotton shipments from Nacogdoches, Sabine, and San Augustine counties increased from 3,500 to 5,500 bales.[65] By 1843, cotton production in Nacogdoches County alone had reached 8,000 bales, almost "twice as large as that of the previous year...," with approximately 50,000 bales expected to be raised in the counties between the Trinity River and Louisiana.[66] Also by 1843, the river's cotton shipments enabled at least two steamboats to engage in the Trinity River trade full-time, although another circumstance forced the vessels to probe farther and farther upriver in search of cargoes. Despite the wagon-freighting costs, the high tariff rates of the Texas Republic on merchandise imported through Galveston kept many upcountry growers tied to the overland New Orleans market. Due to the large quantity of wares smuggled across the Sabine River, the Houston Telegraph observed in 1843 that:[67]

...the planters even as far west as Crockett on the
Trinity River have been furnished with goods from
the Shreveport market at a lower rate than they
could purchase them at Galveston or Houston...

The marketing of cotton, obviously, was a two-way trade, for the Trinity planter needed not only to market his cotton, but also to receive the necessary imports that would sustain his household for the next twelve months. Hence, it was entirely possible to pay the high wagon-freighting costs on cotton and still save significantly on imported wares by avoiding the high Texas tariff rates.

In 1843, Colonel Elliott travelled by canoe to all of the upriver landings beyond Magnolia, reporting that, except for the shoal areas, obstructions to Trinity navigation were negligible. He added that "if two or three small rafts {logjams} and a few leaning trees were removed, steamboats could ascend with little difficulty to the Three Forks {25 miles southeast of Dallas}, a distance of 300 miles above Magnolia."[68]

During the two years or more after 1842, the packets Ellen Frankland and Vesta became the work horses of the Trinity River trade, and each would suffer the misfortune of sinking twice, either in Galveston Bay or in the turbulent waters of the river. Frankland arrived at Galveston in November, 1842, and immediately made two voyages in the river. The Houston Telegraph noted that the steamer had been built for the "trade of the Tabasco River ...but was sold at New Orleans and was purchased by Jones and Company of Galveston, ...intended for the trade of the Trinity River."[69]

The steamer remained in the river throughout its career. The vessel traveled often to the upper ports on the Trinity River, and while he was aboard at Cincinnati in January, 1844, William Bollaert observed that "there is much more cotton ready than there are boats to take it down the river."[70] Three months later, and only two weeks after the Vesta sank for the second time, the Ellen Frankland, loaded with cotton and freight, foundered on Redfish Bar in Galveston Bay.[71]

Because of a number of river accidents that season, the Dayton, in the Galveston Bay trade, and the Colonel Woods, "employed exclusively in the trade of the Sabine River," were for the moment the only inland steamboats left in Texas.[72] Although it is not known how long the Ellen Frankland remained under water, by the following November, the packet had been raised and was being repaired at the Emerson and Lufkin Shipways on Galveston Island. In August, 1846, the steamboat "Columbia, formerly the Ellen Frankland, was snagged and sunk in the Trinity River a few days since and is considered a total loss."[73]

Following her initial sinking in the Trinity River in December, 1840, the steamboat Vesta was raised, and appears to have carried or to have been known by two different names thereafter. In 1842, the Houston Telegraph stated that the packet "Alabama, formerly the Vesta, arrived at our landing {Houston} from Galveston. She has been repaired and is now commanded by Captain Robert Lewis."[74] In May of the same year, the steamer carried a cargo of Trinity River cotton from Liberty to Galveston. In November, several newspapers carried advertisements that the Alabama would sail December 1st for all points along the Trinity River. In March, 1843, the Telegraph again reported that the Vesta had ascended the Trinity "to Fort Houston or Magnolia and took away a large quantity of cotton."[75]

After returning to the Trinity trade during the 1844 season, the Vesta (or Alabama) suffered its second dunking in the river's murky depths the following April. By May 11, the steamboat had been refloated and taken to Galveston for repairs. Only one record of the Vesta ever appeared in the newspapers after that date. In November, the Houston Morning Star observed that the Vesta was one of only five river packets flying the Texas flag, and her ultimate fate thereafter is not recorded. The sternwheeler may have been sold and removed from the area, sunk again, or simply (Heaven forbid!) lost her identity a second time under a different name.[76]

Following two voyages in the Sabine River, a new steamboat named Scioto Belle arrived at Galveston from New Orleans on May 7, 1844. The Weekly News recorded that the packet was "intended to run ...on the Trinity, for which trade she is well-adapted, as she is new, substantial, and of light draft."[77] The following November, the Scioto Belle was one of only five steam riverboats still flying the Texas flag. She continued in the river trade in 1845, bringing down a "full cargo of cotton from the Trinity" in April, but the steamer disappeared from the Galveston Bay area thereafter. Since the newspapers carried no record of her sale or sinking, it is probable that the packet was transferred to South Texas to carry troops for the United Stated Army during the Mexican War.[78]

The significance and value of the Trinity River trade became increasingly visible during the 1844-1845 shipping seasons, when four boats, the Oriole, Scioto Belle, Spartan, and Vesta, were engaged in hauling cotton on that stream, while still a fifth steamboat, the Ellen Frankland, was undergoing repairs at Galveston.[79] For a while, the writer thought that the new packet Oriole might be the old Vesta under a different name, that is, until both names began to appear simultaneously in the newspapers. In addition, a new export commodity began making its appearance on the Trinity River as well for, by 1847, one hundred and twenty of the river's plantations were manufacturing sugar and syrup. Large quantities of corn, peltries, and deer hides were also coming down the river, and certainly, the most unusual item ever to be carried on a Texas riverboat, a cargo manifest of 1847 included a quantity of Indian scalps.[80]

The river commerce of 1845 also included a product of heavy industry, the first steamer built on the Trinity River and the fourth steamer built in Texas. Although unidentified by name, there seems to be little doubt that it was the McKinney-Williams and Co. steamer, the Sam M. *Williams*, McKinney-Williams, and Co. had initiated the practice of building its steamers locally when, in 1841, it built the Lafitte at Velasco at a total cost of $19,000, the first steamboat built in Texas. After several voyages in the Brazos River and Sabine Lake, the Lafitte was wrecked in 1843 while in route from the Brazos bar to Galveston. The second steamboat built in Texas was the Red River Planter, built at Berlin, Red River County, in 1842, and the third was built at Soda Lake. The fifth built in Texas, the Kate Ward, was launched at Matagorda in August, 1845.[81]

In April, 1845, Captains Sterrett and Tichenor launched a new steamboat hull, built by a Mr. Clark, at Cincinnati (Texas) and soon floated it downriver with the currents, in the style of the keelboats, to Galveston with 500 bales of cotton on board. The article added that the new boat had a 1,000-bale capacity and was 140 feet long and 26 feet wide. After its arrival at the Emerson and Lufkin Shipways on Galveston Island, the engine, and boilers of the old riverboat Dayton (or Sam Houston) were installed in it. Allowing for the trip downriver and the time needed to install engine, boilers, piping, and related machinery, it seems likely that it might have been late summer or early fall before the new boat was ready to sail under its own power. And despite a slight variance in bale capacity, the writer concludes this to be the packet Sam M. Williams because of the timing. In October, 1845, the Houston Telegraph recounted that:[82]

> ...the new steamboat S. M. Williams started
> yesterday on her second trip to Galveston. This boat
> we believe is the second built west of the Trinity and
> reflects great credit to her builders. She is capable of
> carrying 1,100 bales and ...with her cabins are fitted
> up with admirable neatness and good taste.

In the area of shipbuilding, a second steamer being built on the Trinity River in September, 1847, was "rapidly progressing." The following July, the Houston Telegraph noted that the "new steamboat built on the Trinity by the late Mr. MacDonald is also here {Houston}," but again no name was supplied.[83] Begun in 1847, the new packet Thomas F. McKinney was built by Emerson and Lufkin at Galveston at a total cost of $25,000. Built "expressly for the Trinity River trade," the McKinney could carry 1,000 bales, was 110 feet long, 37 feet wide, and had a 4 1/2 foot depth of hold.[84]

Near the close of the 1844-1845 shipping season, both the Oriole and the Scioto Belle arrived at Galveston with full cargoes of cotton from the upper Trinity landings. The new packet Spartan, whose captain, S. P. McQuown, had just entered the Galveston Bay trade, had "gone up the river with a full cargo of merchandise." The same article stated that the three steamboats would remain in the Trinity River trade, but it appears that the Spartan left the river and went elsewhere during the 1845-1846 season.[85] Since in the spring of 1846, a number of steamers were needed to ferry General

Zachary Taylor's army from New Orleans to Corpus Christi, and the need continued to supply it, it appears probable as well that the Spartan may have chosen to abandon the cotton trade for the more lucrative government contracts.

Two events of 1845-1846 were to have a significant effect on the Texas cotton steamer fleet. Annexation placed the vessels under the flag, laws, and jurisdiction of the United States. The impending war with Mexico was to create an unprecedented demand for transportation facilities along the Texas coast. Two Texas steamboats, the Dayton from Galveston Bay, and the Sabine from the Sabine River, quickly left for the South Texas region, where the former soon exploded and the latter wrecked and sank in the Rio Grande River.

The Mexican War was also to have a tremendous effect on the Trinity River trade, for one of its landings, Robbins' Ferry, was soon selected to become a quartermaster and supply depot for American troops moving overland to the Rio Grande River. In pre-Texas Revolution days, it was also the point where "El Camino Real" (King's Highway) crossed the Trinity River in route from Natchitoches, Louisiana, to San Antonio, and in 1775, it was one of two places, then known as "Spanish Fort" or Presidio Bucarelli, in East Texas garrisoned by Spanish troops. The United States Army soon chartered the new sidewheeler Sam M. Williams and another recent arrival in the Galveston Bay trade, the packet Gazelle. In June, 1846, the Williams left Galveston "to convey military stores to the upper landings on the Trinity River where the dragoons and mounted riflemen from the Western States are expected to cross." While descending the river from Robbins' Ferry, the Williams passed the Gazelle, loaded with a full cargo of "military supplies" and bound for the new quartermaster depot. In April, 1849, the Williams was wrecked in the Gulf while in route from the Brazos to Galveston.[86]

After the war ended, Captain S. P. McQuown purchased the Rio Grande steamer Monroe for the Trinity River trade, but while in route to its new assignment, the steamboat wrecked, "a total loss," at the mouth of the river.[87] Since McQuown had formerly owned and commanded the Spartan, the announcement strongly suggested that the latter vessel had also been sacrificed to the war effort, but no newspaper account to that effect has ever been located.

In January, 1847, Captain Tichenor brought the steamboat Reliance. commanded by D. S. Kelsey, to Galveston Bay. Described as about one year old, 130 feet in length, and 26 feet wide, her physical description very nearly matches that of the steamer built by Tichenor and Sterrett at Cincinnati, the river port on the Trinity River, in 1845. Another account, however, eliminates that possibility, for Reliance did not make her first Trinity voyage until March of 1848, although the packet remained in the Trinity permanently thereafter.[88]

Four boats, the Williams, the T. F. McKinney, the Billow and Reliance, were engaged in the river's commerce during the 1847-1848 shipping season, but the former soon transferred to the Brazos River. Apparently four steamers were not enough transportation to export that year's cotton output. In April, 1848, Polk County planters assembled and complained about the insufficiency of Trinity River packets, and in May, 1848, there were still 3,000 bales of the 1847 crop awaiting shipment from the landings.[89] Since the McKinney's horsepower was considered insufficient to challenge the Trinity's shoal currents on the upper river, the owners had already decided to transfer the packet to the bay trade. In the face of the Polk County complaint, they relented, however, and agreed that:[90]

> *...if the stage of the water will permit, she {the McKinney} will be kept permanently in the trade between the Trinity and Galveston. The planters of the Trinity Valley have displayed a great degree of anxiety to test the practicability of navigating that stream {farther upriver}, and many of them are confident that the steamer T. F. McKinney can navigate it at least two-thirds of the year...*

Although the packet Billow is reported as having entered the Trinity River on two or more occasions in 1848, no newspaper account survives concerning the volume of cotton carried on that vessel. On Reliance's first Trinity voyage in March, 1848, Captain Thomas Webb brought down 973 bales of cotton, 975 bushels of corn, 479 hides, and 41 bales of furs. The Reliance being considerably overloaded, the steamer Billow had to lighten a part of the cargo in order to enable the Reliance to cross the Trinity's shallow bar at its mouth. Late in May of that year, the Reliance was reported as being above Swarthout, and "when last heard from, she was on her way to Leona."[91]

When the McKinney reached Galveston on April 25, 1848, the packet carried 22 passengers, 606 bales of cotton, and a "large quantity of corn, hides, etc."[92] Another account noted that the McKinney made a number of Trinity River voyages that season, "bringing out on one of them a cargo equal to 1,000 bales of cotton, consisting of various articles, deer skins, and Indian scalps being a portion of it." During April, 1848, another 2,000 bales reached Wallisville, near the river's mouth, on flatboats.[93]

During the 1848-1849 shipping season, the owners of the McKinney withdrew the steamer to the Galveston Bay trade. The Trinity cotton carriers of that season included the Reliance, the Brownsville, the Galveston, and Ogden, as well as a "new boat {unidentified}, under Captain (Wash) Clark, built by the planters for the Trinity River trade."[94]

During the late 1840's, several vessels abandoned the Trinity River even though the volume of cotton commerce there was among the most profitable to be found in Texas. The obvious reason was that, like the McKinney, the steamers' engines lacked sufficient horsepower to confront the rapid shoal currents that were upstream. In some instances, the high rate of steamer accidents in the river may have discouraged some captains, all of which probably increased the costs of insurance for both cotton and ships.[95]

The ill-fated Brownsville, under Captain H. A. Broadman, enjoyed a lucrative career on Trinity. No record appears concerning the number of cotton cargoes she carried out, but on one of the packet's voyages to Jones' Bluff in March, 1848, the steamer struck a snag and foundered on the return journey.[96] However, the steamboat was soon raised, repaired, and remained on the river until 1850 or later. The small steamer Galveston, built on Buffalo Bayou and commanded by Captain J. F. Harrell, made one trip in the Trinity River in October, 1849, but soon abandoned that river for the Brazos trade.[97]

Likewise, it appears that the steamboat E. A. Ogden, under Captain James Havilland, also abandoned the Trinity River after its first voyage. And perhaps the packet initiated another branch of pioneer steam transportation, that of carrying Texas cattle to market in New Orleans. After her Trinity voyage, the Ogden sailed for the Sabine River, where Captain Havilland purchased a load of cattle for the Crescent City. Apparently, that voyage was unsatisfactory to the captain, for he soon took the Ogden back to Brazos trade, where the packet sank near Brazoria in October, 1850. Later, some of the machinery from the Ogden was salvaged.[98]

The Reliance remained the Trinity River's work horse throughout the 1849-1850 season and made several voyages as far north as Parker's Bluff, 600 miles upriver, which meant the steamer had to challenge the four worst shoal rapids in the upper river. She was also described as the only "temperance steamer" in Texas since the packet had no bar or saloon aboard.[99] In February, 1850, both the Reliance and the Brownsville returned to Galveston after successful voyages, each with a 600-bale load from points 650 miles or more upriver, after which the Brownsville returned to Jones' Bluff on the Trinity for another cargo.[100]

During the 1840's, the Trinity River trade grew from a position of insignificance—in fact, from virtual non-existence—to a thriving commerce, which could support several steamers. That decade also witnessed the passing of an era when Galveston merchandise could barely compete with the smuggled wares from the Red River trade in Louisiana; and of course, for a time it could not compete at all. At the end, the ten-year span was still plagued by a shortage of transport facilities, which left many upriver planters still dependent on the Red River, either via Jefferson, in Harrison

County, Texas, or via Grand Ecore, Louisiana, and hence, a market still un-weaned from its New Orleans mother.

The Trinity Valley planters soon realized the logical solution to their problems. With the valley's cotton production grown to about 20,000 bales or more annually, there was no longer any cause to depend on the whims of the independent steamboat owners, whose boats moved from river to river at will in search of better profits. Although their steamers usually possessed profitable cotton bale capacities, they sometimes lacked the engine horsepower necessary for the upriver shoal-region navigation, so turbulent during the winter freshets. There is simply no other logical explanation for boats abandoning a river whose remunerative potential was equal to or greater than any other river in Texas. The obvious solution would entail an organization of planters and the pooling of planter resources to lobby for the clearing of rafts, snags, and shoals, and to purchase a fleet of plantation-owned steamers that was equal to and responsive to the Trinity Valley's needs, as well as committed to move cotton until every bale at the Trinity River landings had reached Galveston.

Plantation owners could foresee that, dollar-wise, the only logical route to market was via the Trinity River. The only alternative was a system of railroads which would require financing in the Northern States, staggering expenditures of capital, and many years to build. In the end, the planters chose the river route, but they did not succeed in lowering the stream's steamer-mortality rate, probably the highest of any Texas river. Being first and foremost plantation owners, rather than steamboatmen, they would also choose to stifle and annihilate the river trade when the railroads arrived in the vicinity of their plantations.

Endnotes—Chapter 10

[31](Galveston) *Daily News,* November 26, 1892, and January 11, 15 and February 26, 1893.

[32]*Ibid.*, June 11, 1893.

[33](Houston) *Telegraph and Texas Register*, June 9, 1838.

[34]*Ibid.*, June 16, 1838.

[35](Galveston) *Daily News,* April 26, 1893; (Houston) *Telegraph and Texas Register*, June 9, 30, 1838.

[36]Manuscript Census Returns, Schedule IV, Products of Agriculture, Liberty County, Texas, 1860, Eighth Manuscript Census of the United States.

[37](Houston) *Telegraph and Texas Register,* July 21, 1838; (Galveston) *Daily News*, April 26, 1893.

[38](Galveston) *Commercial Intelligencer*, January 12, 1839.

[39](Houston) *Morning Star,* November 4, 1840.

[40](Galveston) *Daily News*, April 23, 1893.

[41](Houston) *Telegraph and Texas Register,* February 5, March 31, June 9, and September 1, 1838.

[42](Houston) *Morning Star,* March 16, 1840.

[43](Houston) *National Intelligencer*, June 20, 1839; (Galveston) *Daily News,* April 26, 1893.

[44](Richmond, Tx.) *Telescope*, April 4, 1840; T. J. Lee, Texas-United States Joint Boundary Commission, "Map of the Sabine River," 1840, Texas General Land Office; "Entrances and Clearances," March 31, 1840, Port of Sabine Bay Customs Records, File 4-21/10, Texas State Archives.

[45](Houston) *Morning Star*, March 17, 21, 1840.

[46](Houston) *Telegraph and Texas Register,* June 9, September 15, and December 20, 1838; January 12, 1839.

[47]*Ibid.*, January 8, 1840.

[48]*Ibid.*, July 15, 1840; (Houston) *Morning Star*, May 13, 1840; (Galveston) *Daily News*, April 23, 1893.

[49](Houston) *Morning Star,* December 10, 1840; (Houston) *Telegraph and Texas Register*, January 27, 1841.

[50](Houston) *Weekly Times*, April 9, 1840.

[51](Houston) *Morning Star*, March 10, 1840; (Galveston) *Daily News*, April 23, 1893.

[52](Houston) *Morning Star,* June 15, 1840.

[53](Houston) *Telegraph and Texas Register*, August 24, 31, 1842.

[54]*Ibid.*, November 21, 1842.

[55](Houston) *Morning Star,* January 31, March 23, and November 25, 1843; (Houston) *Telegraph and Texas Register*, December 14, 28, 1842; March 29, June 21, and October 18, 1843.

[56]*Telegraph and Texas Register*, July 30, 1852.

[57]*Ibid.*, December 29, 1841.

[58](Houston) *Telegraph and Texas Register,* June 1, 1848; (Galveston) *Civilian and Galveston Gazette*, June 9, 1848.

[59](Nacogdoches) *Chronicle*, April 5, 1853; John A. Caplan, "Early Steamboat Days," (Galveston) *Daily News,* January 7, 1900; (Houston) *Telegraph and Texas Register*, January 21, 1853.

[60](Houston) *Morning Star,* March 1, 1842; (Houston) *Telegraph and Texas Register,* October 27, 1841; January 12, March 9, and August 24, 1842; November 19, 1844; February 8, 1849.

[61]*Telegraph*, December 6, 1843.

[62](Houston) *Morning Star,* January 9, 1844; (Houston) *Telegraph and Texas Register,* December 27, 1843.

[63](Galveston) *Daily Advertiser,* February 26, 1842; (Houston) *Morning Star*, April 10, 1841; February 14 and March 18, 1843; April 22, 1845; (Houston) *Telegraph and Texas Register*, March 9, May 11, and December 14, 1842.

[64](Houston) *Telegraph and Texas Register*, April 12, and June 12, 1843; William R. Hogan, *The Texas Republic: A Social and Economic History* (Norman: University of Oklahoma Press, 1969), p. 76; "Abstract of Imposts," January 31, 1843, Port of Sabine Bay Customs Records, File 4-21/10, Texas State Archives.

[65]Letter, Power to Saligny, June 20, 1842, as reprinted in E. D. Adams (ed.), *British Diplomatic Correspondence Concerning the*

Republic of Texas (Austin: Texas State Historical Association, 1917), p. 77. During the 1844-1845 cotton season, the Port of Houston shipped 11,359 bales. See *Telegraph,* August 31, 1845.

[66](Houston) *Telegraph and Texas Register*, August 2, 1843.

[67]*Ibid.*

[68]*Ibid.*, June 28, 1843.

[69](Galveston) *Texas Times,* November 30, 1842; (Galveston) *Daily News,* December 1, 1842; (Houston) *Morning Star*, December 1, 1842; (Houston) *Telegraph and Texas Register*, December 7, 1842.

[70]Hollen and Butler, *William Bollaert's Texas,* p. 313.

[71](Houston) *Morning Star*, April 2, 18, 1844.

[72]*Ibid.*, April 27, 1844.

[73](Houston) *Morning Star*, November 19, 1844; (Houston) *Telegraph and Texas Register,* August 8, 1846.

[74]*Telegraph and Texas Register,* October 19, 1842.

[75]*Ibid.*, May 4, October 16, and December 7, 1842; February 1 and March 8, 1843.

[76](Houston) *Morning Star,* April 2, May 11, and November 11, 1844; *Telegraph and Texas Register*, November 15, 1843. Shortly afterward, the packet *Oriole,* whose origin in unknown to the writer, appeared on the Trinity River. There is no evidence, however, for assuming that she was the former *Vesta* under a new name.

[77](Galveston) *Weekly News,* May 11, 1844; (Houston) *Morning Star*, May 11, 1844.

[78](Houston) *Morning Star*, November 19, 1844; *Telegraph and Texas Register*, April 2, 1845.

[79]*Ibid.*

[80](Galveston) *Daily News,* April 23, 1893; *Telegraph and Texas Register*, March 9, 1848.

[81](Galveston) *Daily News,* January 30, 1893; (Houston) *Morning Star*, July 3, 1841; *Telegraph and Texas Register*, October 19, 1842; January 4, 1843; August 16, 1845.

[82]*Morning Star*, April 22, and October 18, 1845; *Telegraph and Texas Register,* October 22, 1845.

[83](Houston) *Telegraph and Texas Register,* November 23, 1847; June 22, 1848.

[84]*Ibid.*, March 2 and June 1, 1848; (Galveston) *Daily News*, April 23, 1893.

[85]*Telegraph and Texas Register,* January 31, April 2, and December 31, 1845.

[86]*Ibid.*, July 1, 8, 1846; (Galveston) *Weekly News,* April 13, 1849.

[87]*Telegraph and Texas Register,* December 9, 1847

[88](Galveston) *Civilian and Galveston Gazette*, May 5, 1848; *Telegraph and Texas Register,* January 18, 25, 1847.

[89]*Telegraph and Texas Register*, April 27, and May 8, 1848.

[90]*Ibid.,* April 27, 1848.

[91]*Civilian and Galveston Gazette*, May 5, 1848; *Telegraph and Texas Register*, April 11, and June 1, 8, 1848.

[92]*Telegraph*, May 4, 1848.

[93](Galveston) *Daily News,* April 23, 1893; *Telegraph and Texas Register*, May 4, 1848.

[94]*Telegraph*, October 29, 1849.

[95]The volume of cotton on the Trinity River for the 1849-1850 season was estimated at 22,000 bales. See *Telegraph*, December 20, 1849.

[96]*Telegraph and Texas Register*, December 20, 1849; February 18 and March 11, 28, 1850.

[97]*Ibid.*, October 25, 1849.

[98]*Ibid.,* September 6, 1849; November 13, 29, 1850.

[99]*Ibid.*, December 13, 1849; January 10 and November 11, 1850.

[100](Galveston) *Weekly. News,* February 18, and March 11, 1850.

Chapter 11—The Trinity River and the Prosperous 1850's

If the decade of the 1840's (when a sluggish cotton market generally prevailed) in Texas had significant economic improvement over its predecessor, it in turn was destined to be dwarfed by its successor, the decade of the 1850's. During the years 1845 and 1846, cotton dropped to four and five cents a pound, and for the next four years, remained only slightly above those figures. During the 1850's, however, cotton prices advanced sharply due to increased demand in Europe, and for years, the supply was never equal to the demand.

Also, emigration to East Texas continued to increase, and cotton production flourished, limited only by the pace at which new land could be cleared. Much of East Texas continued to be tied to the New Orleans market. Some of the largest cotton-producing counties, including Red River and Harrison, had direct water-shipping facilities via the Red River, and nine of every ten bales shipped at Sabine Pass went to New Orleans as well. Yet despite those facts, cotton shipments from Galveston reached almost a half-million bales by 1877. During the 1876-1877 season, although only 753 bales came direct from the Brazos River and only 2,034 bales came direct from the Trinity, Galveston still managed to ship 488,970 bales, nearly all of it received by rail from Houston.[101] The Trinity Valley shared in every aspect of agricultural increment, and even the Civil War proved to be only a tragic and unfortunate interlude which stifled the rate of plantation growth only temporarily. After the war ended, the bankrupted survivors in the war-torn states and soil-eroded plantations in the Southeastern States had all the more cause for migrating to East Texas.

While other regions of East Texas may have found it more economical and feasible to ship cotton via the Trinity River as well, twelve counties, as follows, lay directed on the river, and constitute the Trinity Valley counties, that is, as far north as Ennis and Athens: Chambers, Liberty, Polk, Walker, Trinity, San Jacinto, Madison, Leon, Houston, Freestone, Anderson, Navarro, and Henderson.

While the eastern-most planters in Trinity, Houston, Anderson, and Henderson counties were also adjacent to the Neches River, that route terminated at Sabine Pass, where shippers were wholly dependent upon the intermittent sailings of a fleet of New Orleans-based and bound schooners.

As the mid-nineteenth century dawned, Trinity planters moved ahead with their plans to own their own fleet of river steamers. Their first effort in that direction came in October, 1849, when the plantation owners purchased the "new boat...under Captain Clark."[102] In January, 1850, Trinity planters subscribed jointly to the sum of $10,000 in order to purchase the new steamer, Jack Hays. The Hays was one of many Trinity steamers which enjoyed long careers and made profits for the owners during the 1850's. However, a mishap to the Hays in 1854 and other sinkings during the first years of that decade discouraged further investment, and the envisioned fleet of plantation-owned packets did not reach fruition until after the Civil War. Indirectly the series of mishaps also contributed to the chartering of the New Orleans, Texas, and Pacific Railroad Company, eventually to become the Texas and New Orleans, and that line's subsequent building.[103]

Although many early vessels had sunk in the Trinity, most of the accidents had occurred on the upper stretches of the river, where the shoals and snags were plentiful and perhaps some mishaps were expected. In May, 1851, the packet *Elite* was brought from the Brazos "to run in the Trinity River," and the following February, the steamboat sank near Smithfield, "a complete wreck."[104] Also in 1851, the Galveston Bay steamer, *Judge McLean*, made a trip in the river, but was snagged and foundered, an unsalvageable wreck, near Moore's Bluff, only a few miles above the river delta. The lower region of the Trinity was deep at all seasons of the year, and snags had not been considered a menace to navigation in that area.[105]

When the *Jack Hays* first arrived at Galveston, one account noted that the new packet had exactly the same dimensions as the steamer *Reliance*.[106] In February, 1851, the *Hays* left Hall's Bluff (which was located due west of Crockett and 456 river miles from

Galveston) with 1,100 bales aboard and expected to load another 300 bales while in route downriver.[107] Other vessels reported as being in the Trinity River during that year included the steamers *Reliance, Magnolia, Buffalo, McLean, Elite,* and *Star State.*[108] In 1852, another account stated that the *Hays*, under Captain Peter Menard, "will run regularly between Galveston and the several landings on the Trinity River. This steamer has just received the most thorough repairs; her boilers have been enlarged and various other improvements added."[109]

Shortly after entering the Trinity River on January 1, 1854, the packet *Jack Hays* struck a snag and foundered at the exact location where the *McLean* sank three years earlier. Because the *Hays'* hull filled with water within five minutes, the pilot barely had time to ram the steamer's prow into the shore before the stern began to settle in the river. Fortunately, no lives were lost, but the steamboat's $125,000 cargo of freight, only a portion of which was insured, was badly damaged. The Trinity River sternwheeler *Guadalupe* picked up 1,000 barrels of the damaged freight, after which the Jack Hays was refloated and towed to Lynchburg shipyard by the packet Eclipse. By February 28th, the Hays had "been refitted" and was back in service.[110]

Commenting on the steamboat accident, the Galveston Weekly News observed:[111]

> *...The recent loss of the steamer Jack Hays...the discouraging effect this must have on the ascent of other boats...force upon us the consideration whether there may not be some remedy for these evils. A project for a railroad from Lynchburg to Trinity would immediately concentrate and control the trade from above. With the aid of such a railroad, the navigation of the river would be sufficient to meet the wants of the country for years to come.*

Shortly afterward, the Weekly News added that "northward from Lynchburg in a distance of about 60 miles, a railroad would reach the richest part of the country on the Trinity...The railroad would of itself complete the system of internal communications..."[112] Within two months after the sinking, the Texas legislature chartered the line to Liberty which subsequently became the Texas and New Orleans Railroad.

Among the additional vessels engaging in the Trinity River trade during the 1851-1852 season, the new packet Star State arrived at Houston in December. At the end of her second Trinity voyage in March, 1852, the steamboat "arrived at the mouth...with 1,258 bales of cotton, where she will remain until the receipt of another load of freight for up the river. The steamer-lighter Dr. W. R. Smith brought over one load of cotton from the Star State with her passengers yesterday."[113] Most of the Dr. Smith's career on the Trinity consisted of off-loading cotton at the shallow Trinity River bar in order for the cotton steamers to get over the bar and into Galveston Bay. The Star State was still in the Trinity trade as late as the 1855-1856 season.

In April, 1852, the new steamboat Nick Hill ascended the river all the way to Taos or Porter's Bluff (50 miles southeast of Dallas and 754 river miles from Galveston), which Trinity voyage stood as the record river ascension by any steamer until the Job Boat No. 1 sailed to Dallas in 1868.[114] Having negotiated every major shoal rapid successfully on the upstream trip, the vessel was less fortunate while returning, as evidenced in the following surviving letter:[115]

Steamboat *Nick Hill*, May 4, 1852

3 miles above Green's Landing

N. S. Hill, Dear Sir:

Last evening about 1/2 past 6 we struck a snag, knocking a hole in the side of the boat, which made it necessary to throw overboard 75 or 100 sacks salt to enable us to get at the leak, which was soon stopped by forcing beds and bedding into the hole sufficiently to enable us to keep her nearly free of water through the night. We have taken out some of the freight and she is not leaking at present, with a fair prospect of repairing it as soon as we could expect. Upon examination we find the freight in the hold damaged but very little.

H. H. Spencer, Clerk

Early in January, 1854, the Nick Hill was wrecked at the mouth of the Trinity River during a freak winter storm so severe that it drove the 1,800-bale Josiah H. Bell, anchored at Lynchburg and the largest of the Trinity steamboats, 300 yards into the adjacent prairie. The packet Star State was left "in a very critical condition" as a result of the storm.[116] The Bell could only be refloated by digging a canal.

In 1852, General T. J. Chambers built a long wharf and two warehouses near the mouth of the Trinity River for the convenience of keelboatmen and steamers.[117] The accommodations were a boon to the steamboat captains who could then lighten enough cotton ashore to enable them to negotiate the Trinity's shallow bar. Keelboatmen could turn their cotton over to a shipping agent or commission merchant and avoid the long waits for the cotton schooners or some steamer captain to buy their cargoes. Large numbers of keelboats continued to arrive during each shipping season, even into the late 1870's when the steamboat trade had officially ended. In 1867, the packet A. S. Ruthven, while ascending the Trinity River, passed fourteen loaded keelboats floating south, in route to the river's mouth.[118]

In January, 1851, the new steamer Magnolia arrived at Galveston for the Trinity River trade. During the next seven years, the packet, like its counterpart, the Jack Hays, reaped considerable profits for her owners and suffered no known mishaps while so doing, bringing down on some voyages as much as 1,075 bales.[119] The Magnolia no longer appeared in the Trinity River marine records after the 1857-1858 season, and her ultimate fate is unknown.

In 1852, the steamboat Brazos joined the Jack Hays, Magnolia, Star State, Nick Hill, Buffalo, Elite, and Reliance in the

Trinity River trade, but soon disappeared from the river thereafter. After the packet reached Galveston in March with 555 bales that were loaded at Magnolia on the Trinity, one account observed that:[120]

> ...the Brazos met with a slight accident coming down
> the river. One of her guards was raised by striking a
> snag, and the cotton on that side precipitated into
> the river. When she took a list, and to lighten her, the
> cotton on the other side had to be thrown overboard,
> all of which was picked up again...

In April, 1853, the packet Washington, under Captain Henry Quick, left Galveston for the Trinity River, but it remained there for only a part of one season.[121] Yellow fever may have caused both the Brazos and the Washington to return to the Brazos River where they were usually based. The year 1853 was a poor time and choice for any captain to enter the Galveston Bay and Trinity River trade, for a very virulent form of yellow fever struck the Island City and throughout the length and breadth of the Trinity Valley between July and November of that year. In a two-weeks period, there were 17 deaths at Cincinnati, Walker County, alone, and between August 7 and October 17th, four doctors, six priests (there were only 11 in all of Texas), and 403 other persons died of yellow fever at Galveston.[122]

On November 1, 1853, the owners of the Angelina-Neches packet Kate moved to the Trinity River and opened a cotton brokerage business, known as Bondies-Roehte and Co., at Magnolia, southwest of Palestine, in Anderson County. During the four years beginning in 1849, Captain George Bondies and his partner, Theodore Roehte, who was also the Kate's clerk, operated four stores scattered over East Texas, at San Augustine, Pattonia, Nacogdoches and Sabine Pass, but apparently were of the opinion that the Trinity River offered a more remunerative potential for profit. For three years the partners did prosper, Kate bringing down as much as 1,026 bales on some voyages. In April, 1856, the Kate rammed a snag and sank, "a total loss," but its cotton cargo was insured. Apparently, Bondies and Roehte chose to abandon the river thereafter, for their names do not appear on subsequent crew lists or steamboat arrivals in later years.[123] In 1867, the Kate was reported as still being a "total wreck," though still visible beneath the water, "lying just above Wheeler's Landing."[124]

In January, 1854, while in route from New Orleans to the Trinity River trade, the new steamboat Magyar ran ashore and wrecked on the beach near High Island, a total loss.[125] Other packets, however, the John Jenkins, Swan, Guadalupe, Eclipse, Clifton, and Josiah H. Bell, arrived to share a part of the river's economic plums with the Hays, Magnolia, and Kate. No figures are available for the 1854-1855 shipping season on the Trinity. There is every indication, however, that it was a banner year that may have seen 20,000 bales shipped downstream, and certainly, another 20,000 bales were expected to be shipped down the Trinity River during the succeeding season.[126] During the week ending April 10, 1854, the packet Guadalupe arrived at Galveston from the Trinity River with 697 bales of cotton aboard; the Kate unloaded 1,026 bales of Trinity cotton there; the Clifton arrived at Galveston with 1,213 bales aboard; and the Magnolia with 1,075 bales, a total of 4,011 bales for the four steamers.[127] In July, 1854, well beyond the normal shipping season, the Swan arrived from the Trinity with 823 bales, certainly an indication of the fantastic amounts of cotton that were reaching the banks of the stream quite late in the season.[128] No figures were located for the Jenkins or Eclipse. The latter was a Brazos steamer that probably made only one trip to help clean up the cotton at the landings. The Jenkins arrived from the Sabine River trade in April, 1854, and one article noted that the following September, while undergoing repairs at San Jacinto, the Jenkins "sank at the stern."[129]

The career of the deep sea steamer Josiah H. Bell was a most unusual one and warrants special attention. While being interviewed about the old steamboat fleet, W. A. Bowen, an old Trinity River steamboatman, stated that:[130]

...An old Trinity riverboat was being fitted out at the close of the war as the most formidable gunboat on

the Texas coast. This was Josiah Henry Bell. She ran the Trinity trade from about 1854 to 1860 and having a deep sea hull she paid little attention to snags and willows, but rushed right on, breaking past them like weeds, and shoving snags and sawyers out of the way. It was the Bell which first made the new channel going out of the Trinity into Galveston Bay at Anahuac. The river had begun to spread over the flats, sluggishly pushing its way across shallows, and had deposited a bank of soft mud. The J. H. Bell, after soundings, took a run and would plow as far as her momentum would take her and then back out and try it again. Thus, she finally went through. It was also the Bell that first started what is known as the "cut-off" some distance above Liberty. She came up there during a very high water. The pilot, the late Captain McCormick, who also was pilot of the gunboat Bayou City at the Battle of Galveston, saw the water running across from a narrow place, and he suggested the idea of running the Bell over it—only a few hundred feet—thus saving ten or 15 miles. The captain agreed and it was done. Her keel rubbed the earth and plowed a great ditch, and when the river went down, that plowing had grown to a considerable channel. The channel was dug out on a 'low-water,' and the next rise went through. The Bell began clearing away small rafts and thus worked herself higher and higher up the river, and the other boats, meeting obstructions, would wait until she came along, when she would "snatch snags" out of the way and thus allow rafts to float down. The other boats would pay for this. The Bell was being fitted out for sea at Orange when Lee surrendered, and our people sank her there.

During the 1855-1856 shipping season, four new vessels, the Grapeshot, the Betty Powell, San Antonio, and Fort Henry, showed up on the river, and along with the Hays, Dr. W. R. Smith, Magnolia, Jenkins, and Star State, constituted the Trinity cotton fleet for that season. There is no record that the Dr. Smith ever sailed beyond Liberty, and apparently it remained near the river's mouth in order to execute its primary function, serving as a 'steamer-lighter' for the Trinity bar.

In October, 1855, the new Grapeshot, under Captain S. P. McGuire. reached Galveston. Built at Louisville, Kentucky, for the Brazos trade, the packet was 150 feet in length, 28 feet wide, and could carry 1,500 bales. The owners, McGuire, and his clerk, entered the Trinity River trade instead, but after one voyage sold the vessel to Captain H. R. Dawson of the Trinity-Liberty Steamboat Company.[131]

The unsure newspaper accounts reveal that during three weeks of the 1855-1856 shipping season (one week each in December, February, and May), the Trinity carriers unloaded 9,025 bales at Galveston. No information is obtainable for the months of January, March, and April, each of those months being also an integral period of the shipping season. With the foregoing information as a yardstick, that season's cotton shipments may have exceeded the years 1870-1871, which was the 'golden year' of the post-bellum Trinity trade, when nearly 28,000 bales reached Galveston.[132]

Kate completed at least three voyages, bringing down 3,000 bales, and had another 1,000 bales aboard when she sank.[133]. During the last week of February, the Jack Hays arrived with 1,000 bales; the Star State with 1,200; the Kate with 1,000; and the Grapeshot carried 275 bales.[134] Late in May, the Grapeshot brought down 1,100 bales to Galveston; the Dr. W. R. Smith carried 450 to the Island City, probably off-loaded at the Trinity bar; the Jack Hays arrived from Parker's Bluff with 1,175 bales; and the Star State unloaded 1,109 more at Galveston. Although Betty Powell and J. Jenkins were reported as navigating the river throughout that season, no figures were located for those vessels.[135]

Captain Joseph Boddeker of Galveston, a veteran Trinity navigator, once recalled in later years that he:[136]

>...first began steam boating on the Trinity in 1855 on the Grapeshot, which was a 1,200-bale boat commanded by the late Captain William Jenkins. Pine Bluff, about 600 miles from Galveston, was considered the head of navigation during high water, and boats seldom went beyond that point and Magnolia. Some of the old time boats I can recall were the Josiah Bell, 1,800 bales; Gov. E. M. Pease, 1,500 bales; Star State, 1,500 bales; Grapeshot, 1,200 bales; John F. Carr and Colonel Stell, about 1,000 bales each; and Swan, 1,000 bales. Navigation was always open as far up as Liberty, and the A. S. Ruthven was the regular mail packet between Galveston and that point. She carried 1,000 bales of cotton, and I have taken her up as far as Parker's Bluff...

The years 1857-1858 appear to have been perhaps less lucrative, and they were also marred by the burning of the steamers Governor E. M. Pease and Grapeshot. By 1857, the Jack Hays had disappeared from the Trinity River, but two new packets, the San Antonio, and the Welshman, entered the river trade in addition to the regular Trinity River carriers, which included the Pease, Magnolia, Grapeshot, Betty Powell, J. H. Bell, John Jenkins, Fort Henry, Dr. Smith, and Swan. Since the San Antonio's master, Peter Menard, formerly had commanded the Hays, it would indicate that the latter (the Hays belonged to the coalition of planters) may have been sunk or sold, but no record of its fate was ever recounted in the newspapers.

Two new steamers were also built on the Trinity during those years also. John F. Carr, one of the Trinity's largest planters and cotton traders, launched an unidentified steamboat at Smithfield, Polk County, in August, 1858. Described as "the largest built in Texas to date," the vessel was 143 feet long, 26 feet wide, and carried 1,500 bales.[137] Strangely, the packet John F. Carr appeared on the Trinity the following year, but it had different dimensions, a different owner, and was built in Pittsburgh, Pennsylvania.[138] In December, 1857, A. P. Rice and Llewellyn of Magnolia launched the Welshman, a 600-bale, light draft steamboat, designed to reach the upper landings on the Trinity River.[139]

The 1857-1858 season was marked by low water due to lack of rain, which trapped some vessels in the river, and packets arrived at Galveston, carrying no more than one-half of their bale capacities because they could not get to the cotton on the upper landings. This certainly indicates an abnormally-dry season to the writer, and possibly one accompanied by sharply-curtailed cotton production. By December, 1857, the Grapeshot was able to reach Parker's Bluff (west of Palestine), where it loaded 611 bales, but earlier the Magnolia, with 877 bales aboard, was trapped in the river and had to await a river freshet before it could descend.[140]

In March, 1858, the San Antonio docked at Galveston with 490 bales of cotton from the Trinity River. This may have been that packet's only voyage, for during a subsequent gale, the San Antonio "was blown ashore near Smith's Point, but after several months was gotten off."[141] After three successful but lightly loaded voyages, the Grapeshot sailed for the Trinity on May 9, 1858, when another impending gale forced the vessel to anchor in Galveston Bay. The high winds soon broke the anchors, destroyed the chimneys (smokestacks), and while the crew sought to extinguish the boiler fires, a strong draft carried the flames outside and ignited the adjacent cabins. The Grapeshot soon burned to the waterline, but no lives were lost, the crew and ten passengers having escaped to a nearby barge. The $50,000 cargo of freight aboard was largely covered by insurance.[142]

Two months earlier, Gov. E. M. Pease was loaded with 1,400 bales at Alabama landing when flames, apparently from a smoldering bale of cotton, quickly enveloped the steamer. The packet burned to the waterline so rapidly that crewmen had only four minutes of time to throw themselves and 29 bales of the

$50,000 cargo overboard. The manifest showed that 981 bales were not insured.[143] On other voyages of that season, the Betty Powell was reported as arriving at Galveston with 770 bales aboard, the Swan with 101 bales, the John Jenkins with 1,000 bales, the Fort Henry with 850 bales, and the J. H. Bell with 836 bales.[144]

Between 1859 and 1861, many new packets, including the John F. Carr, Pathfinder, A. S. Ruthven, Alice M., Belle Sulphur, Mary Hill, Lucy Gwin, and Lone Star, joined the old fleet of Trinity River cotton carriers, whereas many of the old steamers, the Magnolia, J. H. Bell, Betty Powell, San Antonio, and others disappeared. Josiah Bell made one voyage in May, 1859, the same month that Betty Powell caught fire and burned to the waterline with a full cargo of cotton. The Bell was then purchased by the Texas and New Orleans Railroad and transferred to the Neches River to haul rails, crossties, and other construction materials.[145] The other vessels may have been sunk or sold, or possibly moved to the bay or Brazos trade, but at this writing, their fates are unknown.

W. J. C. Powell of Legg's Prairie, Kaufman County, recalled in 1893 that he had served as:[146]

...mate on the steamboat Pathfinder, Captain Jules Poitevent, commanding, which in the year 1861 made two trips up the Trinity as far as Porter's Bluff {Taos, 50 miles southeast of Dallas}. On the second return trip the Pathfinder struck a snag just after leaving Porter's Bluff and went to the bottom. She was running after night when snagged, trying to make the shoals before the river fell. The Pathfinder was a keel-bottomed boat and drew 6 1/2 feet of water when loaded heavily...

Before and after the Civil War, the Alice M. made scheduled semi-weekly runs between Galveston and Liberty, carrying passengers, mail, and small amounts of cotton, usually 25 or 30 bales picked up at the landings south of Liberty, but never more 311 bales.[147] The new 1,200-bale John F. Carr belonged to Captain Charles Gearing and measured 140 feet long and 22 feet wide, its equipment including three boilers and a 21-foot stern wheel, the latter still being somewhat of a novelty in Texas waters. By 1863, the Carr was an armed, cottonclad gunboat in Matagorda Bay.[148]

On two voyages of the Mary Hill from the Trinity in 1859, the packet arrived at Galveston with 1,200 and 456 bales, respectively.[149] The new, 1,200-bale Lucy Gwin, under Captain A. W. McKee, arrived in Galveston in December, 1859, bound for the Trinity River trade. The following March, the Gwin was loading cotton at Magnolia landing when four keelboats, carrying 1,200 bales, passed her in route downstream to Wallisville.[150]

The Belle Sulphur, under Captain Henry Quick, was a new boat when it arrived in Houston in September, 1859. Within a month, the captain completed his first Trinity River voyage, arriving in Galveston with 523 bales aboard. In March, 1860, the packet Lone Star loaded 800 bales of cotton at Magnolia and Parker's Bluff in Navarro County before returning to the Island City. Other Trinity steamers which carried cotton to Galveston during the 1859-1860 season included the Swan, John Jenkins, and J. H. Bell.[151] Although the packet A. H. Ruthven carried mail, passengers, and small amounts of cotton between Liberty and Galveston during the 1860-1861 shipping season, the Ruthven did not evolve as a major cotton carrier on the Trinity River until the post-bellum years.[152]

During the fratricidal civil conflict of 1861-1865, many of the Trinity River packets and steamboatmen were soon caught up in the War Between The States, but that record rightfully belongs to a separate manuscript covering the boats and personnel of the Texas Marine Department, under which name the Confederate Navy operated in Texas. Normally, these boats operated with civilian crews, with the artillery manned by Confederate soldiers. In brief, two Trinity River veterans, Colonel Leon Smith, and Captain John H. Sterrett, commanded that department, which was the naval gunboat and water transport arm of the Confederate Department of Texas, New Mexico, and Arizona, commanded by Major General John Bankhead Magruder. Captain Sterrett served as Superintendent of Transports, and Major C. M. Mason served as Chief of Confederate Marine Artillery. Many of Smith's, Sterrett's, and Mason's letters survive in the 158 volumes of the Official Records of the Union and Confederate Armies and Navies. Steamboat clerk H. N. Connor, whose father and brothers commanded the Reliance, Sunflower, and other steamers, has left a 90-page account of his service in the Confederate cavalry in Texas, Louisiana, and Arkansas.[153] Exactly how many Trinity navigators fought or died in the conflict is unknown, but undoubtedly, many of them manned the Confederate gunboats, tenders and blockade-runners which were based along the Texas coast. Perhaps a few of them possessed unwavering Union sympathies and may have gone north to serve in the Union forces. The J. H. Bell, the Uncle Ben, the Bayou City, and the John F. Carr, all of them old cotton boats, became key gunboats used in the defense of Sabine Pass, Galveston Bay, and Matagorda Bay.

In the history of the Trinity Valley cotton trade, only the fabulous and "golden" post-bellum years can compare with the prosperous 1850's. By 1859 cotton production in the twelve Trinity Valley counties was enumerated as follows, and it is safe to assume that the majority of it was going to market via the Trinity River: Anderson County, 8,257 bales; Chambers County, 151 bales; Freestone, 6,913 bales; Henderson, 2,026 bales; Houston, 7,011 bales; Liberty, 1,565 bales; Leon, 5,783 bales; Madison, 1,436 bales; Navarro, 2,340; Polk, 9,313 bales; Trinity, 2,945 bales; and Walker, 11,970 bales. The aggregate of cotton bales produced in the twelve counties lying on or adjacent to the Trinity River was 59,710.

Some planters and aspects of their cotton-growing in the Trinity Valley deserve special mention. The greatest concentration of production was at the Waverly community, Walker County, where 3,887 bales were grown. Generally, planters there grew quantities in excess of 75 bales each, and the seven largest producers averaged 368 bales each. The largest Trinity Valley grower, also a Walker County resident, but not from Waverly, was I. A. Thomason, who grew 603 bales. In Navarro County, three brothers, Hugh, Washington, and A. Ingram, produced 812 bales, or more than one-third of that county's production.[154]

For many of the steamboatmen and planters of the Trinity Valley, the guns of Fort Sumter, South Carolina, were soon to signal a new and tragic way of life. The carefree life of the packet crews on the river came to an end, as many of them tied up their boats and enlisted in military companies bound for Virginia. And many of them were destined to fill nameless graves in distant places. However, the valley's cotton production, centered as it was upon the labor of slaves, did not cease, but its supervision was soon transferred to the women and to others too old or unfit for military service. For those embittered, but fortunate to be alive, ex-Confederates who returned in 1865, the slave labor was gone. Perhaps other aspects of the slave-plantation economy came to an end as well, but the fields, the oxen, the cotton sacks, the gins, the steamboats that needed only a restoking of their boiler fires, and most of all, the challenge to rebuild the Trinity River valley's economy were awaiting their arrival.

Endnotes—Chapter 11

[101]*Ibid.,* June 18, 1877.

[102]*Telegraph and Texas Register,* October 29, 1849.

[103]H. P. N. Gammel, *The Laws of Texas, 1822-1896* (Austin, 1898), IV, 55-58, 744-749, 1301; *Telegraph and Texas Register,* January 10, and February 18, 1850.

[104]*Telegraph,* May 9, 1851 and February 27, 1852.

[105](Galveston) *Weekly News,* January 3, 1854.

[106]*Telegraph and Texas Register,* January 10, 1850.

[107](Galveston) *Weekly News*, February 11, 1851.

[108]*Telegraph and Texas Register*, January 31, May 9, and December 5, 1851.

[109](Galveston) *Semi-Weekly Journal,* February 9, 1852.

[110](Galveston) *Weekly News,* January 3, 10, and February 28, 1854.

[111]*Ibid.,* January 10, 1854.

[112]*Ibid.,* February 28, 1854.

[113](Galveston) *Semi-Weekly Journal,* March 22, 1852; *Telegraph and Texas Register*, December 5, 1851. In May 1852, the *Star State* arrived at Galveston with 628 bales, described as "the largest load ever brought from Houston." She belonged to the Houston Transportation Company. See *Semi-Weekly Journal*, May 10, 1852.

[114]*Telegraph and Texas Register,* June 25, 1852.

[115](Galveston) *Semi-Weekly Journal,* May 10, 1852.

[116](Nacogdoches) *Chronicle*, January 10, 1854.

[117]*Telegraph and Texas Register*, December 3, 1852.

[118](Galveston) *Weekly News,* March 28, 1867.

[119](Houston) *Telegraph and Texas Register*, January 17, 1851; (Galveston) *Weekly News*, April 11, 1854.

[120](Galveston) *Semi-Weekly Journal,* March 22, 1852.

[121](Galveston) *Weekly News*, April 19, 1853.

[122](Nacogdoches) *Chronicle*, October 25, and November 15, 1853. For an excellent account of the Galveston yellow fever

epidemic of 1853, see also P. F. Parisot, *The Reminiscences of A Missionary Priest* (San Antonio: 1899).

[123](Nacogdoches) *Times*, March 24, 1849; (Nacogdoches) *Chronicle*, August 7, 1852, and November 8, 1853; (Galveston) *Weekly News*, April 11, 1854, and April 8, 1856; Lois F. Blount, "The Story of Old Pattonia," *East Texas Historical Journal,* V (March, 1967), 19-20.

[124](Galveston) *Weekly News*, March 28, 1867.

[125](Nacogdoches) *Chronicle,* January 24, 1854.

[126](Galveston) *Weekly News,* March 11, 1856.

[127]*Ibid.,* April 11, 1854.

[128]*Ibid.,* July 11, 1854.

[129]*Ibid.,* February 28, 1854; (Nacogdoches) *Chronicle,* April 4, 1854; (San Augustine, Texas) *Redlander,* September 9, 1854.

[130](Galveston) *Daily News,* June 11, 1893.

[131](Galveston) *Weekly News*, October 30, 1855, and May 17, 1856.

[132]*Ibid.,* June 12, 1871.

[133](Galveston) *Tri-Weekly News,* December 27, 1855, and February 9, 1856; *Weekly News,* April 8, 1856.

[134](Galveston) *Weekly News,* February 26, 1856.

[135]*Ibid.,* May 20, 27, 1856.

[136](Galveston) *Daily News,* April 23, 1893.

[137](Galveston) *Weekly News,* August 31, 1858.

[138](Galveston) *Tri-Weekly News,* November 20, 1860.

[139]*Ibid.,* December 19, 1857.

[140](Galveston) *Weekly News,* March 3, and December 15, 1857.

[141]*Ibid.,* April 6, 1858; (Galveston) *Daily News,* April 27, 1893.

[142](Galveston) *Weekly News*, May 11, 1858.

[143]*Ibid.,* March 9, 1858.

[144]*Ibid.,* February 6, April 6, and November 23, 1858.

[145]*Ibid.,* May 31, 1859.

[146](Galveston) *Daily News*, April 28, 1893.

[147](Galveston) *Weekly News,* February 1, and November 22, 1859; March 21 and April 5, 1867.

[148](Galveston) *Tri-Weekly News*, November 11, 1860.

[149](Galveston) *Weekly News,* May 31, and October 25, 1859.

[150]*Ibid.*, December 6, 1859; March 3, 1860.

[151]*Ibid.*, May 31, September 6, 27, 1859; March 3, 1860.

[152](Galveston) *Tri-Weekly News,* November 20, 1860.

[153]MSS, "Diary of First Sergeant H. N. Connor," unpublished, 90 pages, copy owned by Dr. Haskell Monroe, University of Missouri.

[154]Manuscript Census Returns of 1860, Eighth Census of the United States, Schedules IV, Products of Agriculture, for Anderson, Chambers, Freestone, Henderson, Houston, Liberty, Leon Madison, Navarro, Polk, San Jacinto, Trinity, and Walker counties, Texas, Microfilm Reels 1 and 2, Lamar University Library.

Chapter 12—The Trinity River's Thriving Post-Bellum Commerce

When General E. Kirby Smith surrendered the Confederacy's Trans-Mississippi Department to Union General E. R. S. Canby at Galveston on June 4, 1865, the occasion was a mere formality. Most of the Confederate troops in Texas had either gone home or been mustered out of service, and many of them had returned to the fields to do their spring plowing. By July 10, many points in East Texas had already been or were in the process of being occupied by Union troops, and civilians were soon subjected to military rule and edict.[155] Federal commanders were immediately ordered to seize all remaining stocks of Confederate government-owned cotton, weaponry, and quartermaster goods. The suspension of local government and its replacement by martial law are quite visible in the archives of Jefferson County, where the commissioners' court did not meet from the spring session of 1865 until ordered to do so by General A. J. Hamilton, the provisional governor of Texas, in January, 1866.[156]

The unsure newspaper accounts for the immediate post-bellum years, 1865-1867, and the corresponding small volume of cotton reported as reaching Galveston from the Trinity Valley could easily induce one to deduct that the cotton industry there was a corpse that had received insurmountable setbacks as a result of losing the war. The maritime columns of two Galveston newspapers repeatedly list two steamers as arriving with small quantities of cotton from Liberty,[157] but only a few instances where larger cargoes reached Galveston from other points on the river. During the same period, however, thousands of bales arrived at the Island City daily via the Galveston, Houston, and Henderson Railroad or aboard the bay steamers plying between there and Houston.

The writer is thus led to believe that the Trinity shippers were continuing a practice that was certainly instituted no later than October, 1862, when both Sabine Lake and Galveston Bay were occupied by Federal fleets. Any Trinity Valley cotton moving south by steamer or keelboat could go no farther than Liberty, at which point the cargoes would have to transfer to the Texas and New Orleans Railroad for trans-shipment elsewhere. From October through December, 1862, both Beaumont and Houston were threatened by the nearby Federal forces, but after the Battle of Galveston on January 1, 1863, either town, as well as Orange, would have been a safe point for the storage of cotton.

During 1866, the largest Trinity River cotton cargo noted as arriving at Galveston consisted of 288 bales aboard the packet Colonel Stell, a boat with a 1,000 bale capacity.158 By 1867, the packets were reaching there with full cargoes, and others, some of which had plied between Galveston and Houston consistently for years, abandoned the Galveston Bay trade for the Trinity. To the writer, the obvious conclusion regarding cause was the state of disrepair and subsequent closing of the Texas and New Orleans Railroad, which remained inoperative between Houston and Liberty from 1867 until 1872 (and between Houston and Beaumont and Orange until 1876). In 1869, the Galveston Weekly News stated that "after the Civil War, the Texas and New Orleans Railroad to Beaumont was permitted to go to decay, and will require new crossties, new bridges, and in places, some new grading."[159]

During 1866, it is likewise apparent that South and East Texans were planting cotton to the detriment of the food and grain crops, and that cotton prices were fair, even in the face of a declining and unstable market. On May 2, the Weekly News observed that:[160]

...the late continued and heavy decline in cotton will be likely to admonish our planters ...of the folly of attempting to raise large crops of cotton under the present embarrassments and at a cost of probably fifty percent more... At this moment large amounts of corn are being brought from New Orleans on every steamer and shipped by our railroads to supply the best corn country in the world in the vicinity of Oyster Creek, the Brazos, and the Trinity ...

Four weeks later, the editor's comment about Walker County, where "planters think that not more than half a crop of cotton will be made," suggests that a prolonged drought was in progress.[161] During the same month, the cotton prices at Galveston ranged from 22 cents to 25 cents for the lowest grades to above 30 cents for 'middling' and up, whereas the New York cotton market was reported as "dull at 37 cents."[162]

During the fall of 1865, two ill-fated steamers engaged in the Trinity trade, and each brought out sizeable cargoes, although far below their bale capacities. In September, 1865, the Lone Star wrecked on Redfish Bar with 450 bales of Trinity cotton aboard.[163] In November, the packet Sunflower reached Galveston from Liberty with 352 bales. During 1866, the latter, a 1,000-bale boat and former Confederate tender from the Neches River trade, was intermittently in both the Galveston Bay and Trinity River trade. In January, 1867, however, the Sunflower, under Captain D. E. Connor, sank at Patrick's Landing, north of Swarthout, with 553 bales aboard, "a total loss," and there is no subsequent record of its refloating.[164]

A new steamer, the likewise ill-fated Colonel Stell, engaged in the Trinity cotton commerce during the late 1865-1866 season and returned to the river the following December. In January, 1867, while descending the stream near Cincinnati, Walker County, the Stell was snagged and quickly foundered in the river. At first, Captain Luke Falvel was of the opinion that the packet could be refloated. He later returned to the site with a Galveston salvage crew, but soon abandoned the project as becoming too costly. On March 28, the Weekly News reported that "the Stell is a total wreck near Cincinnati. Her chimneys are gone and very little of the hull can be seen." Farther downstream, another mishap of 1867 left the steamboat S. J. Lee "entirely covered with water, and nothing of her could be seen."[165]

The Liberty-to-Galveston run was always a profitable venture for the holder of a mail contract, and two round-trips could be easily accomplished in one week. Neither Wallisville, Moore's Bluff, Moss Bluff nor the other landings on the lower Trinity River had rail facilities and were wholly dependent on the mail steamer for passenger, freight, and produce traffic. Beginning with the closing of the Texas and New Orleans Railroad in 1867, the passenger traffic mushroomed along that route, much of it bound to and from Sour Lake.

By 1856, the Sour Lake springs and hotel had become the fashionable "watering place" (spa or mineral bathing resort) of Texas, and between 1861 and 1867, the Texas and New Orleans Railroad derived much of its revenue from the affluent families of Galveston and Houston, comprised principally of the rising cotton aristocracy, who travelled to and from that point. As of 1857, the spa's facilities included 25 cabins in addition to the large hotel, and the mineral and sulfur-scented springs were believed to contain curative powers, in fact, magic "cure-alls," for all ills. The closing of the Texas and New Orleans line rerouted the Sour Lake passenger traffic via steamer to Liberty, and via "Mr. Mintar's line of hacks connecting with the steamer at a cost of $5."[166]

During 1866, the steamboat Royal Arch travelled the route from Galveston to Liberty, carrying small amounts of cotton shipped from the intermediate points on the lower Trinity. By 1867, that vessel had transferred to the Brazos River,[167] and was replaced as the mail contractor by the Alice M., which returned in the fall of 1866. Between October and the last week of February, 1867, the Alice M. carried small amounts of cotton, seldom move than fifty bales, on each trip to Galveston, but by March, its shipments suddenly mushroomed to more than 300 bales on each voyage. The sudden change strongly suggests that the Texas and New Orleans line had abruptly withdrawn rail service between Liberty and Houston.[168]

Besides Alice M., Colonel Stell, Sunflower, and Royal Arch, there were three other steamboats in the Trinity during the late 1866 season. In April and May, the packet T. J. Emory reached Galveston with 140 and 263 bales, respectively, but abandoned Trinity for the Sabine River after that season. The Indian Queen No. 2 (usually referred to as the Indian, or the Indian No. 2, under Captain Byrd Grace) arrived from Liberty with 28 bales late in March, 1866 and began loading freight for Parker's Bluff. In August,

1862, the Indian No. 2 was running the blockade at Sabine Pass when it was captured, with 48 tons of bacon and flour aboard, by the U. S. S. Hatteras. In May, the A. S. Ruthven reached Galveston with 148 bales aboard.[169]

From 1866 until the cotton commerce finally folded, the plantation-owned A. S. Ruthven, under Captain Wash Rose, remained one of the work horses of the Trinity River trade. During the 1866-1867 season, the packet made three successful voyages, bringing out, respectively, 725, 755, and 775 bales on those trips, and under the most adverse of weather circumstances. The Weekly News recorded in March that the steamer had reached Parker's Bluff on the 11th with:[170]

> ...a large cargo {of freight} ...Coming up the Ruthven met 14 flatboats at various points, all loaded with cotton for Galveston. We understand that the Ruthven will go as high up as Wild Cat Bluff {640 miles} and will return up the river and remain above Magnolia till next fall ...The snow, sleet, and hail fell on the deck of the boat to a depth of six inches...The cold was so severe that the steam pipes of the steamers and steam sawmills were frozen and burst. Such severe cold weather in the month of March was never before known ...

Over a ten-year span, "the historic old A. S. Ruthven" suffered no mishaps and possibly became the most profitable vessel ever to engage in the Trinity trade. To determine how fortunate the steamboat was, one need only recall that during the years Ruthven was on the Trinity (1860-1873), the other Trinity. packets Lee, Stell, Sunflower, Black Cloud, Kate, Mustang, and Mary Conley all sank in the river; the steamers Grapeshot, Betty Powell, Governor Pease, and H. A. Jones all burned; and the Mollie Hambleton sank in a hurricane. In 1893, W. A. Bowen recalled that after Dr. Young's Houston and Great Northern Railroad had completed trackage to Crockett in 1872, the plantation-owned Ruthven was tied up and was "finally torn to pieces at Parker's Bluff, and her machinery was utilized for mills and gins, and her cabin, the finest ever in Texas, was made into a magnificent residence."[171]

During the 1866-1867 shipping season, two new steamboats, the Como, and Black Cloud, joined the Ruthven, Alice M., Indian No. 2, Sunflower, Stell, and S. J. Lee in the Trinity cotton trade, and the cargoes reaching Galveston soon equaled the pre-war levels once again. During the week ending February 27, the Alice M. made three trips from Liberty, carrying 40, 58, 79 bales, respectively. The Como brought down 1,011 bales from the upriver landings; the Indian No. 2 carried out 681 bales to Galveston, and the Ruthven reached the Island City with 754 bales aboard.[172] During the week ending March 12, 1867, the Alice arrived with 272 bales, and the Black Cloud brought down 724 bales of cotton from the Trinity.[173] The Como made two more voyages, carrying out on each trip 1,051 and 975 bales, respectively. On subsequent trips in March and April, the Black Cloud arrived at Galveston with 658 bales from the upper river; the Alice arrived with 864 (on three trips); and the Indian carried 667 bales.[174] In view of the Weekly News figures that Galveston received 9,118 bales direct from the Trinity between February 20 and April 16, it becomes apparent that the Daily News report of 1893 (see Ch. IX, Fn. 30)—that only 6,415 bales arrived during the year ending August 31, 1867—is grossly understated. This trend of understatement follows through the 1872-1873 shipping season, but the 1893 report for the last five years, 1873 to 1878, is accurate to the bale.

According to one account, the Black Cloud was another plantation-owned steamer, whose career was both long and profitable, but the river would eventually claim the proud packet as a victim in 1872. Over a span of thirty years, her master, Thomas Peacock, probably captained more Trinity River steamboats than any other person. In 1893, W. A. Bowen, the old Trinity River sailor-turned-journalist, recalled that the Black Cloud was:[175]

...built especially for the Trinity trade, with a view to go over the Anahuac mud flats at any stage, and to run over snags and into willows with impunity. She was a scow in build, with an extra strong hull, plenty

of boiler and cylinder power, and a large stern wheel.
Captain Joe Rogers was her first pilot. The Black
Cloud made a number of upriver trips and always
paid (profited). She could go over Cannonball, White
Rock, and Kickapoo Shoals when no other boat could

...

In recent years, wreckage of the Black Cloud was located in a silted-over portion of the river near Robinson's Bluff. Some artifacts from the wreckage, including the anchor, can be seen at the Sam Houston State Regional Library at Liberty.

There also began in 1867 an 8-months trip that eventually reached Dallas, a voyage that had long been the dream of Trinity steamboatmen. As early as 1852, when the Nick Hill reached Taos or Porter's Bluff, north of Corsicana, the feasibility and eventuality of such a voyage was foreseen, but the upper river beyond Taos contained a myriad of obstructions to navigation. Captain James McGarvey, who carried the dream to fruition, planned prudently for the trip, purchasing a snag boat especially-built and designed for removing navigational impediments. By September, 1867, McGarvey was prepared to sail, and this surviving record observed that he:[176]

...left Galveston for Dallas in a little stern wheel
steamboat named Job Boat No. 1, which was 85 feet
long, 18-foot beam, and a thirty-inch draft of water.
He had a cargo of goods on board, and preceded up
the river leisurely, trading with the inhabitants along
the banks as he passed by, cutting away overhanging
limbs, pulling up snags, and worrying over sand bars.
Dallas was reached in May, 1868, after an eight-
months trip, and the captain was warmly received by
the citizens. On the up trip, he cut out twenty-eight
rafts formed by the lodged drift {logjams} between
Liberty and Magnolia, and from that point to Dallas
the trip occupied only a month ...

Twenty-five years later, when the Dallas Board of Trade and the Trinity Navigation Company united in a strenuous effort to canalize the 800-mile river route via a series of locks, Captain McGarvey accompanied Captain Joseph Rogers aboard the snag boat H. A. Harvey, Jr., the second and last occasion when a steamboat travelled the entire 890 river miles from Galveston to Dallas.

Primary sources are unsure, in fact almost non-existent, for the 1867-1868 season, but several new packets joined the fleet of Trinity carriers at that time. With the Texas and New Orleans Railroad inoperative, and a corresponding reduction in the volume of cotton reaching Houston, the bay steamers Era No. 3, T. M. Bagby, and the J. H. Whitelaw quickly abandoned Buffalo Bayou for the Trinity River. Other new packets of that year included Orleans, Mustang, Ida Reese, Fleta, Justice, Mollie Hambleton, Royal Arch, and Early Bird.

The steamboats Early Bird and W. J. Poitevent, captained respectively by Jules and Adoph Poitevent, belonged to a wealthy family of Navarro County planters, who operated the vessels primarily for the own convenience, to carry theirs and their neighbors cotton to market. Earlier Poitevent had also owned the Pathfinder, which sank in the river. When the Trinity shipping season ended early, which it sometimes did with so many steamboats in the river, the Poitevent brothers sometimes took the packets to carry cotton on the Neches and Sabine Rivers, where around 1870 the banks often had 5,000 or more bales at the landings awaiting transportation. Another newspaper account once recounted that:[177]

> ...Captain Jules Poitevent, the son of an extensive
> planter in Navarro County, went over to Louisiana
> and bought the Early Bird, a small sidewheel steamer
> with a capacity of 600 bales, to run up the Trinity and
> bring out his cotton to Galveston ...The Early Bird
> first demonstrated that the river could be
> successfully navigated as high as Dallas. She never

*came to Dallas, but she made a number of trips
above Lockridge's Bluff ...The captain made a fortune
out of the Early Bird. She ran from 1868 to about
1871 or 1872 {actually 1873}, and was finally laid up
near his plantation and her machinery was taken out
and used for gins and mills ...*

Among the voyages of 1868, Ruthven made a 543-mile voyage to Parker's Bluff and returned to Galveston with 290 bales of cotton. A month later, the Early Bird arrived there with 526 bales from Magnolia on the Trinity, followed by the Fleta with 255 bales from West Point.[178]

By 1869, the Houston and Texas Central Railroad had reached Huntsville, and by 1873, had built its trackage almost to the Red River. The line appears to have offered only minimal competition to the Trinity carriers at first, since a total of fifteen packets operated on the Trinity River during the 1869-1870 shipping season, followed by seventeen steamers during 1870-1871. Quite obviously, the plantation owners of the steamboats were in no hurry to tie up their boats, and the reason was soon revealed. In noting one planter's reaction to the railroad, a Huntsville resident complained in 1869 that he represented:[179]

*...a large majority of the people in Walker County in
a wish to get some other channel of trade to
Galveston except through Houston and by the
Central Railroad. Their prices are over high and
onerous ...*

The steamer Orleans, captained by Lewis King, operated in Trinity for only a short period of time. In 1869, the packet was purchased by Keith and Vaughn, commission cotton merchants of Sabine Pass, where that vessel sank during the hurricane of September, 1871.[180] A small steamboat, the Justice, served as the Liberty mail packet for a season, and in 1868, reached Galveston on three occasions, carrying cargoes of 356, 334, and 146 bales, respectively. The steamer was subsequently sold to Captain James

Patrick, but it remained in the Trinity River trade until the 1870 season ended.[181]

In 1868, the 1,200-bale Ida Reese reached the Trinity River and brought out cargoes of 1,052 and 661 bales during that year. She remained in the river through the 1871-1872 season, arriving in Galveston in 1871 with an 804-bale load and again in 1872 with 1,029 bales. While docked at Beaver's Landing to load cotton in March, 1870, her master, Captain T. J. Stubblefield, was murdered during an altercation with a passenger.[182] In February, 1873, a time when most of the cotton on the Trinity had already been marketed, the Ida Reese was purchased by David R. Wingate of Orange and transferred to the Sabine River, where the packet sank near Stark's Landing on its first return voyage, with 385 bales aboard, in March, 1873. After the Reese had lain submerged for four years, Wingate hired a marine salvage crew in 1877 and succeeded in recovering the packet's engines, boilers, shaft, piping, and other machinery, which were subsequently used in Wingate's Orange sawmilling industry.[183]

Also in 1868, the Mustang, the second steamer of that name to ply the Trinity, entered the river trade and for a time served as the Liberty mail contractor. In July 1869, the Mustang sank at Moore's Bluff, the exact place where Jack Hays and the McLean had foundered, south of Liberty, several years earlier, from an undetermined cause. The Liberty Gazette complained that the loss of the Mustang "leaves us {Liberty} without a Galveston packet."[184]

Among the voyages of 1868-1869, the Mustang carried cargoes of 678, 880, and 361 bales respectively to Galveston. Other voyages and cargoes of that season included the Ida Reese, 1,052 and 661 bales; Early Bird, 788 and 634 bales; Indian No. 2, 1,028 and 669 bales; Justice, 356, 334, and 146 bales; and the Fleta, 444 and 448, for a grand total of 10,344 bales of Trinity cotton reaching Galveston during the months of January, February, and March, 1869.[185]

The three succeeding seasons, 1869 to 1872, would witness the largest number of steamboats operating in the Trinity during any one year and what the writer believes to have been the greatest volume of cotton ever to move down that stream. The 1871-1872 season, however, would forecast the impending doom of the river trade as well, the removal of the plantation-owned fleet, and the further encroachment of the railroads as trackage reached Palestine, Crockett, and other points in the Trinity Valley. It likewise appears that, although many planters disliked the "over high and onerous" rail rates, they in time came to prefer that mode of movement that depended solely on rails rather than rainfall and river freshets. Hence, for many, the railroads undoubtedly provided a fast route to market, as opposed to the frequent and long waits for cotton or a river freshet at the river landings, and correspondingly, a faster return of the planter's yearly income.

During 1869-1870, the bay steamers T. M. Bagby, J. H. Whitelaw, and Era No. 3, along with the new packets Caddo, Henry A. Jones, Cleona, Mary Conley, and Mollie Hambleton joined the Reese, Justice, Early Bird, Mustang, Black Cloud, and Indian No. 2 as the Trinity River's fleet of steam-driven cotton carriers — a total of fifteen boats. Three of the new steamers were ill-fated from the beginning, however, as the following records reveal.

In March, 1870, a newspaper account observed that Captain P. F. Cooper's new sidewheeler, the Mary Conley, was a "welcome accession to our fleet of river transports." In February, 1873, the Conley, while in route downstream with a large cargo, was snagged and sank near Nevill's Landing, but the Early Bird was able to salvage 140 bales from the wrecked steamboat.[186] Early in June, during the first of two severe hurricanes in 1871, the Mollie Hambleton, under Captain Calvin Blakeman, capsized and sank, "a total wreck from the storm at Galveston."[187] On February 14, 1873, the Henry A. Jones, loaded with Trinity River cotton, burned in Galveston Bay with a loss of three officers' lives as well as the entire cargo. Most of the crew were fortunate to escape to the barge that was being towed by the packet.[188]

According to the Galveston Weekly News and Tri-Weekly News, which kept week-by-week accumulative total of cotton receipts during 1869-1871, 22,896 bales reached Galveston direct from the Trinity River between September 1, 1869 and June 12,

1870. The Trinity River trade was still ascending, whereas the Daily News (for comparative purposes) report of 1893 noted only 17,584 bales as having arrived during that shipping season, down 8,000 bales from the reported peak year of 1868-1869 (See also Ch. IX, Fn. 30).[189] Other accounts point out that the Era No. 3, Reese, Bagby, and Whitelaw unloaded 2,738 bales (or more) at Houston; hence, the Trinity carriers exported a minimum of 25,632 bales during that season.[190]

The Mollie Hambleton made two voyages to Magnolia during that period, returning with 852 bales on the first trip and a "full cargo" on the second.[191] Captain J. H. Hailey's 600-bale Cleona arrived twice, carrying 514 and 600 bales of cotton, respectively. Captain Caesar Burgess sailed the Caddo twice to the Island City, bringing down full cargoes. Among other shipments of Trinity cotton for 1869-1870, the keelboats George Wright, J. Crisp, and Roes arrived at Wallisville in April, carrying down an aggregate 950 bales.[192] At the close of that season, the plantation-owned Hambleton, Cleona, H. A. Jones, and Indian No. 2 solicited freight for their final voyages to West Point and Magnolia, where the vessels would be "laid up" until the following December.[193]

The available records point out that Trinity River cotton shipments reached their zenith during the 1870-1871 season, when seventeen steamboats carried a total of 27,728 bales to Galveston.[194] The volume arriving at Houston by rail and steamer may well have swelled the Trinity Valley's cotton exports beyond the 50,000 bale mark. In retrospect, it seems inconceivable that the Trinity River's cotton trade could have plummeted so rapidly, from almost 28,000 bales in 1871 to only 1,732 in 1874, but these are substantiated facts. The following quote certainly implies that such brisk competition from the railroads was not immediately expected, and that whatever conveniences the rails offered were counterbalanced by the increased shipping costs. It is an inescapable fact, however, that shipment by rail probably reduced insurance rates, for that mode of movement disgorged no cotton cargoes into the Trinity River's murky depths. In May, 1871, the Weekly News stated that Captain Jameson of the packet Colonel D. S. Cage had arrived at Galveston with:[195]

...350 bales of cotton from Lockridge's Landing in
Navarro County, some 600 or 700 miles up the river.
The navigation is and has been for some time
excellent. On the next trip, he {Jameson} proposes to
go to Porter's Bluff {Taos}, some 200 miles above ...
Were it not for the overhanging limbs, he thinks he
could go as high as Dallas. The people are all looking
to the steamers to bring their cotton to Galveston as
they thereby save some $6.00 or $7.00 per bale, as
compared with the cost of sending it to New Orleans,
and $4.00 or $5.00 per bale, as compared with the
cost of sending it to Galveston by Central Railroad.
Captain Jameson informs us that flour, when taken
to Navarro County by the railroad, costs $14.00 or
$15.00 a barrel, but that he can deliver it by his
steamer at a cost of $10.00 per barrel ...

During the 1870-1871 season, ten new boats, the Beardstown, H. F. Matthews, Twelfth Era (also known as Era No. 12),[196] Nora, Colonel D. S. Cage, S. J. Lee,[197] Wren, C. K. Hall, Belle of Texas, and Emily P. joined the old remnant of Trinity River carriers, the Mary Conley, Era No. 3, Hambleton, Ida Reese, Black Cloud, and Early Bird, in the cotton trade. Four Trinity steamers docked at Galveston during the hurricane of June, 1871, were sunk or damaged. The Hambleton sank, the packet Emily P., "loaded with cotton," was left "a total loss;" the D. S. Cage had her pilot house and stacks blown away, and the Belle of Texas lost a chimney.[198] The hurricane of September, 1871, sank the steamboat C. K. Hall at Galveston.[199] Despite that statement, the Emily P. would be salvaged to serve a long period of service in the Sabine River before finding its watery grave in the Brazos.

The 339-ton, 800-bale Beardstown (which had only a 16-inch draft unloaded) arrived as the new Liberty mail contractor. Under Captain J. H. Matthews, E. S. Bell of Waco owned the packet. A brother, Captain H. F. Matthews, owned the new steamer which bore his name.[200] Another brother-captain duo also arrived on Trinity at that approximate moment. Earlier, Captains Frank and James H. Maratta had brought the new Henry A. Jones, built in 1869, to the river, but soon sold that vessel to an upriver plantation owner. During 1871-1872, Frank Maratta sailed the 1,200-bale Belle of Texas in the Trinity cotton trade, and was joined in 1872 by J. H. Maratta, who owned the new Liberty mail packet, the Tobe Hurt. After transferring to the Sabine River as a mail contractor, the Tobe Hurt was "entirely consumed" by fire, with one life lost, while docked at Orange in April, 1873.[201]

During 1870-1871, the Twelfth Era made five upriver voyages, returning on two of them with "full cargoes" and on the remainder with 758, 677 and 1,000 bales of cotton, respectively.[202] The Black Cloud reached Galveston on five occasions, unloading cargoes, respectively, of 700, 800, 1,056, 598, and 348 bales. The D. S. Cage made six trips to the Trinity River during that season, but none of its cargoes exceeded 378 bales.[203] Among other cotton reports located by the writer, the Early Bird made four upriver voyages; the Nora, Reese, and Hambleton, three trips each; the Belle of Texas, two; and the S. J. Lee and Conley, one voyage each.[204]

The year 1872 witnessed the first significant decrease in the Trinity River cotton cargoes. The Daily News' 1893 report (3,211 bales) is again erroneous, for the unsure records compiled for that season by the writer indicate that at least 6,583 bales reached Galveston aboard the Trinity steamboats. When compared to the previous year, the growth of rail competition and the volume of cotton reaching the river landings during 1872 were in sharp diametric proportion. And although thirteen packets entered the river trade at the beginning of the 1871-1872 season, half of that number would have sufficed. By March 1, the shipping season had ended, and the few cotton carriers that remained after that date usually arrived at Galveston carrying no more than forty or fifty bales.

During 1872, 1,000 men were engaged in the rebuilding of the Texas and New Orleans Railroad. They soon reopened the line to Liberty and expected to reach Beaumont within a year (it was actually 1876). The completion date at Liberty was apparently subsequent to May, for passengers to Sour Lake were still embarking at Galveston aboard the mail packet Tobe Hurt, which was making semi-weekly trips to Liberty as of that month.[205] By 1872, the Houston and Great Northern line had reached Crockett and (soon renamed the International and Great Northern) had completed trackage to Troupe, 50 miles north of Palestine, by March, 1873.[206] By February, 1873, rail communication via the Texas and Pacific line was opened between Longview and Houston, and the Houston and Texas Central Railroad was rapidly approaching the Red River.[207] Although cotton shipments to Galveston via the Trinity River steamers dropped from 27,728 bales in 1871 to 1,732 in 1874, the volume received from Houston by rail or by Galveston Bay steamers mushroomed from 235,201 bales to 368,089 bales during the same time span.[208]

During the 1872 shipping season, three new cotton boats, the Anne S., Tobe Hurt, and W. J. Poitevent, joined the Beardstown, Matthews, Belle of Texas, Nora, Early Bird, Conley, Reese, Wren, Cage, and Black Cloud for varying periods of time. At the season's beginning, Galveston cotton traders and merchants apparently anticipated a repetition of the previous year, the Tri-Weekly News reporting that "great activity is thus given to the Trinity trade, and quite a number of our grocery dealers have as much as they can do to fill orders."[209]

During January and February, 1872, several steamboats reached Galveston with large cargoes, apparently with no inkling that that year's river commerce would abruptly cease. During January, the Cage unloaded 400 bales at the Island City; the Nora arrived with 559; the H. F. Matthews brought down 1,000 bales of cotton, and the Belle of Texas arrived at Galveston with 281 bales. In February, the Beardstown arrived there with 728 bales; the Early Bird unloaded 654; and the Ida Reese and W. J. Poitevent carried, respectively, 1,029 and 1,.001 bales from Magnolia to Galveston.[210]

From March 1 until the shipping season ended, it appears that no more cotton arrives at the landings, and the packets probed farther and farther upstream in a fruitless search for cargoes. During

March, the Nora brought 198 bales from Pine Bluff; the Wren carried 63 bales from Magnolia to Galveston; and the Beardstown unloaded 204 at the Island City, each one carrying only a small fraction of its bale capacity. In April, the Nora sailed all the way to Lockridge's Landing in search of cotton but located only 23 bales along the return route. The Belle of Texas unloaded 51 bales from Magnolia, and the Poitevent arrived from the Trinity River with only 59 bales.[211] One by one, the boats of the plantation-owned fleet were tied up at the upriver landings, and other boats soon abandoned the stream as a result of that season's experiences.

During the 1872-1873 shipping season, a number of the old boats were no longer present, but the new propeller-driven Kate from the Neches River joined six of the old steamer fleet, the Ida Reese, Tobe Hurt, H. A. Jones, Mary Conley, Wren, and the Early Bird., in pursuit of cotton on the Trinity River. If anything, that year was to prove more of a disaster than the previous one, for by the end of the season, five of the seven vessels had either sunk or burned. During January and February, the H. A. Jones burned in Galveston Bay with the loss of some crewmen, and the Mary Conley sank near Nevil's Landing in the Trinity River. During March, the Tobe Hurt and Ida Reese transferred to the Sabine River, where the latter snagged and sank on its first return voyage, and the Tobe Hurt burned at Orange. In December, the Kate sank at Moore's Bluff, following a collision with sunken logs.[212] In February, the Early Bird made one of the only two voyages of consequence recorded during 1873, carrying out 587 bales, but it was subsequently "laid up" at Lockridge's Landing, Navarro County, by its owner, Jules Poitevent, and was later dismantled. In March, 1873, the W. J. Poitevent (the writer believes it to have been the old J. J. Warren from the Sabine River), the last of the planter-owned packets, unloaded 922 bales of Trinity River cotton, and at the season's end, joined its sister ship at the upstream "boneyard" of plantation-owned steamers at Lockridge's Landing.[213]

During 1874, the propeller steamer Kate was refloated and repaired, and along with Wren, continued on for perhaps three years in the almost-extinct Trinity trade. In April, 1872, Captain James Roach had purchased the Wren for $3,882, when the steamer, because of an admiralty court decree, was sold at auction by the United States marshal.[214] In 1877, Roach sold the Wren to Davis, Call and Son of Orange, where the steamboat remained in the cotton and lumber trade for only a season before sinking in the Sabine River.[215]

With the sale of the Wren, the writer considers the cotton trade as officially ended. The aggregate of Trinity River cotton shipments during the 1877-1878 season was only 979 bales, mostly picked up in small quantities at Moore's Bluff, Moss Bluff, and Wallisville, the latter community being at that time the Chambers County seat. All the landings south of Liberty had no access to rail facilities and no other route to market except on the Liberty mail steamer's semi-weekly voyages. Throughout the 1880's, the Galveston Weekly News and Daily News, as well as the Liberty Vindicator after 1887, failed to mention anything about the Trinity River steamboats, and the writer surmises that whatever steamboat trade remained on the river was of minute importance or else in support of the lumber trade. But despite three sawmills, a stave mill, and a barrel factory on the lower Trinity River, the lumber trade there never remotely approached the size of that industry at either Beaumont or Orange. Since no rail facilities existed south of Liberty, the Liberty-to-Galveston mail packets were probably continued for years afterward, the passenger trade from the county seat community of Wallisville being an important factor as well.

In 1893, the Vindicator noted that, despite the intersections of the International and Great Northern, the Texas and New Orleans, and the Houston East and West Texas rails with the river, "still steamboats plied the Trinity, carrying freight and passengers from points below Liberty, and making occasional trips to points beyond."[216] The principal cause for the steamer's survival was the rising lumber and timber products industry. Logs were floated downstream to sawmills erected at Anahuac, Wallisville, and Liberty. During 1893, the packets Poor Boy and Alice Blair carried loads of barrel staves from a mill located on the Trinity River near Goodrich, Texas, to the barrel factory at Liberty. By 1898, Blair, along with another former Trinity steamboat, the Emily P., lay sunken, rotting and abandoned in the graveyard of river boats that were accumulating at Columbia landing on the Brazos River.[217]

During the summer of 1891, the L. Q. C. Lamar, formerly of the Sabine River trade and perhaps the last of the old cotton boats to be interred in the Trinity's depths, joined the river's growing graveyard of ships. On its first voyage for the lumber industry, the Lamar was snagged and foundered nine miles below Liberty. During the previous ten years, the steamer had carried cotton on many successful voyages on the Sabine River. In October, 1886, the Lamar was the first relief vessel to succor the surviving hurricane victims after Sabine Pass was destroyed, and later the vessel transferred to the Brazos River for a short time. Two early efforts to refloat the Lamar failed, and the third and last attempt, in February, 1892, ended in disaster, when Andrew Wilson, a Galveston salvage diver, fouled his air lines and died.[218]

Over a span of forty years between 1838 and 1878, a number of other steamboats are credited by Charles N. Eley as having carried cotton or other items in the Trinity River trade, but the writer located no verifying records to that effect among the few surviving newspapers. Many of the boats are well known to the writer because of their periods of service on the other Texas rivers. William Penn was a Brazos River steamer during the antebellum period and sometimes participated in the Galveston Bay trade. During the 1870's, James L. Graham plied the Sabine and Neches Rivers. In 1873, the Graham salvaged most of the cargo of the Ida Reese, sunk in the Sabine, and later, the Graham transferred to the Brazos trade. In the spring of 1876, the steamer won a contract to haul bridge timbers for the Texas and New Orleans Railroad at Liberty, and while in route there with 30,000 feet of oak lumber, the packet sank in a storm near the Vingt et Un Islands in Galveston Bay.[219] Between 1866 and 1874, the Camorgo was in the Angelina-Neches River trade. Owned variously by Captain Andrew F. Smyth of Bevilport, C. H. Alexander and Co. of Sabine Pass, and Crain and Griffith of Johnson's Bayou, La., the Camorgo sank near Townsend's Landing on the Angelina in January, 1874, with 229 bales of cotton aboard.[220] In 1871, the iron steamship Stonewall belonged to Norris and Company of Galveston and engaged in the offshore Sabine Pass, Galveston, Calcasieu River, La., trade. The packet also made weekly visits to Orange, Texas on the Sabine and to Bunn's Bluff on the Neches.[221] At the time of the Trinity River cotton trade's demise, the steamboats Stonewall and J. H. Sellers were making intermittent voyages between Galveston and the Brazos River, but both packets probably made one or more voyages in the Trinity that the writer was not able to document.[222]

Except for Chapter 13. which follows, an account of the snag boats H. A. Harvey, Jr. and the Dallas, and the extensive effort put forth by the Trinity Navigation Company to raise funds and canalize the river from Dallas to the Gulf, the story of some one hundred and twenty Trinity River steamboats comes to an end. If it were possible to line the steamers end-to-end and parade them in procession bound upriver, the Trinity's cotton fleet over the forty year span would stretch for four miles downstream from the northern-most point. By 1875, however, what had once been so thriving a commerce that seventeen packets were engaged in it at one time, had dwindled away to nothing, bowing once more to the railroads they had helped to build. And in time, only the memories of the cotton bales, the keelboats, and the sternwheelers lingered on, with the silence of the Trinity forests no longer shattered by the blast of the steamer's shrill whistle. Today, even the memories are lost in the mists of time, the steamboatmen are long since dead, and the echoes of the cotton boats' whistles are silenced. Only the various old newspaper accounts and similar records survive, and of course, a few old rotting steamer hulks in the depths of the stream remain to testify in silence of an age when ships of wood and crewmen of steel navigated in the cotton trade of the Trinity River.

Endnotes—Chapter 12

[155]Official Records of the Union and Confederate Armies in the War of the Rebellion (Washington, D. C.: 1880-1901) Series I, Vol. XLVIII, Part 2, 1062-1075.

[156]Volume C, pp. 188-191, Commissioners Court Minutes, Jefferson County, Texas, Archives.

[157]The instances are too numerous to cite in detail. See Weekly News, May 9, 23 and November 2, 9, 22, 1866.

[158](Galveston) Weekly News, May 9, 1866.

[159]Ibid., December 20, 1869. See also "The History of the Texas and New Orleans Railroad," (Galveston) Tri-Weekly News, December 22, 1869; also S. G. Reed, A History of the Texas Railroads (Houston: 1941), 85-86.

[160](Galveston) Weekly News, May 2, 1866.

[161]Ibid., May 30, 1866.

[162]Ibid., May 2 and January 10, 1866.

[163](Houston) Tri-Weekly Telegraph, September 15, 1865.

[164](Galveston) Civilian and Galveston Gazette, November 18, 1865; (Galveston) Weekly News, January 11, 1867; (Houston) Tri-Weekly Telegraph, February 23, 1866.

[165](Galveston) Weekly News, May 9, 1866; February 1 and March 28, 1867.

[166](Galveston) Tri-Weekly News, May 29, 1872. See also 1852 ad of the Sour Lake Hotel and Spa, then owned by Byrd, Holland, and Co, in (Galveston) Semi-Weekly Journal, March 22, 1852; also "Letter From Hal," Weekly News, September 30, 1856.

[167](Galveston) Weekly News, May 9, 16, and June 6, 1866; April 12, 1867.

[168]Ibid., November 2, 9, 22, 1866; February 15, 22, and March 7, 14, 21, 1867; Official Records, Navies, in The War of The Rebellion, Series I, Vol. XIX, 225-229.

[169](Galveston) Weekly News, March 1, 28, April 4 and May 9, 16, 1866.

[170]Ibid., March 28, 1867.

[171](Galveston) Daily News, June 11, 1893; (Galveston) Tri-Weekly News, March 5, 1873.

[172](Galveston) Weekly News, March 1, 8, 1867.

[173]Ibid., March 14, 1867.

[174]Ibid, March 21, 28 and April 5, 12, 1867.

[175](Galveston) Daily News, June 11, 1893.

[176]Ibid., April 23, 1893; May 22, 1892.

[177](Galveston) Daily News, June 11, 1893. While the Trinity snag boat H. A. Harvey was in route to Dallas in 1893, her captain recalled that: "...In 1873, I came up on the Early Bird to a point called Spivey's Ferry...I made a dozen trips on the same boat to Lockridge's Bluff in Navarro County ..." See Ibid., May 16, 1893.

[178](Galveston) Daily News, April 23, 1893.

[179](Galveston) Tri-Weekly News, May 31, 1869; March 7, 1873.

[180](Sabine Pass, Texas) Beacon, June 10, 1871; MSS, Sumpter Keith, "History of the K. D. Keith Family," unpublished, 1907.

[181](Galveston) Daily News, April 23, 1893; (Galveston) Tri-Weekly News, January 28, February 18, and March 23, 1870; December 24, 1869.

[182]Daily News, April 23, 1893; (Galveston) Tri-Weekly News, January 5, and March 9, 1870; February 1 and March 10, 1871; February 12 and December 11, 1872; February 7 and August 7, 1873.

[183](Galveston) Weekly News, November 5, 1877; (Galveston) Tri-Weekly News, March 14, 1873; Daily News, June 11, 1893.

[184](Galveston) Tri-Weekly News, August 4, 1869, quoting Liberty Gazette.

[185](Galveston) Daily News, April 23, 1893.

[186](Galveston) Tri-Weekly News, February 26, 1873.

[187](Galveston) Weekly News, June 19, 1871; (Sabine Pass, Texas) Beacon, June 10, 1871.

[188](Galveston) Tri-Weekly News, February 21, 1873.

[189](Galveston) Weekly News, June 12, 1871.

[190](Galveston) Tri-Weekly News, December 13, 27, 31, 1869; January 5, 23, 31; February 16, 23, and April 29, 1870.

[191]Ibid., December 13, 1869; January 23, 1870.

[192]Ibid., December 31, 1869; January 31, April 27, 29, 1870.

[193]Ibid., May 4, 1870.

[194](Galveston) Weekly News, June 12, 1871. The Daily News report of 1893 listed only 5,440 bales as arriving during the same time span.

[195]Ibid., May 1, 1871.

[196]Many vessels of the "Era" class were built on the Red River at Shreveport and named identically, but in numerical sequence. Several of them operated on the Texas rivers. Era No. 8 plied the Sabine River for ten years and sank there in 1881. See (Sabine Pass) Beacon, June 10, 1871, and (Beaumont) Enterprise, November 6, 1881.

[197]The writer believes this to have been a new boat named S. J. Lee, rather than the wrecked vessel of the same name. It seems highly unlikely that the sunken S. J. Lee would have been refloated after three years lying submerged and out of sight.

[198](Sabine Pass, Texas) Beacon, June 10, 1871; (Galveston) Weekly News, June 19, 1871.

[199](Galveston) Tri-Weekly News, October 11, 1871.

[200]Ibid., September 6, 11, 1871.

[201]Ibid., December 1, 1869; February 24, March 1, 24, 1871; April 4 and December 11, 1872.

[202](Galveston) Tri-Weekly News, February 12, March 1, 6, 15 and April 5, 1871.

[203]Ibid., December 28, 1870; January 4, 27, March 10, 13, 31, April 10, May 5, 8 and June 7, 1871.

[204]Ibid., December 27, 1870; January 4, 27, February 12, 22, 24, March 13, 17 24, April 14, 19, May 3, 5, 8, and June 7, 1871.

[205]Ibid., April 28 and May 29, 1872.

[206]Ibid., March 5, 30, 1873.

[207]Ibid., February 10 and March 7, 1873.

[208](Galveston) Weekly News, June 26, 1871, and June 29, 1874.

[209](Galveston) Tri-Weekly News, January 10, 1872.

[210]Ibid., January 12, 21, 24 and February 4, 7, 12, 14, 23, 1872.

[211]Ibid., March 11, 13, 15 and April 12, 14, 24, 1872.

[212](Galveston) Tri-Weekly News, December 19, 24, 1873.

[213]Ibid., February 26 and March 10, 1873.

[214]Ibid., April 24, 1872.

[215]Ibid., December 3, 1877, quoting the Orange Tribune; (Orange, Texas) Tribune, September 12, 1879.

[216](Liberty, Texas) Vindicator, April 28, 1893.

[217]Ibid., February 3, 1893; (Galveston) Daily News, January 9, 1898.

[218](Beaumont) Enterprise, December 18, 1880; (Liberty) Vindicator, March 18, 1892; (Galveston) Daily News, October 14, 15, 16, 1886.

[219](Galveston) Weekly News, May 8, and June 12, 1871; (Galveston) Tri-Weekly News, August 16, 1869, and February 23, 1870; (Sabine Pass, Texas) Beacon, June 10, 1871.

[220] (Galveston) Weekly News, February 2, 1874. See also William Seale, Texas Riverman: The Life and Times of Captain Andrew Smyth (Austin: 1966); File 45-B, Estate of C. H. Alexander, Probate Record, Jefferson County, Texas, Archives; (Sabine Pass) Beacon, June 10, 1871.

[221](Sabine Pass, Texas) Beacon, June 10, 1871.

[222](Galveston) Tri-Weekly News, December 20, 1871, and March 8, 1871.

Chapter 13—On to Dallas!

The Trinity's Grand Scheme that Failed

After lying dormant for many years, the subject of Trinity River navigation all the way to Dallas came to the forefront again in the year 1892. The main promoters for the canalization of the river via a series of about twenty locks were the Dallas Board of Trade and the principal shippers of Dallas who, in furtherance of the project, organized at that time the Trinity Navigation Company. Its purpose was to clear the river of all obstructions, demonstrate the practicability and navigability of the Trinity River all the way to Dallas, solicit funds for expenses, and to prepare, publicize, and lobby for legislation that would eventually underwrite the costs of building and operating the series of locks or dams along the river, as well as "guarantee the free navigation of the Trinity." Its stated objective was:[223]

> ...to build up north Texas and the country tributary to the river much of which is virgin. This, when accomplished, will make Dallas the largest manufacturing center in the south, and benefit the counties on both sides of the river immeasurably by opening up sources of wealth dormant and undreamed of ...

Between 1880 and 1890, Dallas had grown from a city of 10,000 people to a bustling shipping center with a population of 25,000 inhabitants. Its growth rate among Texas cities during that decade (250%) was second only to that of El Paso, which seemed to guarantee to Dallas its place in the economic "sun" of Texas. With its railroads fanning out in all directions, the cotton and grain crops of North Texas found their way into its markets, and only one factor threatened to stunt its growth potential. Dallas, like most of the agricultural Southland in that "age of the robber barons," was saddled with prejudicial freight rates which favored the Northern and seacoast cities. In fact, a railroad, the Kansas City Southern, was being built toward the Gulf of Mexico at that very moment and for the same reason. No solution to their problems was visible until the Dallas shippers' sights were focused upon a Dallas-owned and built sternwheeler, the Dallas, which at that moment was transporting crossties and rails for the chief economic enemy of the steamboat, the Houston, and Texas Central Railroad.

Captain W. C. Husung, who owned the steamer Dallas, had sailed downstream for the first time on December 7, 1891, bent upon clearing the upper one hundred miles of the river in order to execute his railroad contract, and as a sideline, to conduct excursion voyages.[224] His activities called attention to the small and silent stream, the commercial potential of which had not been previously noticed or else was regarded as being only in the category of pleasure. Certainly, its latent possibilities for making Dallas an inland seaport, and hence, an instrument for reducing freight rates through heavy competition, had remained unforeseen. There extended for hundreds of miles north and west of Dallas a vast wheat-growing region, including the Texas Panhandle, the Indian Territory, Northeast Texas, and Kansas, which had created for Kansas City many of the same problems which Dallas experienced–high freight rates, and for Kansas City, total dependency on the monopoly of the East-West Railroads. The need to break that monopoly had already caused one entrepreneur, Arthur Stilwell, to organize the Kansas City, Pittsburgh, and Gulf Railroad, now the Kansas City Southern, which by 1893 had laid rails as far south as Siloam Springs in northwest Arkansas, the destination of which was a terminus on the Gulf of Mexico. It occurred to the Dallas businessmen that, with a Trinity River canalized via a series of twenty locks and blessed with deep water to the sea at all seasons, the railroad builder might be induced to terminate his line at Dallas and save the immense building costs for 300 additional miles of track.[225]

During 1892, the Dallas promoters met and organized the Trinity Navigation Company, with C. A. Keating, its chief instigator, as president; and Leo Wolfson (of the Board of Trade), S. W. S Duncan, J. W. Griffith, J. P. Murphey, W. H. Prather, James Moroney, F. G. Moore, Philip Sanger, and W. C. Padgitt comprising the principal officers and board of directors. The officers immediately engaged Colonel R. V. Tompkins as the company's general manager. Captain J. H. McGarvey, the steamer captain who had made the steamboat voyage to Dallas in 1868, was also employed to supervise the company's activities at Galveston.[226]

One immediate objective of the company was to build an especially equipped snag boat (also to be name the Dallas) to clear obstructions while in route downriver, and to purchase or build a similar snag boat at Galveston to work upriver from Anahuac. The new Dallas (under construction at Dallas' Lamar Street Dockyard during the fall of 1892) contained 60,000 feet of the stoutest timbers and was 100 feet long and 25 feet wide. Her equipment included 45-horsepower, locomotive-type driving engines; 25-horsepower steam hoisting engines for the derrick crane used to lift out logs, rocks, and other obstructions; a powerful pump for cutting away sand bars and overhanging trees, as well as a dynamo which supplied lighting for night work and power for the electric motors. The snag boat Dallas was launched in January, 1893 and was ready for service a month later.[227]

In March, the new company bought H. A. Harvey, Jr., a photograph of which appears elsewhere, which was a 113-foot sternwheeler identically equipped with the new Dallas, for $6,000. Built early in 1892, the vessel had spent the previous year cleaning out Louisiana's Mermentau River under contract with the United States Corps of Engineers. Upon her arrival in Galveston, Captain Joseph Rogers, a veteran Trinity River "pilot of many years' experiences, was placed in command,"[228] and by March 15, 1893, the Harvey was in route to Dallas.

The enthusiasm that the navigation plans engendered is quite evident in the Galveston, Liberty, and Dallas newspapers, the pages of which gave wide coverage to the project over a long six-months span. One Dallas backer predicted that "we will handle 500,000 bales of cotton in Dallas when we get this river working."[229] With a gradual elevation decline of only six water inches per mile of length, the Trinity was regarded as an ideal and excellent stream for the company's promulgated planning, as evidenced by the statement, which follows, of Captain Husung in Dallas:[230]

...a dam (lock) ten feet high will throw the water
back about thirty miles. Twenty dams would convert
the Trinity into one of the finest canals in the world—
a canal with permanent banks and formed perfectly
by nature. There would not be a yard of leveeing
required, and the locks and dams placed in position
would not probably exceed $6,000 each ...

Husung's enthusiasm was also shared by Captain McGarvey, who believed that Trinity navigation to Dallas was a practical project of year-round worth. "The river is better above Magnolia," he noted, "than below. There are a number of shoals in the river ...and I think it would take fifteen or twenty locks and dams to give five feet of water all the year round between Galveston and Dallas ..."[231]

As the H. A. Harvey worked its way slowly upstream, pulling snags, cutting out overhanging trees and other navigation impediments, plans were in progress to stage a mass celebration (with Governor James Hogg attending) upon the steamer's arrival in Dallas.[232] During the vessel's seven weeks in route, some 38 days were consumed overcoming travel obstructions, principal of which was the delay experienced when a section of each railroad bridge had to be removed and then replaced. On June 2, one newspaper observed that:[233]

Perhaps the biggest, most enthusiastic, and
important demonstration ...of a people directly
interested, was that at Dallas last week in
celebration of the steamboat Harvey, an event
practically demonstrating to the world that the
Trinity was a stream that could be navigated ...

A week later, the Harvey was "running with ease and safety from Dallas down the river" in route to Galveston, and the Liberty Vindicator challenged all of the East Texas legislators to take up the issue of Trinity navigation and support the project until its successful canalization was a reality.[234]

Newspaper silence after July 1st, however, suggests that the project's failure was soon a recognized fact, despite $60,000 of funding, much spending, and a network of supporters who were among the most influential businessmen of Texas. The causes of the failure were unclear and were widely speculated about. Perhaps the rural communities regarded the project as only another scheme that would enhance and enrich the Dallas shipping interests and would have no economic value elsewhere. Others thought the Eastern railroads had blocked any hope of favorable legislation. Logic, however, seems to conclude that the depression of 1893-1895, a period when river and harbors legislation had little hope of enactment, was the underlying reason. And although pleas for Trinity canalization would arise during the twentieth century, they were but mere "cries in the wilderness" when compared to the well-funded planning and promotion of 1893.

During the twentieth century, the majestic river has assumed the role that undoubtedly it will play for an indefinite period in the future. Under the United States Corps of Engineers, flood control dams have been built on the Trinity and some of its tributaries, and man-made lakes such as Lake Livingston now impound millions of acre-feet of water to feed a growing population and the mushrooming industries of East Texas.

In retrospect, the river and its cotton boat fleet served the Trinity Valley inhabitants well and faithfully for over a forty-year span. For thousands, the stream was the only route which moved cotton and other commodities to market and in turn, carried the wares and necessities needed to sustain frontier living throughout East Texas. The many elegant steamboats provided accommodation that enabled passengers to travel in relative comfort and at reasonable rates. A high accident rate, however, resulted in the loss of many vessels and cargoes of cotton, and hence, was a factor in the ultimate demise of the river trade.

Whenever and wherever the writer gazes at length upon the serene, yet oftentimes turbulent, Trinity River, his antebellum nostalgia surfaces immediately and visions of cotton bales appear. For a moment, the forgotten river ports thrive again, and a dozen sternwheel steamboats pass in mental revue. Those which are cotton bale-bedecked head downstream in the direction of Galveston, bending gracefully as they steer around each meander or horseshoe bend of the stream. The other vessels churn northward in search of that fluffy, white commodity which once ruled the Trinity Valley's economy with an iron fist. Yes, these are fleeting but pleasant thoughts, indeed, quick to give way to the realities of everyday living, but always a part of the never-ending romance which characterizes and entwines the history of nineteenth century Texas.

Endnotes—Chapter 13

[223](Galveston) *Daily News,* February 13, 1893.

[224]*Ibid.*, January 1, 1893.

[225]W. T. Block, "Tulip Transplants to East Texas: The Dutch Migration to Nederland, Port Arthur, and Winnie," *East Texas Historical Journal*, XIII (Fall, 1975), p. 36.

[226]"Trinity River Navigation," (Liberty) *Vindicator,* February 3, 1893; (Galveston) *Daily News,* December 5, 1892, and February 13, 1893.

[227](Galveston) *Daily News,* December 5, 1892; January 1 and February 13, 1893.

[228](Liberty, Texas) *Vindicator*, March 24, 1893.

[229](Galveston) *Daily News*, December 5, 1892.

[230]*Ibid.*, January 1, 1893; (Liberty) *Vindicator*, April 21, 1893.

[231]*Ibid.*, April 23, 1893.

[232](Liberty) *Vindicator*, April 14, 1893.

[233]*Ibid.*, June 2, 1893. See also *Vindicator*, June 2, 1893; (Dallas) *News*, June 16, 1893; and (Galveston) *Daily News*, May 16, and June 11, 1893.

Index

N

O

P

Y

Made in the USA
Monee, IL
10 May 2023

c425066f-724a-4126-8dad-c2f37eca5a50R01